Convergences

Convergences

Transactions in Reading and Writing

Edited by

Bruce T. Petersen

With an introduction by

Marilyn S. Sternglass

National Council of Teachers of English
1111 Kenyon Road, Urbana, Illinois 61801

To Jill, Ian, and Quentin.

Staff Editor: Lee Erwin

Book Design: Tom Kovacs for TGK Design

NCTE Stock Number 08563

Library of Congress Cataloging-in-Publication Data

Convergences: transactions in reading and writing.
   Bibliography: p.
    1. English language—Rhetoric—Study and teaching—
Addresses, essays, lectures.   2. English language—
Composition and exercises—Study and teaching—Addresses,
essays, lectures.   3. Reading—Addresses, essays,
lectures. 4. Language arts—Addresses, essays, lectures.
I. Petersen, Bruce T.
PE1404.C634   1986   808'.042'07   86-2368
ISBN 0-8141-0856-3

Contents

III Using the Writing of Others

IV Using Literature and Teaching Literacy

Preface

When Bruce Petersen died from liver cancer suddenly at the age of thirty-seven, he was nearing completion of this manuscript. Bereft as we still are, we are deeply pleased to have been able to finish what little work remained and to see this project through to publication.

The title Bruce chose for his book, *Convergences,* aptly characterizes his short but promising scholarly career. He believed in the liberating power of education, and for him language was the primary alchemical force. As such, it stood at the center of his teaching and scholarship, and many areas of intellectual inquiry converged upon it, including semiotics, reader-response criticism, reading and rhetorical theory, psycholinguistics, politics, and literature, especially the novels of Charles Dickens.

This talent for making connections affected many of us with whom Bruce worked. He was an excellent reader of colleagues' papers, able to provide a global perspective that brought all loose ends together. He was tactful and savvy about gathering together groups of scholars for panels, presentations, and books. And running through his efforts at integration, there were always integrity and ambition, in the very best sense of the term—ambition to know, ambition to contribute meaningfully to the professional dialectic, and ambition to teach and respect whole students, to lead them beyond concerns about GPA to ennobling habits of mind.

As a friend, Bruce encouraged convergence as well. Here in the northern reaches of Michigan's rugged and isolated upper peninsula, where two-hundred-inch yearly snowfalls are the norm rather than the exception, where sense of community is the only antidote to severe bouts of cabin fever, Bruce helped things to make sense for his friends. His home and family were a source of solidarity, his woodstove a place around which to meet for drinks and conversation and laughter when the snow and wind had frayed our patience and the temperature hovered at zero.

We remember Bruce on the racquetball court giggling (and that is the right word) over his impossible kill shots. We remember him bent over his piano, those grand *appassionato* stretches of Beethoven or

rousing medleys of Scott Joplin. We remember his incomparable choc-
olate mousse, his homemade pasta and Chinese food. We remember
the lessons he taught us about family, about loving, about loyalty and
honesty. We remember his outspoken defenses of principles, both
professional and personal. We remember, and now we walk just a bit
more softly for fear that we will say or do something to a friend that
sudden, capricious loss might prevent us from undoing.

We speak here of loss and memories out of our own need to embody
in words the person behind this collection of essays. We have all lost a
colleague and a friend. But the work remains, and we are happy and
honored to make it available to the profession, both for the person
implicit in these pages and for the vision they sustain.

Randy Freisinger
Cynthia Selfe
Billie Wahlstrom

Michigan Technological University

Introduction

It has become acceptable, even fashionable, to speak of the paradigm shifts that have occurred in reading (from a skills model to a psycholinguistic model) and in writing (from a product orientation to a process orientation). What has been examined less frequently is the paradigm shift that has been occurring in the relationships among reading, writing, literature, and literacy. The relationships among these language processes have undergone shifts from being treated as parallel processes (e.g., see the correlational studies reviewed by Stotsky[1]), or as interactive processes,[2] to being treated as transactive processes.[3] In selecting the title for this collection, *Convergences: Transactions in Reading and Writing,* the late Bruce Petersen understood that the time had arrived to bring together the insights gained through current research, particularly in transactional studies, and apply them to classroom activities in ways that would bring together not only researchers but teachers of reading, writing, literature, and literacy.

In an early draft of an introduction to this volume that Bruce Petersen began but never completed, he explained the relationships he felt needed to be explored and the timeliness of this conjunction:

> Recently a number of theorists and researchers have noted important convergences between composition research and research into the ways people read. They find that writers are constrained by both the text they produce and by the texts they read to inform their writing; they find that reflective and critical reading of our own texts plays an important role in revision; they find that writing plays a perhaps unique role in helping students think about and comprehend texts; they find that the cognitive strategies and schemata we learn by expansive reading may be reflected in the schemata and strategies we are able to develop for generating texts; and they find that various old and new theories of discourse (classical rhetoric, reader-response criticism, and speech-act theory) have direct applications to what they are learning about reading and writing. These convergences of theory and research about reading and writing point to the need for discussion, analysis, and clarification of what is currently known about the connections between the processes of reading and writing. One purpose of *Convergences: Transactions in Reading and Writing* is to provide that forum.

To understand the significance of bringing these disciplines together, it is useful to look briefly at features of the paradigms from which reading-writing relationships have been viewed. In a comprehensive review, Sandra Stotsky describes early correlational studies, which fell into three categories: (1) those correlating measures of reading achievement with measures of writing ability; (2) those correlating measures of reading experience with measures of writing ability; and (3) those correlating measures of reading ability with measures of syntactic complexity in students' compositions.[4] Although most of these studies concluded that there was a statistically significant relationship between reading ability and writing quality, what is interesting from the perspective of this volume is that the underlying premise of all such studies is that the processes of reading and writing are parallel and that examining them discretely allows one to draw conclusions about interactive effects.

Even more recently, although arguing that text production is much more than a simple reversal of comprehension, Walter Kintsch asserts that a model of text production will have to deal with the same levels of processing as a model of comprehension: analysis of surface structure, construction of a semantic representation, integration of knowledge, and formation of the macrostructure, the gist of the text.[5] Again, the formulation of the relationships suggests the use of parallel strategies.

James R. Squire argues that composing and comprehending are "two sides of the same process." Although his description of the "two sides" treats them as discrete entities, he sees them both as critical to thinking processes and interactive in their operations: composing is a process "which actively engages the learner in constructing meaning, in developing ideas, in relating ideas, in expressing ideas. Comprehending is critical because it requires the learner to reconstruct the structure and meaning of ideas expressed by another writer. To possess an idea that one is reading about requires competence in regenerating the idea, competence in learning how to write the ideas of another."[6] Though moving toward a more interactional perspective, this approach still contains many of the characteristics Jerome C. Harste pointed to in his review of paradigm shifts in reading comprehension research. Harste calls this view of reading "information transfer," stating that in such studies "the difference between a good and not so good reader is the degree to which they can answer questions or reproduce the text verbatim in a retelling." He notes, though, that even when this assumption is operating implicitly or explicitly in a study, the researcher is also "typically looking at other background information, text structure, lesson frameworks, and ability to infer, as to why differences exist among multiple choice test scores and retellings."[7]

Studies examining the relationships between reading and writing from an interactive perspective have had two major orientations: (1) looking at the role of reading while writing was occurring and (2) the more indirect effect that reading has on a writer. From the first perspective, Margaret Atwell explored the role of reading while composing. In examining the performance of basic writers and better writers, she found that better writers could produce more coherent and better organized texts when their emerging texts were masked than could remedial writers.[8] From the second perspective, Frank Smith argues that reading influences writing skills because readers unconsciously "read like writers." He goes on to say that

> to read like a writer we engage with the author in what the author is writing. We anticipate what the author will say, so that the author is in effect writing on our behalf, not showing how something is done but doing it with us. . . . Bit by bit, one thing at a time, but enormous numbers of things over the passage of time, the learner learns through *reading* like a writer to *write* like a writer.[9]

This explanation could account for the studies cited in Stotsky's review in which students who were asked to do additional reading instead of extra writing[10] or reading instead of grammar activities[11] performed better in writing than the control groups in these studies. Arguing from a similar perspective in "Reading Teaches Plans for Writing," Bonnie J. F. Meyer describes a study in which students who wrote reports on readings using the same plan as the reading's author used remembered far more content than those who did not organize their reports along the same plan used by the author. She then argues that composition teachers should teach rhetorical planning because it will assist readers to remember more content and expend less time and effort doing it.[12]

A more active concept of interaction, as it relates to reading, is one proposed by Harste as involving an active reader contributing some things in the reading of a text while the text contributes some other things.[13] This type of interaction then makes inferring possible for readers. And it leads directly to the idea that composing is something done by both readers and writers, as is developed more fully in the transactional models currently being proposed.

Robert J. Tierney describes the shift in the focus of attention from interaction to transaction: interaction deals with how reading and writing influence each other in terms of achievement, while transaction explains how reading and writing are interfaced. From one perspective, he is interested in the transactional relationship that readers and writers are involved in as text is being created.

> Writers consider their readers as they compose text—they consider the transactions in which readers are likely to engage. At the same time, writers act as their own readers—they read and review what they have written as if they (the writers) assumed they were their own audiences [what Donald Murray (1982) has called inner readers]. Readers, as they comprehend text, respond reflexively and actively to what writers are trying to get them to think or do. These readers use knowledge of the world and the text cues to compose meaning: they recognize these cues to meaning making are provided by an author who is trying to get them to think or do something.[14]

Tierney and P. David Pearson reiterate in another article the relationships of reading and writing as "essentially similar processes of meaning construction." They argue that "there is no meaning on the page until a reader decides there is."[15]

In a review of the assumptions underlying their study of literacy and learning processes of preschool children, Harste, Woodward, and Burke argue that in a transactional model the "coming together of learner and environment affects what is learned." They question the notions of developmental stages, readiness, and emergent reading and conclude that similar types of psycholinguistic and sociolinguistic activity affect the literacy processes of both children and adult language users.[16]

Another transactional model is presented by David Bleich.[17] As Petrosky describes it, "for Bleich, the only way to demonstrate comprehension is through extended discourse where readers become writers who articulate their understandings of and connections to the text in their responses. Response is, then, an expression and explanation of comprehension; and comprehension means using writing to explicate the connections between our models of reality—our prior knowledge— and the texts we recreate in light of them."[18] Petrosky then adopts Bleich's response model as a way of urging a conjunction of reading, literary theory, and composition. He is concerned that it is not enough to understand the transactive model of reading as proposed by, for example, Louise Rosenblatt,[19] but that "writing about reading is one of the best ways to get students to unravel their transactions so that we can see how they understand and, in the process, help them to elaborate, clarify, and illustrate their responses by reference to the associations and prior knowledge that inform them."[20]

Still another instructional model proposing to bring reading and writing into a transactional relationship is set forth by Ann E. Berthoff, who describes a double-entry journal in which reading notes and observational notes are recorded on one side and notes about these notes on the facing page.[21] In this way, a dialectic is set up that fosters speculative thinking and makes students see that both reading and writing are processes of meaning making, as Tierney and Pearson point out. Berthoff's dialectic also anticipates the cognitive stereoscopy proposed by Bleich in this volume.

Harste sees the shifts described to this point as a movement from transfer to transaction. No longer is the primary focus on the transfer of information from the writer to the reader, from the text to the reader. Rather, in a transaction, meaning is composed both by readers and writers, so that what emerges is a "new event, larger than the sum of its parts."[22]

But Petrosky best summarizes the relationships among reading, writing, and literacy that must have led Bruce Petersen to his notion that the next step in examining these relationships must deal with their convergence:

> One of the most interesting results of connecting reading, literary, and composition theory and pedagogy is that they yield similar explanations of human understanding as a process rooted in the individual's knowledge and feelings and characterized by the fundamental act of making meaning, whether it be through reading, responding, or writing. When we read, we comprehend by putting together impressions of the text with our personal, cultural, and contextual models of reality. When we write, we compose by making meaning from available information, our personal knowledge, and the cultural and contextual frames we happen to find ourselves in. Our theoretical understandings of these processes are *converging* . . . around the central role of human understanding—be it of texts or the world—as a process of composing. (Emphasis added)[23]

Thus, in this collection, the insights offered by a transactional model of reading, writing, and literacy are explored from a perspective from which they can converge in literature, language, and composition classrooms to build understandings transcending any that could be gained by treating these processes discretely.

The essays in this collection have been grouped into four general categories: Becoming Readers and Writers, Reading and Writing as Social Activities, Using the Writing of Others, and Using Literature and Teaching Literacy. As a guide to reading the collection, I will briefly review the individual essays.

Becoming Readers and Writers

The first chapter opens with an essay by Robert J. Tierney and Margie Leys, "What Is the Value of Connecting Reading and Writing?" Tierney and Leys address an issue popular in correlational studies, i.e., whether improvement in reading performance contributes to improvement in writing performance and vice versa, but they treat it from a perspective entirely different from the one taken in correlational studies. They argue that it is impossible to address these processes separately because the processes are confounded, the writer reading, and the reader often writing. They see reading and writing working together as tools for information storage and retrieval, discovery and logical thought, communication, and self-indulgence.

The next three essays explore the role of reading during writing from a transactional perspective. In "Reflective Thought: The Connection between Reading and Writing," June Birnbaum points out that good readers and good writers are more likely to reflect on their own texts than are poor readers and poor writers. Better readers and writers seem to take control of written language, formulate better questions and solutions about the unfolding text, and continually monitor their success or failure in constructing meaning in or from print. She urges teachers to promote reflective thinking by asking questions that demand higher reasoning and predicting. The following essay, Cynthia Selfe's "Reading as a Writing Strategy: Two Case Studies," addresses writing apprehension as a factor in writing. Selfe examines the protocols of two students, one a proficient writer and the other a less proficient and highly apprehensive writer. She finds that the two students differed markedly in their uses of reading while writing, with the more apprehensive student neither extracting information from the reading of assignments nor using the reading of his own text as an opportunity to explore the effectiveness of his material or to discover new directions for it. This study confirms the importance of reflective thought postulated by Birnbaum in the previous essay. An implication of Selfe's article is picked up in the next essay, "The Writing/Reading Relationship: Becoming One's Own Best Reader," by Richard Beach and JoAnne Liebman-Kleine. Beach and Liebman-Kleine detail the cognitive requirements involved in becoming what they term "one's own best reader." They maintain that a writer must think as a reader, that is, adopt the reader's perspective. They propose activities that will help writers infer audience attributes and use these attributes to assess their writing.

In the last essay in this section, "Writing Plans as Strategies for Reading, Writing, and Revising," Barbey Dougherty expands on the approach taken by Meyer.[24] Dougherty presents eight ways to structure information, plans that he sees as cognitive structures rather than content. If these structures for composing text can be learned, they can be helpful for directing the future reading of texts.

Reading and Writing as Social Activities

The next section begins with David Bleich's "Cognitive Stereoscopy and the Study of Language and Literature." Bleich maintains that two or more perspectives on any experience must be solicited and that, furthermore, these perspectives must be examined in a collective, social environment. He argues that new knowledge comes about only when at least two people share their perspectives on some event or experience. Through multiple perspectives in a classroom, authority can be distributed and all forms of language, literature, and composition can be equally valued. In "Social Foundations of Reading and Writing," Deborah Brandt takes up the importance of the social environment, noting that meaning-making in writing is like meaning-making in oral interactions. She argues that a writer must attend to the here-and-now that will be shared by an (eventual) reader in the same way that a speaker must attend to a listener in their dialogue. Writing thus becomes a social act, as does reading, for readers must also adopt a stance of "weness." Reading and writing then lead to the establishment of meaning by transcending the individual mind. Dorothy Augustine and W. Ross Winterowd, in "Speech Acts and the Reader-Writer Transaction," also imply a relationship between readers and writers that is similar to the relationship assumed between speakers and listeners. They assert that writers are attempting to address and satisfy what they project as the response of the reader to the speech act underlying the surface structure of the communication. In other words, the writer's invention of the reader is part of an implicit theory of speech acts—of projecting the hypothetical responses and questions of a reader to an emerging text and, thus, of constraining the direction of that text.

Using the Writing of Others

The next section of essays treats the issue of writers depending on resources which lie outside of themselves. In the first essay, "Writing Based on Reading," Marilyn Sternglass deals with the ways in which the writing process is constrained when writers must depend on outside sources of information to create their new texts. She also deals with the corollary problem of how readers of a text are constrained when they lack some of the knowledge the writer has used. Patricia Sullivan and Linda Flower, in "How Do Users Read Computer Manuals? Some Protocol Contributions to Writers' Knowledge," take up the issue of whether watching what readers do can lead to better writing of instructions.

They study the way readers use computer manuals and conclude that protocol analysis of actual use can lead to recognition of functional changes required by readers and users of such materials.

In the next essay, "Using Nonfiction Literature in the Composition Classroom," Maxine Hairston provides a pedagogical function for outside reading, i.e., using essays to teach the process of writing. She argues that nonfiction can be used in the composition classroom as an adjunct to teaching the writing process because reading experiences can sensitize writers to the factors in the rhetorical context which students are often unaware of. Hairston observes that too often literature and essays are taught in writing classes not in order to see how writers work or how the writing processes of class members interact with other texts, but rather to provide "content" for a course. Jill Burkland and Bruce Petersen, in "An Integrative Approach to Research: Theory and Practice," take up the issue of using literature in the research process. Examining the problem of how students respond to outside reading required for their writing through an analysis of composition theory and reader-response criticism, they demonstrate how the use of personal responses to reading can be used to help students learn each others' research processes and to write a variety of research-based papers. Their approach fosters the composing of active questioning and writing as the basis for developing strategies for exploring their own experience and the experience of others.

The last essay in this section deals with the use of technical and scientific texts in the classroom. In "Combined Reading-Writing Instruction Using Technical and Scientific Texts," Anne Eisenberg first summarizes findings in psycholinguistics and linguistics research and then shows how to use technical and scientific discourse to teach both reading and writing. Eisenberg wishes to encourage teachers of reading and writing who are not scientifically trained to use technical and scientific materials with their engineering and technical students. She offers an extensive list of titles and three methods for teaching (by historical period, by rhetorical model, and by thematic content) which should be of particular use to teachers interested in the teaching of technically oriented students.

Using Literature and Teaching Literacy

In his draft for an introduction, Bruce Petersen aptly described the conflict that is dealt with in this last section of the book: "Few things make literature professors more wary than the proposal that they teach composition in their literature classes. What happens, they ask, to our reverence for the literary work? Few things make composition professors more wary than the proposal that they teach literature in their composition classes. What happens, they ask, to our students' emerging sense of process?" The three essays in this section react to these legitimate concerns and forge responses that demonstrate the convergences this book reflects. Joseph Comprone, in "Integrating the Acts of Reading and Writing about Literature: A Sequence of Assignments Based on James Joyce's 'Counterparts,'" proposes that expressive writing is the key to designing a sequence of assignments that will encourage an ongoing give and take between subjective and objective perspectives in the experience of reading, a perspective similar to that taken by Berthoff and Bleich. His essay details how expressive writing exercises can help students synthesize this initial dichotomy of response into a whole. In her essay, "The Self and the Other in the Process of Composing: Implications for Integrating the Acts of Reading and Writing," Katharine Ronald also takes up the role of expressive writing in the classroom. Ronald argues that expressive writing as a response to literature allows students to function initially as spectators (in Britton's sense[25]), thus uniting their initial reading and writing experiences. As students learn to undertake the roles of both the self and the other, and become part of an interpretive community, they become more fluent readers and writers.

In the final essay in this section, Stephen Tchudi looks at "Reading and Writing as Liberal Arts." Tchudi notes that reading and writing should be used within a curriculum that fosters students' growing emotional, psychological, and linguistic needs. Rather than using classics, periods, or genres as the basis for reading and writing activities, teachers should develop curricula based on the experiential needs of the students themselves.

The final chapter in the collection is an annotated bibliography prepared by Patricia Stock and Karen Wixson. These sources should provide readers with a basis for further research, writing, and thought.

Concluding Thoughts

The conception of this book by Bruce Petersen underlines the realization in our multiple fields—reading, writing, literature, and literacy— that the understanding of transactional language processes leads us to a natural and productive convergence. Various perspectives have been delineated in the essays—psycholinguistics, ethnography, reader-response criticism, speech-act theory, linguistics, discourse analysis, protocol study, case study, process-oriented composition research, and others. What these perspectives share is the belief that transactional language processes lead to the creation of new meanings, new meanings initiated by conscious learners who reflect what literacy truly is.

Marilyn S. Sternglass
City College of the
City University of New York

Notes

1. Sandra Stotsky, "Research on Reading/Writing Relationships: A Synthesis and Suggested Directions," *Language Arts* 60 (1983): 627–42.

2. Margaret Atwell, "The Evolution of Text: The Interrelationship of Reading and Writing in the Composing Process" (Ph.D. diss., Indiana University, 1981).

3. David Bleich, *Subjective Criticism* (Baltimore, Md.: Johns Hopkins University Press, 1978); Anthony R. Petrosky, "From Story to Essay: Reading and Writing," *College Composition and Communication* 33 (1982): 24–25; and Jerome C. Harste, "The Winds of Change: Examining Assumptions in Instructional Research in Reading Comprehension" (Paper presented at National Council of Teachers of English Conference, Detroit, Michigan, November 1984).

4. Stotsky, p. 628.

5. Walter Kintsch, "The Role of Strategies in Reading and Writing," *Fforum III* 67 (1982).

6. James R. Squire, "Composing and Comprehending: Two Sides of the Same Basic Process," *Language Arts* 60 (1983): 581–82.

7. Harste, p. 19.

8. Atwell, "The Evolution of Text."

9. Frank Smith, "Reading Like a Writer," *Language Arts* 60 (1983): 553–64.

10. F. Heys, "The Theme-a-Week Assumption: A Report of an Experiment," *English Journal* 51 (1962): 320–22; and T. Devries, "Reading, Writing Frequency, and Expository Writing," *Reading Improvement* 7 (1970): 14, 15, 19.

11. E. V. Bagley, "A Critical Study of Objective Estimates in the Teaching of English," *British Journal of Educational Psychology* (1937): 57–71, 138–55.

12. Bonnie J. F. Meyer, "Reading Teaches Plans for Writing," *Fforum III* (1982): 69–70.

13. Jerome C. Harste, Virginia A. Woodward, and Carolyn L. Burke, "Examining Our Assumptions: A Transactional View of Literacy and Learning," *Research in the Teaching of English* 18 (1984): 21.

14. Robert J. Tierney, "Writer-Reader Transactions: Defining the Dimensions of Negotiation," in *Fforum: Essays on Theory and Practice in the Teaching of Writing,* ed. Patricia L. Stock (Upper Montclair, N.J.: Boynton/Cook, 1983), 150.

15. Robert J. Tierney and P. David Pearson, "Toward a Composing Model of Reading," *Language Arts* 60 (1983): 568–69.

16. Harste, Woodward, and Burke, pp. 90, 105.

17. Bleich.

18. Petrosky, pp. 24–25.

19. Louise Rosenblatt, *The Reader, the Text, the Poem: The Transactional Theory of the Literary Work* (Carbondale, Ill.: Southern Illinois Univ. Press, 1978).

20. Petrosky, p. 24.

21. Ann E. Berthoff, "How We Construe Is How We Construct," *Fforum III* (1982): 84–86.

22. Harste, p. 22.

23. Petrosky, p. 16.

24. See Meyer, "Reading Teaches Plans."

25. James Britton, Tony Burgess, Nancy Martin, Alex McLeod, and Harold Rosen, *The Development of Writing Abilities (11–18),* Schools Council Research Studies (London: Macmillan Education, 1975).

Becoming Readers
and Writers

What Is the Value of Connecting Reading and Writing?

Robert J. Tierney
Center for the Study of Reading at the University of Illinois
at Urbana-Champaign

Margie Leys
Riverina College of Advanced Education, Wagga Wagga, Australia

In recent years there has been an upsurge in the number of journal articles and conference presentations discussing the relationships between reading and writing. In general, these articles and papers have stressed the theoretical links between reading and writing processes. But a central question remains unaddressed: What are the benefits or learning outcomes that arise from interrelating or connecting reading and writing? When researchers considered reading-writing relationships in the past, they often focused upon the correlation between reading and writing or the improvements in reading due to writing instruction and vice versa. More recently, research in reading-writing relationships has expanded and so too has our view of the learning outcomes arising from their interconnections. For example, recent studies of readers' past writing experiences—overall achievement, attitude, genre preferences, or sense of audience—show that such experiences can contribute to the reader's selection of books, attitude, and sense and appreciation of authorship. We are beginning to see how reading influences revision, how readers use writing during studying, and how writers use reading during the preparation of a critical essay.

In this paper we explore some of the learning outcomes we have noted from past research and from our own observations of elementary-grade students.[1] Specifically, we address these questions:

1. Do gains in overall reading performance contribute to gains in overall writing performance and do gains in overall writing performance contribute to gains in overall reading performance?

2. How does writing influence reading and how does reading influence writing?

**In What Ways Do Gains in Overall Reading Improvement
Contribute to Gains in Overall Writing Improvement
and Vice Versa?**

Can we expect students who are successful readers to be successful
writers, or students who are successful writers to be successful readers?
When we read studies which show that good readers are also good
writers we are not surprised, for we intuitively feel that reading and
writing skills develop together or are so entangled that they appear
inseparable. In contrast, if we read research suggesting that good
readers are not necessarily good writers, we might initially question
such a finding. For example, we might ask: What definition of reading
and writing is being used? Or, What instrument was used to measure
reading and writing performance? On further reflection, we can all
recall individuals who were good readers, even good editors, but poor
or only fair writers. Alternatively, we have greater difficulty accepting
that there are good writers who are poor readers (surely good writing
demands a fair amount of reading ability). One way to reconcile this
apparent contradiction is to adopt a more pragmatic point of view
based upon what we know about how thoroughly separated reading
instruction and writing instruction are in schools. They are commonly
taught as individual subjects, and in quite different ways, and the way
they are tested is usually also quite different. Reading performance is
often scored with multiple-choice test items as either right or wrong;
writing performance is often scored using qualitative comparisons.

Having considered the possible relationships between reading and
writing performance, we should not be surprised to learn that most
correlational studies of reading and writing suggest a modest general
correlation between overall reading performance and writing achievement. Such studies have also shown that there are fluctuations in the
magnitude of this correlation because of factors such as age or the
measures employed. Thorough examination by T. Shanahan of the
reading-writing relationships of children in grades 2 and 5 suggested
that, as students moved through the grades, the correlation between
reading and writing varied erratically depending upon the measures
which were employed.[2] Similarly, an extensive study by W. Loban found
that the relationship between reading achievement and ratings of writing increased across grades 4, 6, and 9. In terms of students for whom
there were marked differences in reading and writing achievement,
Loban reported that approximately 40 percent of the students were
either good readers and poor writers or good writers and poor readers.[3]
In our own research, with three third-grade classrooms in three different schools, we found that students ranked as good readers were not

necessarily the same students ranked as good writers and vice versa. In particular, approximately 20 percent of the students ranked in the first quartile for reading or writing were given a rank much lower (usually toward the bottom of the second or in the third quartile) for writing or reading, respectively.

Studies of the overall impact of reading upon writing and writing upon reading are not necessarily restricted to achievement. In our work with third graders, we have looked at the extent to which attitudes to reading and writing are correlated. Our analyses of attitudes parallel our findings for achievement. There are some students who maintain a high or low value for both reading and writing; others vary from reading to writing.

Can we reach any conclusions, then, about the extent to which reading and writing achievement are related? If we take these data at face value, we might conclude that reading and writing appear to be either strongly or weakly related for some individuals, depending upon the measures which are employed to assess reading and writing performance. Changes in the strength of this relationship by individuals suggest that other factors may intrude—such as a reader or writer's instructional history, the extent to which students have opportunities to read and write, or the extent to which reading and writing opportunities are coordinated.

Conclusions such as these are not without their limitations. For example, there is the problem of determining what should be measured, that is, which of the different reading and writing experiences to which an individual is exposed should be sampled. Or perhaps we need to examine the correlations more differentially within genre and by task. Unfortunately, coming to grips with specific reading and writing tasks as well as measurement issues is not a straightforward matter. For what is *not* generally addressed in examinations of reading and writing is that the two processes are confounded. When an individual writes he or she also reads, and when an individual reads he or she often writes. Certainly, the impossibility of avoiding the intrusion of reading upon writing and sometimes writing upon reading suggests that we need to consider a more detailed examination of when and how reading and writing interact with each other. That is, we should address how writing influences reading and how reading influences writing.

How Does Writing Influence Reading?

As far back as 1908, Edmond Huey reported the use of a sentence method that used students' writing as the basis for reading instruction.

Since that time, various educators have advocated numerous practices in which writing is incorporated into the reading lesson. We would like to review some of these suggestions and to discuss some of their possible benefits.

C. Chomsky, who together with Charles Read[4] introduced us to the notion of "invented spellings," makes a strong case for learning to write before learning to read:

> Children who have been writing for months are in a very favorable position when they undertake learning to read. They have at their command considerable phonetic information about English, practice in phonemic segmentation, and experience with alphabetic representation. These are some of the technical skills that they need to get started. They have, in addition, an expectation of going ahead on their own. They are prepared to make sense, and their purpose is to derive a message from the print, not just to pronounce the words.[5]

More recent analyses of the attitudes, strategies, and understandings of children during their first five years by Ferriero and Teberosky[6] and Harste, Woodward, and Burke[7] have substantiated and extended this argument. Through writing samples collected from children aged four to six, they show how varied writing experiences (e.g., notes, stories, picture captions, etc.) provide children with the opportunities to develop, test, reinforce, and extend their understandings about text. As Harste, Woodward, and Burke argue, writing allows children the opportunity to test their "growing understanding of storiness, of wordness, of how one keeps ideas apart in writing, how the sounds of language are mapped onto written letters, of how one uses writing to mean and more."[8]

Such notions are not novel. The suggestion that children might actually learn to read by writing is consistent with the basic tenets underlying the language-experience approach as well as selected "creative" writing approaches.[9] There appear to be more than enough affidavits and research evidence regarding the effectiveness of these approaches to warrant accepting them as credible at least some of the time for some children. For example, such approaches have been shown to contribute substantially to improved concept development, word recognition, and vocabulary and comprehension development, as well as to heighten the students' awareness of the author's role and craft. One of the third-grade students in our study recounted how early opportunities to write contributed to his learning to read:

> I learned to write before I could read. I just wrote and then I
> started reading books because my mother taught me letters and

how to spell and showed me all kinds of words. I started making words and I started making them spelled right, and then I decided to read books because I knew I could read right with the words all spelled right. So I started reading books and I could understand books more because I wrote first.

The claim that writing contributes to a reader's sense of the author's craft is consistent with the findings offered by a number of other researchers.[10] They suggest that students involved in a rich writing curriculum develop a keen sense of why something they are reading was written, as well as its strengths and weaknesses. Furthermore, unlike students who are allotted little time to write, the students who write frequently and discuss their writing will approach reading with what might be termed the "eye of a writer." Questions and comments from children who have received extensive opportunities to write provide evidence for these claims. Lucy Calkins recorded questions such as "[I wonder] why the author chose the lead he did?" and "I wonder if these characters come from the author's life?" during discussions about various texts in a classroom where children write extensively. A quotation from a young author illustrates his change in understanding the writing process:

> Before I ever wrote a book, I used to think there was a big machine, and they typed a title and then the machine went until the book was done. Now I look at a book and I know a guy wrote it and it's been his project for a long time. After the guy writes it, he probably thinks of questions people will ask him and revises it like I do.[11]

Some educators suggest that we should take even greater advantage of how writers make meaning and revamp our approach to teaching reading in such a way as to treat our readers as if they were writers.[12] That is, readers should be encouraged to approach reading with the same playfulness and some of the same strategies that writers use when they research a topic, develop a draft, reread and redevelop their texts, and revise and distance themselves from their own thinking. But as Tierney and Pearson have suggested, these suggestions are not part of current instructional practices or student behavior:

> It seems that students rarely pause to reflect on their ideas or to judge the quality of their developing interpretations. Nor do they often reread a text either from the same or a different perspective. In fact, to suggest that a reader should approach text as a writer who crafts an understanding across several drafts—who pauses, rethinks, and revises—is almost contrary to the well established goals readers proclaim for themselves (e.g., that efficient reading is equivalent to maximum recall based upon a single fast reading).[13]

Occasionally, however, students do apply strategies from their writing to their reading, and they do this quite spontaneously. For example, one of the good readers and writers in our study sometimes referred to procedures he used in his writing that he had also found useful in reading. When discussing what he did when he got "stuck" on a word he suggested: "What I do is I just think of what I do when I'm writing . . . I remember that mistakes aren't everything." This is an extension of an earlier commentary he made about mistakes, when he said "If you thought making mistakes was everything, like say they were dumb, so you would get more bored with the book . . . I have learned to make another draft and correct them [mistakes] and then go on to a final [draft] after I have corrected them."

There are a variety of other ways in which writing has been shown to contribute to a reader's experience. B. M. Taylor and R. W. Beach were able to improve students' reading of expository text by involving them in writing paragraphs with the same structures.[14] A. R. Petrosky found that having students write essay responses to stories they had read enhanced the quality of their reading.[15] In a similar vein, both Nancy Atwell and J. Staton attribute the development of a sense of the communicative purposes of writing to the use of dialogue journals (i.e., the opportunity to have a written dialogue with a teacher through a journal).[16]

At times writing will be used primarily as an adjunct to reading and studying. For example, often a reader will respond to a reading assignment with a marginal notation, summary, or some other form of reflective comment intended as an aid to staying on task or as a critical reaction to the author's ideas. Indeed, there are a number of different note-taking strategies and other procedures that incorporate the use of this type of writing as an aid to studying.[17] Not surprisingly, research suggests that if students are capable note takers or summary writers and if the purpose for reading the text warrants this type of response, such activities are worthwhile.[18]

Although there are numerous writing activities that may contribute to reading, there are some that do not. For example, the research on sentence combining has yielded quite mixed results in terms of carry-overs to reading.[19] This should not be surprising since sentence combining, especially if it does not extend beyond exercises which require combining sentence pairs, can be viewed either as an end unto itself or a skill with rather limited transfer value to reading. Those studies in which benefits for reading have been accrued might be, as both Combs and Stotsky have suggested, due to indirect influences, for example the extent to which a student is forced to attend to text.[20]

In summary, although there may be writing activities that do not contribute to reading, there are many writing activities that *do*. But even this is a limited view, for there are other aspects to this issue. In particular, we need to consider how reading can influence writing, and, moreover, how reading and writing might work together.

How Does Reading Influence Writing?

Reading may contribute to writing in a variety of ways. You may speculate that the type and amount of reading material to which writers are exposed may influence their choice of topic, genre, writing style, and vocabulary, as well as affecting the values they hold regarding writing and heightening their understanding of the author's craft. From a slightly different perspective, we might consider when reading is tied more directly to writing, as, for example, when writers research a topic prior to writing, review their notes during writing, compare their style or format with that of another author, revise their work, or rethink and evaluate their own thoughts and arguments. Writers often put reading to a number of different uses as they develop drafts or take part in everyday exchanges of information. As will become apparent in our forthcoming discussion, research offers a great deal of support for such speculations.

Selected experimental studies that have looked at the influence of selected reading experiences upon writing suggest that, for better or worse, what students read does indeed influence what they write. Studies by C. N. Dixon and by B. Eckhoff have provided evidence of the negative impact of being exposed to the stilted language and format often found in first-grade readers.[21] For example, Eckhoff looked at two second-grade classes using two different basal series. She found that children who used a series that had stilted language and format tended to produce writing that was also stilted in language and format.

Research by E. Geva and R. J. Tierney and by C. Bereiter and M. Scardamalia has demonstrated the influence of selected formats of text and rhetorical features upon the writing of students at various levels.[22] Geva and Tierney had high school students read different types of compare/contrast texts and then write either summaries or recalls. They found that the format of the text read by the students influenced the format of the students' writing. Bereiter and Scardamalia had a range of students, from third grade to graduate school, read single examples of literary types and then write in the same form. They found that students of all ages exhibited evidence of acquiring rhetorical knowledge from their reading. It should be noted, however, that this knowledge was biased at all ages toward discrete elements of language and content.

In a similar vein, C. J. Gordon and C. Braun found that students' writing improved if the structural characteristics of stories were highlighted.[23] They taught one group of fifth graders about the structural characteristics of stories while another group simply read and discussed the stories, and found that the instruction helped the students' comprehension of stories as well as their writing of stories.

In our work with third graders, we have received similar confirmation of the effects of reading upon writing. We have observed that students will initiate writing in a certain genre, or write a certain report, or use an alternative format, based upon what they have read. In addition, we have found, as have other investigators, that with encouragement to do so students will compare their own writing with the plot or character development in what they are reading. Students will begin using their reading as a rich resource for considering possible topics, ideas, and stylistic options. One boy in our study, for example, was particularly fond of the Encyclopedia Brown books by Donald Sobol. When the student was asked how he had started writing a piece called "The Mini-Sub" he replied,

> I got that chapter out of an Encyclopedia Brown book—I was reading a chapter called, "The Flying Submarine." And it's a little bit similar to the chapter I am writing right now. That's how I got the name of the chapter, it's very similar, but I got this topic because I made up a character named Brad Wilson and he's supposed to be a detective. . . . I wanted to copy down things [from "The Flying Submarine"] but I decided that that's like stealing, so I made different characters, sentences and all that, and I think mine is better than the book I just read.

The children also told us that they learned about the author's craft and about new words from their reading:

1. *Interviewer:* "I noticed . . . at the beginning of Chapter 5 [you wrote] 'Meanwhile, at home' . . . how did you know how to do that?"
   Child: "I have seen it in other books."
   Interviewer: "What are some of the other things that you use?"
   Child: "Words and dedications, dialogue, ways to show people that you are going back to something else."

2. "[A good book has] showy words, action, dialogue . . . things like that."

3. "I think my reading helps my writing because when I read I get new words for my writing and when I read I also get new ideas

like I dedicate now and I put feelings and details and better titles and that's how I think reading helps writing."

The influence of reading upon writing may also extend to strategies. Studies by Spivey and Birnbaum have dealt in part with this question.[24] Spivey had college students read three articles on the same topic and then write essays. She found that the essays written by the more able comprehenders were better organized, more connected, and of higher content quality than those written by the less able comprehenders. Birnbaum found with fourth and seventh graders that more proficient readers tended to know *how* to think and *what* to think about while they were reading and writing. She also found that the quality of writing produced by these students was related to the quality of their reading during writing. That is, the more proficient writers were less localized or sentence-bound in their reading, tending to reread larger chunks of text than did the less-proficient writers. Apart from Spivey's and Birnbaum's work, we have very little research exploring other transfer possibilities. For example, will readers who can self-question, focus their reading, and relate what they are reading to other materials they have read prove able to transfer their strategies to their writing? Similarly, will readers who are critical of the author's craft and have a sense of audience prove to be writers who have a rich sense of their own readers? While this area is only starting to be explored, these questions point toward an important, overlooked area for reading and writing instruction.

Our discussion to this point might suggest that we believe that reading and writing are largely linear operations that follow one after the other. On the contrary, we hold that writers use reading in a more integrated fashion, for, as writers write, they are constantly involved in reading their own writing, reading other material, and using understandings they have acquired from past readings. Consider the following statements taken from third graders as they discussed how they approached the stories and reports they had written.

1. "Sometimes I imagine that I am the one who is going to read it, and I think about what other people would think."
2. "I read my work as another person. I like to have a hint of what the other people may say about it."
3. "If something doesn't make sense [I can always tell] because . . . this little person in my head tells me."
4. "I wrote it down and then I read it over, and the parts that I didn't think were right or where I needed more information, I crossed it

out and put it on the side, this is a second draft and first draft put
together."

5. "Well, some people don't know what elliptical means, so [on my
   second draft] I just decided to put that there [a definition] so that
   they wouldn't get mixed up."

6. *Interviewer:* "How did you think of the ideas (for your book
                Natasha's Runaway Imagination)?"

   Child: "Well, I read this other book, and it was about this
                girl's imagination but I just thought about that book
                and I thought it would be a good title for Natasha
                Koren to have a runaway imagination . . . it [the
                other book] wasn't the same . . . she looks at pic-
                tures and stuff and she imagines they are moving
                and stuff like that."

7. Journal entry: "Today I was doing my health book. I'm doing
   blood . . . Can I go to the library on Monday to get some more
   information on blood?"

8. "I did a report on owls, and this chapter right here [in his detec-
   tive novel] is based on owls and [the mystery] is a question
   about owls."

The first five statements give an indication of the type of reading which
occurs in conjunction with reading one's own writing—either for revision purposes or to discover, understand, or enjoy one's own text. Our
data suggest, as do studies by other researchers,[25] that the quality of
writing produced is related to the quality of reading done during writing. Specifically, successful writers have a better sense of the needs of
their audience and tend to be less localized or sentence-bound in their
approach as they read over their own writing. The first five writers refer
to reading their own writing and hint at their sense of audience. What
is particularly noteworthy is the fourth writer's understanding of her
text as a whole and her sense that she is reading it as her own audience;
and whereas the fifth writer is concerned with a specific feature of his
text (the use of one particular word), he is also thinking about an
external audience, in this case, his classmates. The last three statements
represent examples of how writers use texts other than their own or
ones they have written previously for purposes of acquiring additional
ideas to include in a text and for possible stylistic devices. They refer to
the type of reading which often must be done as reports, critical essays,
or scholarly articles are written.

    These influences of reading upon writing upon reading extend
beyond information, behavior, and style to attitude. As Scribner and

Cole and Schmandt-Besserat have noted, attitudes to reading and writing change as societies explore new uses of written literacy.[26] Just as societies' attitudes to writing change with changes in the uses of reading and writing, so do students' attitudes. For example, students will exhibit a change in attitude to writing as a result of recognizing a new use for it. One of our students, Diane, was quite recalcitrant about writing until she began a story, "Do You Like Me?" which was based in part upon her reading of Judy Blume's "Blubber," and in part upon her own experiences of being rejected by her peers. Most of her writing prior to this time had been simple narratives, usually based on things she had experienced (e.g., family trips to the mountains and picking apples); after this time she began to use her writing to explore her feelings (e.g., anger and loneliness associated with trying unsuccessfully to make new friends). Until she began writing on topics such as these, she could see little value in writing and complained, "There's nothing new to write about." In fact, during the interviews she talked about her transition from being a poor writer to becoming a good writer during the writing of her story, "Do You Like Me?" Similarly, students will develop an appreciation of the author's craft as they are exposed both to alternatives in their reading and the chance to consider, as well as explore, these various possibilities in their writing. In our study, for example, a number of the students began to include forewords and/or dedications in their books, after responding positively to another student's use of these features in her books. She, in turn, had decided to include such features after noticing that "published" books contained forewords and dedications.

Conclusion

The goal of this paper has been to address the question: What are the benefits or learning outcomes which arise from interrelating or connecting reading and writing? As we leave our present search we are convinced that numerous benefits accrue from connecting reading and writing. The research to date has substantiated that

—depending upon the measures employed to assess overall reading and writing achievement and attitude, the general correlation between reading and writing is moderate and fluctuates with age, schooling, and other factors.

—selected reading experiences definitely contribute to writing performance; likewise, selected writing experiences contribute to reading performance.

—writers acquire certain values and behaviors from reading and readers acquire certain values and behaviors from writing.

—successful writers integrate reading into their writing experience and successful readers integrate writing into their reading experience.

In the past, what seems to have limited our appreciation of reading-writing relationships has been our perspective, in particular a belief that there exists a general single answer to the question of how reading and writing are related. We are convinced, on the other hand, that the study of reading-writing connections involves appreciating how reading and writing work together in myriad ways as tools for information storage and retrieval, discovery and logical thought, communication, and self-indulgence. Literacy is at a premium when an individual uses reading and writing in concert for such purposes. Indeed, having to justify the integration of reading and writing is tantamount to having to validate the nature and role of literacy in society.

In closing, we would like to pose a question that we think needs to be considered—in our reading and writing instruction, are we preparing students to do the various types of reading and writing that have been discussed in this paper? In particular, are we preparing our students to be proficient readers of their own writing?

Notes

1. The observations of elementary students were made in conjunction with an extended study of reading-writing relationships conducted by Robert J. Tierney and Mary Ellen Giaccobe with the assistance of Avon Crismore, Margie Leys, and others.

2. T. Shanahan, "A Canonical Correlational Analysis of Learning to Read and Learning to Write: An Exploratory Analysis" (Ph.D. diss., University of Delaware, 1980).

3. W. Loban, *Language Development: Kindergarten through Grade Twelve.* (Urbana, Ill.: National Council of Teachers of English, 1976).

4. C. Read, "Pre-School Children's Knowledge of English Phonology," *Harvard Educational Review* 41 (1971): 1–34.

5. C. Chomsky, "Approaching Reading through Invented Spelling," in L. B. Resnick and P. A. Weaver, eds., *Theory and Practice of Early Reading*, vol. 2 (Hillsdale, N.J.: Erlbaum, 1979).

6. E. Ferreiro and A. Teberosky, *Literacy before Schooling*, trans. Karen G. Castro (Exeter, N.H.: Heinemann, 1982).

7. J. Harste, V. A. Woodward, and C. L. Burke, *Language Stories and Literacy Lessons* (Exeter, N.H.: Heinemann, 1984).

8. Harste, Woodward, and Burke, p. 218.

9. R. V. Allen, *Language Experiences in Communication* (Boston: Houghton Mifflin, 1976); S. Ashton-Warner, *Teacher* (New York: Simon & Schuster, 1963); M. Clay, "Early Childhood and Cultural Diversity in New Zealand," *The Reading Teacher* 29 (1976): 333–42; M. Montessori, *The Montessori Method* (New York: Schocken Books, 1964); R. G. Stauffer, *The Language-Experience Approach to the Teaching of Reading* (New York: Harper & Row, 1970); and D. Fader and M. Shaevitz, *Hooked on Books* (New York: Bantam, 1966).

10. M. Boutwell, "Reading and Writing Process: A Reciprocal Agreement," *Language Arts* 60 (1983): 723–30; L. Calkins, *Lessons from a Child* (Exeter, N.H.: Heinemann, 1983); M. E. Giacobbe, "A Writer Reads, a Reader Writes," in T. Newkirk and N. Atwell, eds., *Understanding Writing* (Chelmsford, Mass.: The Northeast Regional Exchange, Inc., 1982), pp. 114–25; and D. Graves and J. Hansen, "The Author's Chair," *Language Arts* 60 (1983): 176–82.

11. Calkins, p. 157.

12. F. Smith, "Reading Like a Writer," *Language Arts* 60 (1983): 558–67; and R. J. Tierney and P. D. Pearson, "Toward a Composing Model of Reading," *Language Arts* 60: 568–80.

13. Tierney and Pearson, p. 577.

14. B. M. Taylor and R. W. Beach, "The Effects of Text Structure Instruction on Middle-Grade Students' Comprehension and Production of Expository Text," *Reading Research Quarterly* 19 (1984): 134–46.

15. A. R. Petrosky, "From Story to Essay: Reading and Writing," *College Composition and Communication* 23 (1982): 19–36.

16. N. Atwell, "Writing and Reading Literature from the Inside Out," *Language Arts* 61 (1984): 240–52; and J. Staton, *Analysis of Dialogue Journal Writing as a Communicative Event,* vols. 1 and 2, Final Report to the National Institute of Education NIE-G-0122, 1982.

17. M. G. Eanet, "An Investigation of the REAP Reading/Study Procedure: Its Rationale and Efficacy," in P. D. Pearson and J. Hansen, eds., *Reading: Discipline Inquiry in Process and Practice,* Twenty-seventh Yearbook of the National Reading Conference (Clemson, S.C.: National Reading Conference, 1978); M. G. Eanet and A. V. Manzo, "REAP—A Strategy for Improving Reading/Writing/Study Skills," *Journal of Reading* 19 (1976): 647–52; R. A. Palmatier, "Comparison of Four Notetaking Procedures," *Journal of Reading* 14 (1971): 235–40, 250; R. A. Palmatier, "A Notetaking System for Learning," *Journal of Reading* 17 (1973): 36–39; and F. P. Robinson, *Effective Study,* rev. ed. (New York: Harper & Row, 1961).

18. T. H. Anderson, "Study Strategies and Adjunct Aids," in R. J. Spiro, B. C. Bruce, and W. F. Brewer, eds., *Theoretical Issues in Reading Comprehension: Perspectives from Cognitive Psychology, Artificial Intelligence, Linguistics and Education* (Hillsdale, N. J.: Erlbaum, 1980); H. F. Arnold, "The Comparative Effectiveness of Certain Study Techniques in the Field of History," *Journal of Educational Psychology* 33 (1942): 449–57; B. H. Bretzing and R. W. Kulhavy, "Note Taking and Depth of Processing," *Contemporary Educational Psychology* 4 (1979): 145–53; B. H. Bretzing and R. W. Kulhavy, "Note Taking and Passage Style," *Journal of Educational Psychology* 73 (1981): 242–50; M. Doctorow, M. C. Wittrock, and C. Marks, "Generative Processes in Reading Comprehension," *Journal of Educational Psychology* 70 (1978): 109–18; C. E. Germaine,

"The Value of the Written Paragraph Summary," *Journal of Educational Research* 3 (1921): 116–23; M. J. A. Howe and L. Singer, "Presentation Variables and Students' Activities in Meaningful Learning," *British Journal of Educational Psychology* 45 (1975): 52–61; R. W. Kulhavy, J. W. Dyer, and L. Silver, "The Effects of Note Taking and Test Expectancy on the Learning of Text Material," *Journal of Educational Research* 68 (1975): 363–65; C. B. Schultz and F. J. DiVesta, "Effects of Passage Organization and Note-Taking on the Selection of Clustering Strategies and on Recall of Textual Materials," *Journal of Educational Psychology* 63 (1972): 244–52; S. M. Shimmerlik and J. D. Nolan, "Reorganization and the Recall of Prose," *Journal of Educational Psychology* 68 (1976): 779–86; B. M. Taylor, "Text Structure and Children's Comprehension and Memory for Expository Material," *Journal of Educational Psychology* 74 (1982): 323–40; B. M. Taylor and S. Berkowitz, "Facilitating Children's Comprehension of Content Material," in *Perspectives on Reading Research and Instruction,* Twenty-ninth Yearbook of the National Reading Conference, ed. M. Kamil and A. Moe (Washington, D.C.: National Reading Conference, Inc., 1980); and W. Todd and C. C. Kessler, "Influence of Response Mode, Sex, Reading Ability and Level of Difficulty on Four Measures of Recall on Meaningful Written Material," *Journal of Educational Psychology* 62 (1971): 229–34.

19. W. E. Combs, "Some Further Effects and Implications of Sentence-Combining Exercises for the Secondary Language Arts Curriculum" (Ph.D. diss., University of Minnesota, 1975); R. Crews, "A Linguistic versus a Traditional Grammar Program—The Effects on Written Sentence Structure and Comprehension," *Educational Leadership* 29 (1971): 145–49; S. M. Howie, "A Study of the Effects of Sentence-Combining and Writing Ability and Reading Level of Ninth Grade Students" (Ph.D. diss., University of Colorado, 1979); B. C. Machie, "The Effects of a Sentence-Combining Program on the Reading Comprehension and Written Composition of Fourth Grade Students" (Ph.D. diss., Hofstra University, New York, 1982); J. W. Ney, "The Hazards of the Course: Sentence Combining in Freshman English," *English Record* 27 (1976): 70–77; A. Obenchain, "Effectiveness of the Precise Essay Question in Programming the Sequential Development of Written Composition Skills and the Simultaneous Development of Critical Reading Skills" (Master's thesis, George Washington University, St. Louis, 1971); and S. B. Straw and R. Schreiner, "The Effect of Sentence Manipulation on Subsequent Measures of Reading and Listening," *Reading Research Quarterly* 17 (1982): 339–52.

20. W. E. Combs, "Examining the Fit of Practice in Syntactic Manipulation and Scores of Reading Comprehension," in D. Daiker, A. Kerek, and M. Morenberg, eds., *Sentence-Combining and the Teacher of Writing* (Conway, Ark.: Univ. of Central Arkansas, 1979); and S. L. Stotsky, "Sentence-Combining as a Curricular Activity: Its Effect on Written Language Development and Reading Comprehension," *Research in the Teaching of English* 9 (1975): 30–71.

21. C. N. Dixon, "Inferences About a Basis for Comprehension: Beginning Reader" (Paper presented at the National Reading Conference, St. Petersburg, Florida, 1978); and B. Eckhoff, "How Reading Affects Children's Writing," *Language Arts* 60 (1983): 607–16.

22. E. Geva and R. J. Tierney, "Text Engineering: The Influence of Manipulated Compare-Contrast Selections" (Paper presented at the American Educational Research Association Annual Meeting, New Orleans, 1984); and C. Bereiter

and M. Scardamalia, "Learning about Writing from Reading," *Written Communication* 1 (1984): 163–88.

23. C. J. Gordon and C. Braun, "Story Schemata: Metatextual Aid to Reading and Writing," in J. A. Niks and L. A. Harris, eds., *New Inquiries in Reading: Research and Instruction,* Thirty-first Yearbook of the National Reading Conference (Rochester, N. Y.: National Reading Conference, 1982).

24. N. N. Spivey, "Discourse Synthesis: Constructing Texts in Reading and Writing" (Ph.D. diss., University of Texas, 1983); J. C. Birnbaum, "A Study of Reading and Writing Behaviors of Selected Fourth Grade and Seventh Grade Students" (Ph.D. diss., Rutgers University, 1981); and J. C. Birnbaum, "The Reading and Composing Behavior of Selected Fourth- and Seventh-Grade Students," *Research in the Teaching of English* 16 (1982): 241–60.

25. M. Atwell, "The Evolution of Text: The Interrelationship of Reading and Writing in the Composing Process" (Ph.D. diss., Indiana University, 1980); Birnbaum, "A Study"; Birnbaum, "Reading and Composing"; S. Perl, "The Composing Processes of Unskilled College Writers," *Research in the Teaching of English* 13 (1979): 317–36; and N. Sommers, "Revision Strategies of Student Writers and Experienced Adult Writers," *College Composition and Communication* 31 (1980): 378–88.

26. S. Scribner and M. Cole, *The Psychology of Literacy* (Cambridge: Harvard Univ. Press, 1981); and D. Schmandt-Besserat, "The Earliest Precursor of Writing," *Scientific American* 6 (1981): 238.

Reflective Thought: The Connection between Reading and Writing

June Cannell Birnbaum
State of New Jersey Department of Education

Why are students who are better writers than their peers also usually better readers, and vice versa? By what means do experiences in one written language process influence experiences in the other? The answer to both questions is suggested by recent independent studies of better readers and of better writers. Investigators in both fields have repeatedly characterized the more proficient as more reflective in their engagements with written language than their less proficient peers. Both better readers and better writers seem to take control of written language, formulating better questions and solutions about the unfolding text and continually monitoring their success or failure in constructing meaning in or from print.

Studies of readers reveal that the more skilled are more aware of their cognitive strategies while comprehending texts. J. A. Langer, who reviewed many of these studies, referred to this ability of watching oneself read as using a "third eye."[1] As A. Brown, J. Campione, and A. Day reported, better readers use the feedback from this mechanism to vary their strategies for improved comprehension.[2] Skilled readers seem to construct more appropriate hypotheses as they read, to carry along better questions, and to recognize more quickly when to abandon incorrect hypotheses or to reread when too many questions remain unanswered.[3] In contrast, less skilled readers seem unaware of their mental processes and unable to vary their strategies in accord with the demands of a text.[4] These studies suggest that better readers are more purposeful in their approach, more aware of alternative strategies and solutions in their reading, and more willing to revise their constructions of meaning. Indeed, E. Lunzer and T. Dolan concluded from their four-year study of several hundred British junior and secondary school readers that comprehension is "merely an index of the ability and willingness to pause and reflect on what one is reading."[5] Moreover, research shows that older readers (fifth and sixth graders) respond to the style, or craft, of writing while younger readers respond more globally.[6]

Similarly, studies of better writers show them more able to pause and deliberate over written language and to see a wide range of alternative solutions to a rhetorical problem. Donald Graves has described the reflective behaviors of more advanced second graders, as opposed to the reactive behaviors of less developed writers at the same age level, as the ability to pause and rehearse a mental plan before beginning to write.[7] His longitudinal study of children in grades 1 through 4 revealed that one mark of development was the extent to which students revised their writing—surely a product of reflecting over their texts.[8] G. Kress, who studied the development of writing ability in Australian children (age 6 through 14), concluded that a critical component was the child's recognition of the need for a shift from the extemporaneous, context-bound characteristics of oral language to the purposeful and more abstract requirements of written language.[9] Studies of secondary and college students underscore the need for this shift. They describe better writers as reflective because they tend to delay longer to develop a plan for their writing; pause at major turning points in their drafts to consider a wider range of rhetorical choices;[10] and view their drafts as tentative and subject to their revision.[11] Linda Flower and John Hayes ascribe to skilled advertising writers, for example, a capacity to set their own rhetorical goals and a monitor that assesses the success of their strategies for attaining them.

That investigators in each field have independently linked reflective behavior, or metacognitive awareness and control, to skilled reading and writing offers strong support for Vygotsky's insistence on the need to make written language the object of deliberate attention in order to elaborate the web of meaning in written texts.[12] And if, as these studies show, reflective thinking is central to proficiency in written language, that explains why so many researchers have found that subjects tend to be at comparable levels in reading and writing.[13] The more proficient readers and writers have developed a stance toward written language that generalizes to most engagements with it, although they might respond negatively to certain contexts. They are simply better thinkers in relation to written language. They know how and what to think about while reading and writing. Moreover, these subjects' tendency to reflect over their experiences allows them to extract more information from those experiences and to further elaborate their schemata for forms and content of discourse. Finally, this same tendency probably accounts for crossovers between the two processes. As their experiences with written language deepen and broaden, young readers and writers gradually develop a positive view of themselves as in control of the processes involved and achieve an aesthetic distance that allows them to read with a "writer's eye" and to write with a "reader's eye." It seems likely that this sensitivity to the dual problems of the writer and reader and their potential solutions leads them to transfer knowledge derived from one process to the other.

It is not enough, however, to identify a characteristic associated with more proficient reading and writing or just to speculate how it might influence these processes. Instead we need to understand the components of the reflective thinking process, how it manifests itself in observed reading and writing behaviors, and, most important, how we can foster its growth in young readers and writers. The purpose of this paper is to examine all of these ambitions.

Reflective Thinking—A Psychological Construct

Although the widespread characterization of better readers and writers as reflective thinkers is a relatively recent one, the importance of reflective thought in problem solving has long been a major theme in the psychological literature. In 1963, J. Kagan, B. L. Rosman, D. Day, J. Albert, and W. Phillips, seeking to explain differences in cognitive styles, or ways of perceiving and processing experiences, found underlying differences among the conceptual tempos of their subjects. They termed these differences the "reflective-impulsive dimension."[14] According to these investigators, reflectiveness is rooted in expectation of mastery rather than anxiety about failure. Reflective thinkers tend to pause and deliberate over alternative solutions to problems when these are simultaneously available and to inhibit incorrect hypotheses before reporting public solutions. In contrast, the impulsives' anxiety over failure leads them to seize the first possible solution to a problem and give it public report. Thus reflectives seem able to exert a control over their cognitive processes that impulsives seem to lack.

Although there has been controversy over the motivations underlying the reflective dimension and the validity of the instruments used to assess it, the relevance of conceptual tempo to reading and writing behaviors seems clear. And there is a large body of literature relating reading achievement to reflectiveness as measured by Kagan's Matching Familiar Figures; few, however, have investigated the relation of reflectiveness to writing.[15]

Consider, as well, John Dewey's description of reflective thought, written nearly a half century ago. He described the influence of prior knowledge upon the problem-solving process and the contribution of reflection to the development of new knowledge. According to Dewey, the reflective thinker defines a problem and identifies a purpose, deliberates over prior experiences in view of the new condition in order to develop an appropriate hypothesis, then tests it and observes the consequences, and finally reflects over the experience to "extract the net meanings which are the capital stock for dealing with further experiences."[16] Dewey's description of reflective thinking translates easily to reading and writing. In fact, if we substitute currently fashionable terms such as "schemata," "scripts," or "stored plans" for "net meanings," we have a description of skilled reading and writing comparable to many advanced today, as well as an explanation of how reflective behavior probably enhances development of schemata for written language.

The Development of Reflective Reading and Writing Behavior

Clearly, the quality of reflective reading and writing changes with cognitive development. However, as findings by Lunzer and Dolan in reading and by Graves and Kress in writing show, reflective stances toward written language can develop very early.[17] As my investigation of fourth and seventh graders revealed, reflective reading and writing are observable behaviors in both age groups but also qualitatively different in terms of the range of concerns addressed by each age group.[18] Furthermore, an ongoing study of college-age readers and writers, both basic and advanced, reveals that reflectiveness is again associated with more proficient reading and writing but manifests itself in awareness of more subtle rhetorical problems of written language. I will illustrate this progression by providing examples from each study.

To watch the reflective mind at work, consider Matthew, a nine-year-old, who read and wrote both silently and orally in a variety of contexts while part of the study. In the following excerpt taken from an oral composing episode, the length of his prewriting pause and his range of deliberations parallel both his observed behaviors and his retrospective explanations of the silent episodes. Therefore, the following protocol seems representative of his normal planning. Before he put pen to paper, he voiced the following concerns:

> Now, should I write a sports story? No—a mystery? Yeah! . . . Now, I'm thinking of a subject. . . . Pick the name Joe—okay? Now a mystery—diamonds? No . . . gold? No—well—maybe gold—I guess so. Okay, the gold is going to be stolen from the New York Bank. How about—what bank? Uhm—let's see—a made-up bank? . . .

Okay! the Eleventh National Bank. All right, now—the robbery of
gold from the Eleventh National Bank. Now who's going to rob it?
Well, that's the mystery. (Sighs) . . . Now, Joe has to be going
somewhere . . . Okay, here it is (begins to write).

As Matthew wrote while voicing his concerns, his longer pauses occurred between major segments of thought during which he reread and
then planned the next section. The following is a typical remark made
when he decided to substitute one segment for another that he had
planned: "No, no—before I can say that, I have to tell how Joe knew
the robbers, otherwise they [the readers] won't understand." Matthew
reveals both a capacity to consider a range of modes and topics and an
ability to distance himself from his text and evaluate it as a reader.

Interestingly, although Matthew's text was subsequently rated high
by independent raters, he rated it as inferior and signaled his judgment
with a giggle and a sardonic use of the formulaic ending "lived happily
ever after." When asked why, Matthew replied, "This isn't my story. I
would have done it differently, but I didn't have time. I should have
fixed it in the middle when I got a different idea, but I couldn't do it
here. I didn't have time." Matthew's evaluation of his writing not only
offered insight into the reflective mind at work but should make us
wary of generalizations about writing behavior based on a single sample.

The reflectiveness revealed by this nine-year-old was magnified in
the more proficient seventh-grade students. Fred, for example, stretched
his oral composing episode over three weeks as he struggled, first to
limit his topic, then to rearrange and rephrase segments of his text to,
in his words, "get it right." In response to my query about the meaning
of "right," he said, "So the ideas are in order and it's worded the way I
like it." Another seventh grader revealed a similar consciousness of
stylistic questions as well as an awareness of her own habitual strategies—
another mark of reflectiveness—in a silent composing episode. As she
composed four paragraphs of her text, her eyes returned repeatedly to
a phrase in the first sentence and she even moved her pen back to it;
yet she did not change it. Finally, she shrugged and turned her attention
to completing her text. Later, she explained that she knew the phrase
"to dinner and to see a play" was not parallel, but she could not revise
it without restructuring the entire sentence. Said Kathy, "That's a bad
habit of mine. I start a sentence one way and then change my mind.
Most times, I leave it until I finish writing and then go back to change it
unless it keeps bothering me like [sic] this one did." Not only does
Kathy's explanation reveal that she monitors her composing behavior
but also that, like Matthew and Fred, she views the text as subject to her
revision and herself as in control of the process.

These students demonstrated a similar control over their reading processes. In comparison to their less proficient peers, they deliberated longer and attended to a wider range of criteria while selecting a text, referred more often to their ongoing predictions concerning the text during postreading discussions, and often cited other experiences with both reading and writing as standards for evaluating texts. Matthew, for example, selected a biography of Elizabeth Blackwell, the first woman doctor, from three texts, and later offered this explanation and evaluation:

> I felt like reading a biography and not a mystery (referring to a historical account of a supposedly haunted house) or a science report . . . this wasn't a very good biography. I've read better ones about players like Willie Mays and Hank Aaron and about politicians like John Kennedy and Robert. They tell more about the people's lives. This one stopped too soon. I wanted to know more about her. . . . The only good part was when they told about how she went blind in one eye.

In fact, at that point in the story, Matthew had physically manifested his engagement in the text by closing one eye as he read. Later he voluntarily referred to his action and explained, "I just wanted to see what it would be like," revealing an awareness of his behaviors while reading. Although the more proficient fourth and seventh graders frequently cited predictions and responses to events in the reading, the seventh graders also tended to incorporate references to the arrangement of ideas and aspects of style, reflecting closer attention to the shape of language. Kathy, for example, slowed her reading rate considerably while reading one passage in a story and frowned when she reached the end. When discussing the story, she mentioned her shift in behavior and explained, "That was an important part and I wanted to get it right. Besides, I liked his style there—the way he used his words. I didn't want it to end." Not only does Kathy's explanation indicate that she is monitoring her behavior and continually evaluating the text but it suggests that her careful attention to her own word choices in writing is paralleled by her attention to other authors' word choices in reading. It seems likely that her consciousness of written language in one process informs her engagement in the other and that her reflective mental behavior promotes this transaction.

The reciprocal influence of the two processes emerged repeatedly in statements made by the more proficient—and reflective—readers and writers, varying in degree with the age of the subjects. The differences that distinguished the two grade levels in their discussion of texts were also evident in their references to experiences in one process that influenced the other. The younger students tended to refer to global characteristics. Yet some were quite sophisticated. For example, Patti, a fourth grader who often incorporated reading experiences into discussion of her writing and vice versa, drew on her knowledge of herself as author to question another author's intention. Having completed a factual narration about a house that suggested it might really be haunted, she said, "But I don't understand this. The author wants us to think that ghosts really exist. I write stories like this all the time—with ghosts and magic—but I make them up. They don't really exist. I know that." Thus Patti imposed her own version of reality, created in her writing, upon the world she encountered in her reading. Fred, a seventh grader, also drew on previous experience in each process but was more willing to suspend disbelief in his reading because of his experiences in writing. In a session where I played, to paraphrase Walker Gibson, "a dumb listener" concerning the psychological motivations of a character, Fred became so agitated about my failure to understand a character's actions in the "Sound of Thunder" that he said: "Look, I know about these things. I read people like Asimov, Clarke, Heinlein, Lewis, and I read *The Martian Chronicles.* And I write stories about Vestuvius [his fictional planet]. It doesn't matter what Travis wants to do—there are rules set and he has to follow them."

Perhaps a statement by Kathy offered the most direct evidence of a reflective user of written language deliberating over experiences in one process and intending to transfer that knowledge to the other. As she completed a third draft of a poem, she commented, "I've been reading a lot of Nikki Giovanni's poems lately, and I'm trying to use images in the same way."

I have drawn my examples from these grades for two reasons: until recently, those were the age groups that I had studied most closely; and they offered concrete examples of reflective behaviors in children before secondary and college age. However, in preliminary findings from a study of twenty college-age basic and experienced readers and writers, the differences evident in younger children emerged again. The better the reader or writer, the more likely he or she is to reflect over engagements in written language. The subjects come from three categories: freshmen, who are required to enroll in a noncredit writing tutorial for one semester before taking regular English 101; students ranging from freshmen to seniors who elect to take a five- or eight-week writing tutorial for credit; and juniors and seniors who have qualified to work as peer tutors in the writing center. The students either work with me on their writing in twice-weekly tutorials limited to four people or, in the case of peer tutors, on developing instructional materials for the center. Because the students write in response to readings or work on papers for other courses, there are opportunities to observe their reading and writing behaviors in a variety of modes. The small-group tutorials also afford opportunities to probe attitudes and obtain reading and writing histories.

Each group displays its own constellations of characteristics regarding the extent and quality of previous reading and writing experiences and the degree to which students have learned to monitor their success in transactions with texts. In addition, the presence or absence of the tendency to reflect over and extract more from experiences in written language seems to have contributed to a gradual perception of self as a good or poor reader and writer and to correlative expectations for success or failure in reading and writing. For example, the freshmen in the noncredit writing tutorial are also enrolled in a noncredit reading course. They report limited reading and even less writing experience in high school and reveal very little knowledge of major historical, literary, scientific, or artistic works or of figures or events that make up our cultural experience and that should inform college reading and writing. Most label themselves as poor readers and writers. Of course, the label may be the result of being placed in remedial classes at the college level; for most, however, the roots go much deeper, and students, initially at least, express preferences for almost any activity other than reading and writing. In contrast, students who elect a writing tutorial for credit have had much more varied and extensive reading and writing experiences and view themselves as good readers and writers, though they are aware of areas in need of improvement—all hallmarks of reflectiveness. That they enroll of their own volition shows that they are seeking opportunities to write rather than avoiding them. The peer tutors share these characteristics, but, in addition, they often express the desire to teach writing in order to learn about their own and others' writing process. Moreover, they view themselves as capable of improving not only their own writing but that of others as well.

At this age level, the more proficient readers and writers again reveal a wider knowledge of the shape and content of discourse that allows them to comprehend and compose a more diverse range of texts. Especially striking is their capacity to read and write texts that require abstraction from particulars and analysis of wholes into parts. On those occasions when they fail, they often signal their prior evaluation of their success by voluntarily alluding to that segment prior to the group discussion of the text. This ability to logically relate superordinate to subordinate ideas, a necessity for most college reading and writing assignments, distinguishes them from their less skilled peers, who tend to cling to chronological organizations. Apparently, the more proficient students' conscious attention to written language has led to a recognition that more often in this mode than in oral language the logical entailment of ideas predominates over a temporal ordering of events. Moreover, even in the latter case, events may be reordered from the original perception of their sequence.

The more skilled also have learned to predict the rhetorical demands of different academic disciplines and to adjust their reading and writing strategies accordingly. For example, Robbie, a junior and a peer tutor, was asked to select two passages of expository prose taken from psychology and history that would be representative of those fields and useful for tutorial readings. When asked what features besides vocabulary led her to select each passage, she replied:

> Well, this looks as if it's for psychology because it gives a hypothesis and then a plan for testing it and then gives the results. . . . This one is history because it gives a general statement about the causes of an event and then talks about each cause in detail . . .

Clearly, the vocabulary of the texts helped, but Robbie was still able to articulate her knowledge of how ideas are arranged in different disciplines. That kind of knowledge, derived from reflection over written texts, enhances the probability of activating relevant schemata and promoting predictive reading and writing.

The more proficient college writers also reveal a wider range of stored plans for different rhetorical purposes and audiences. Sarah, a senior, faced with simultaneous assignments to write an autobiography as part of an application for an internship in Israel and an analysis of Anäis Nin's work, regularly switched purpose and strategy as she talked about each text. Concerning the autobiography, she said:

> I've got to present myself as adventurous, willing to live among different people—but I can't say that. It has to show in the experiences I've had. Maybe I should highlight being an Orthodox Jew from a yeshiva who came to a secular university, kept my religion, but still ended up as yearbook editor and the only roommate who kept kosher in an apartment with Christians. . . . Does this sound too formal? I want me to come through but not be too casual.

Concerning the literary analysis of Nin she said:

> I'm going to ignore her fiction and concentrate on her diaries. But I need a thesis to control my paper and my research. Later I may change it [the thesis], but for now I am going to base it on this quote [about Nin's responsibility to all women as spokesperson]. That sums her up. It might be a good way to start my paper. . . . I have to be careful about how I write this. [The instructor's] a feminist, and some of them don't like Nin. I thought she was wonderful.

Sarah's comments reveal that she has developed a repertoire of writing strategies and varies them in accordance with different purposes and audiences. For the first paper, she adopted an implicit thesis that would guide her choice of which events to include in her autobiography, and settled on an appropriate voice. For the second, she tentatively selected an explicit thesis to develop in her paper and rather pragmatically decided to be guarded in view of her audience. Both comments about her writing reveal a writer who sees herself as in control of her text.

The more skilled freshmen, who elect to enroll in tutorials for credit, lack some of this sophistication because they have less experience in reading and writing college-level texts. Nevertheless, they share a tendency to monitor and evaluate their engagements with written language and often volunteer their assessments of their success with a text. For example, Lisa prefaced her reading of her essay with positive remarks about her choice of topic and organization but then turned to some sentences that she intended to revise:

> I've got a couple of sentences here that are terrible. Listen to this: "What you do is you go to the instructor and ask for help." That's awful—it's think-write! You know? It's the way the idea came into my head and I just put it down the way I'd say it—not the way I should write it. Well, I'll have to fix them.

Lisa offered these evaluations before reading her paper to the group or receiving any feedback, indicating that she could assess her own writing by serving as her first reader, that she knew there was a clear difference between spoken and written language, and that she saw herself as capable of revising her text—again, marks of the reflective writer.

In contrast, her less skilled counterparts who are required to enroll often seem surprised or confused, especially in the first weeks of the semester, when they examine their comprehension of a text in discussion with their peers and tutor or when they read their own texts to the group. They often do not know that they have not comprehended a passage until asked to verbalize their understanding. A typical remark illustrates the problem: "I read it, but now I can't remember what it said." Reading seems to be a passive process in which they cast their eyes over the text but do not assess their comprehension of it. Similarly, when these students read their texts to the group, they often stop and question their own words: "What does this say?" In most cases, it is not illegible writing that gives them pause but the unintelligibility of their writing. Yet they are unaware of the problem until asked to read the text to an audience. Apparently, they become so enmeshed in the demands of written language that they cannot distance themselves from it and pause to evaluate their efforts to create meaning. During the semester, development of the capacity to monitor their reading and writing behaviors, evidenced by their first attempts to volunteer specific comments about texts in advance of the discussion, is an important signpost of their growing control of written language.

A final characteristic shared by the more proficient college readers and writers and almost totally absent in their less proficient counterparts is the tendency to refer to crossovers between the reading and writing processes. Here they often show themselves more like their skilled counterparts in fourth and seventh grade than like their less skilled college-aged counterparts. Because of their age and wider experience, however, they are more analytical and articulate in their explanations of crossovers between the two processes than younger students. In the following excerpt, taken from two sessions, Paul's memories of important experiences with oral and written language underscore the interplay among all language processes that seems to be the foundation for the tendency to reflect over these experiences. Paul is a senior, an English major, and an aspiring novelist.

> Any ability I have to put words together comes from my parents. I still remember those discussions at dinner—we all had to talk up. My mom and dad are great readers so we talked about everything. . . . [Concerning his many literature papers:] I can handle them pretty well. The more you read and write them the better you get and the faster you get. First I need a thesis—that's my map even though I keep tinkering with it as I go along. I can turn out a five- or six-page paper in a couple of hours and get an A or B. . . . [Concerning his reading and writing of fiction:] I wrote my first novel when I was in sixth grade. I go back and read it every so often to see what I was like then. . . . I remember that in eleventh grade we read a book of short stories called *Points of View*.[19] I was fascinated by all the angles a writer could take on a story. I started experimenting, but I really got started in my senior year in a creative writing class. The teacher was pretty good—let you try out different ideas and angles. That's what I'm doing here [points to his fiction manuscript]. Each section has a different point of view and form. The first section is just dialogue—no narrative; the next has some narrative and by the end it's going to be almost Victorian— lots of description. . . . Reading can be dangerous. When I am really impressed by an author, I start to write like him. For a while after I read Proust, I wandered around trying to figure how to write the feel of my memories. . . . But some novels offend me. They are a waste of time. We just had to read two pulp novels for a course. The professor wanted us to see what they are like. They were so dull—no style, just predictable plot.

Paul is quoted at length because at the end of his college career he exemplifies much that we strive for in educating for literacy. He is at home in the world of written language. As he shuttles between reading and writing, he extrapolates from one process and uses that knowledge in the other. Notice how he tends to return to and to reexamine pivotal points in his development as a reader and writer, to underscore those that contributed to his growth, even those that taught him that there were things, like pulp novels, that he could dismiss as a waste of time. Perhaps we might speculate that reflection over the latter led Paul to conclude that there was nothing to reflect upon. Although most of our students will not aspire to be novelists, they do need to develop this kind of mental stance toward written language if they are to become skilled readers and writers. How can we foster these behaviors in the majority instead of the minority of our students? That question raises important issues for research and teaching.

Implications for Research

Although studies of readers and of writers suggest that abilities in both processes tend to develop in tandem, we have too little research on individual development in both processes. First, we need to identify the factors that promote or inhibit growth in each process and to learn whether level of cognitive development places parallel constraints on ability to read and write certain forms of discourse. Second, if, as recent studies in both fields have shown, children move from control of chronological organization to hierarchical organization of ideas, what features within these patterns of organization facilitate or hinder their processing of texts? If we know what children are able to comprehend and compose at each stage—allowing for differences in range of experiences and interests—we can begin to set reasonable goals for children at each level and also begin to prepare them for the next level. Finally, if the capacity to reflect over experiences in written language is a characteristic associated with more skilled readers and writers and is the means by which they develop more elaborated schemata, allowing them to read and write in varied modes about a range of topics, what are its roots and why do some children develop this mental stance while others do not? Many of the recent ethnographic studies of developing literacy in young children have begun to provide answers to these questions. However, we need additional case studies of older students as readers and writers, as well as longitudinal studies like Loban's but designed to specify forms of discourse that students at different ages are able to comprehend and compose and to identify the constellation of personal, academic, and nonacademic characteristics that promote reflective reading and writing behavior. Findings from these kinds of studies will provide a much more specific description of the course of written language development.

Applications for Teaching

Meanwhile, data from recent research suggest three recommendations
for teachers: First, rejoin the teaching of reading and writing, and view
one as a mechanism for developing the other. Second, use current
information concerning the cognitive capacities of students at different
stages, and provide varied written language experiences that will fully
develop those capacities, while also providing experiences that will
begin to move students toward the next level, recognizing that developing new written language skills is somewhat like learning to ride a
bicycle—the learner falls off many times before attaining his or her
balance. Third, promote reflective behavior toward written language,
showing students not only what to think but *how* to think while reading
and writing, by asking questions that demand not just recall but higher-
level reasoning and predicting, and by sometimes demonstrating reflective reading and writing behaviors. To make these recommendations
concrete, I offer the following techniques, none of them new and
certainly not the only ways to achieve these goals, as suggestions for
teaching reading and writing as cognitive processes.

During the prereading stage we can ask students to look at the title
of a text and sample it in order to predict its form and content, then to
recall what they know not only about the topic but about the way ideas
are usually arranged in that mode. We can also provide background
information about the form and content of this type of discourse so that
students can better anticipate what they will be reading. Also, students
should sometimes be given a choice of texts so that they can learn the
value of predictive prereading behavior. We can also occasionally demonstrate the reading process by reading a text aloud with the students,
pausing between major segments to ask not only what the author has
said but why he or she arranged ideas and selected certain stylistic
features rather than others. Then the discussion can move to predictions
concerning the next section, based on the previous passage and the
first words of the next segment. For example, "The author begins with
'In spite of these similarities . . .' What do you think the section will be
about?"

The same type of intervention can be accomplished in silent reading
by developing written materials that contain these kinds of questions
between segments of a text. Following the reading, students can reflect
over their experience through questions that lead them to assess the
accuracy of their predictions and the adequacy of their strategies for
constructing the meaning of the text. As students compare their interpretations of a text with others', they become aware that some texts,

such as literary forms, allow more latitude than others, such as science texts. They also learn to vary their reading strategies to accord with the differing demands of each discipline. Through these types of activities, we not only promote a view of reading as an active cognitive process but enhance writing development as well. By deliberately focusing students' attention on the shape of written language as well as on its content, we make students aware of rhetorical choices that they should consider in their own writing.

Similar techniques can be used to teach students how and what to think about while writing their own texts. During the *prewriting* stage, we can lead students to deliberate over alternative topics, rather than seizing the first idea that occurs to them. We can demystify the process by explaining the different approaches to writing used by skilled writers: e.g., some explore topics on paper, using a first draft analogously to prewriting exploration; others plan mentally prior to writing, creating a map before beginning; both view drafts as tentative and subject to revision. In addition we can show students how to explore the subject for related ideas and possible patterns of organization in view of their audiences by providing heuristics that teach them how to ask appropriate questions concerning the topic and by allowing sufficient time for them to reflect over their texts. During the *composing* stage, teachers can intervene when students pause and seem uncertain of how to proceed. Appropriate questions or comments help writers to re-see what they have written and either recognize the need to rethink it or select and plan the next segment of text. During *postcomposing* discussions, the practice of asking writers to read their texts aloud to a group of peers who respond with written and oral comments seems to enhance both reflective reading and writing behaviors in several ways. First, the knowledge that the writer will have to read his or her text to peers underscores the reality of an audience who will respond with questions and comments. This knowledge causes most writers to deliberate longer over the shape and content of their texts and to attempt to assess them from the reader's viewpoint. Second, well-trained peer groups learn to listen very carefully and to take note of features to be questioned or commented upon, for they know that global responses will not be accepted. Instead, through demonstration and explanation, students learn how to formulate higher-level questions indicative of critical thinking. These are skills required for reading as well as for writing. Third, the writer learns to respond to this level of questioning and to justify choices and arrangements of ideas. Finally, revision, in light of peer and teacher comments, fosters attention to written language from the viewpoints of reader and writer. Students learn to set more inclusive goals that include the multiple considerations of the exploration of ideas, their arrangement, and their presentation in view of the needs of audiences.

Not only the content of teachers' comments but their style and pacing can promote more reflective behavior in students, and in turn develop richer knowledge about the forms and content of discourse in different disciplines. By allowing a sometimes painful silence between questions and answers in the classroom and by allotting sufficient time between assignments and deadlines, we can send the message that it is all right to stop and take time to think or reflect over engagements with written language.

However, in order to demonstrate these kinds of behaviors, we, as teachers, must become more reflective about our own instructional methods. We must begin to monitor our classroom behaviors and constantly assess the effectiveness of our strategies in view of our goals concerning students' development of written language proficiency. Just as we must shift from an emphasis upon the lower-level skills in written language to an emphasis on higher-level cognitive skills, we must shift our primary focus from the daily tasks of classroom management, and from our concern that all students will master the "basics," presently construed as minimal literacy skills, to their mastery of the real basics, the ability to use higher-level cognitive skills in reading and writing and to develop new, more powerful ways of reflecting upon their experiences in reading and writing.

Notes

1. J. A. Langer, "The Reading Process," in A. Berger and H. A. Robinson, eds., *Secondary School Reading: What Research Reveals for Classroom Practices* (Urbana, Ill.: ERIC Clearinghouse on Reading and Communication Skills and National Conference on Research in English, 1982).

2. A. Brown, J. Campione, and J. Day, "Learning to Learn: On Training Students to Learn from Texts," *Educational Research* 10 (1981): 14–25.

3. A. Collins, A. Brown, J. Morgan, and W. Brewer, *The Analysis of Reading Tasks and Texts,* Center for the Study of Reading Teaching Report 43. (Urbana, Ill.: University of Illinois, 1979).

4. E. M. Markman, "Realizing That You Don't Understand: Elementary School Children's Awareness of Inconsistencies," *Child Development* 50 (1979): 643–55.

5. E. Lunzer and T. Dolan, "Reading for Learning in the Secondary School," in A. Cashden, ed., *Language, Reading and Learning* (Oxford: Basil Blackwell, 1979).

6. Thomas L. Hilgers, "Toward a Taxonomy of Beginning Writers' Evaluative Statements on Written Compositions," *Written Communication* 1 (July 1984): 365–84.

7. D. Graves, "An Examination of the Writing Processes of Seven-Year-Old Children," *Research in the Teaching of English* 9 (1975): 227–41.

8. D. Graves, "Patterns of Child Control of the Writing Process," in R. D. Walshe, ed., *Donald Graves in Australia* (Exeter, N.H.: Heinemann, 1982).

9. G. Kress, *Learning to Write* (London: Routledge & Kegan Paul, 1982).

10. L. Flower and J. R. Hayes, "A Cognitive Process Theory of Writing," *College Composition and Communication* 32 (1981): 365–87; and S. Pianko, "Reflection: A Critical Component of the Composing Process," *College Composition and Communication* 30 (1979): 275–78.

11. R. Beach, "Self-Evaluation Strategies of Extensive Revisers and Nonrevisers," *College Composition and Communication* 27 (1976): 160–64; and C. Stallard, "An Analysis of the Writing of Good Student Writers" (Ph.D. diss., University of Virginia, 1972).

12. L. S. Vygotsky, *Thought and Language,* ed. and trans. E. Hanfmann and G. Vakars ([1934] Cambridge, Mass.: MIT Press, 1962).

13. J. C. Birnbaum, "A Study of the Reading and Writing Behaviors of Selected Fourth and Seventh Grade Students" (Ph.D. diss., Rutgers University, 1981); P. Evanechko, L. Ollila, and R. Armstrong, "An Investigation of the Relationship between Children's Performance in Written Language and Their Reading Ability," *Research in the Teaching of English* 8 (1974): 315–26; R. N. Evans, "The Relationship between the Reading and Writing of Syntactic Structures," *Research in the Teaching of English* 13 (1979): 129–35; M. H. Kunz, "The Relationship between Written Syntactic Attainment and Reading Ability in Seventh Graders" (Ph.D. diss., University of Pittsburgh, 1975, ED 113 710); W. F. Lazdowski, "Determining Reading Grade Levels from Analysis of Written Compositions" (Ph.D. diss., New Mexico State University, 1976, ED 127 590); and W. Loban, *Language Development: Kindergarten through Grade 12* (Urbana, Ill.: National Council of Teachers of English, 1976).

14. J. Kagan, B. L. Rosman, D. Day, J. Albert, and W. Phillips, "Information Processing in the Child: Significance of Analytic and Reflective Attitudes," *Psychological Monographs* 78, no. 578 (1963).

15. See Birnbaum, "A Study."

16. J. Dewey, *Experience and Education* ([1938] New York: Collier Books, 1974), 87.

17. Lunzer and Dolan; Graves, "An Examination of the Writing Processes" and "Patterns of Child Control"; and Kress.

18. See Birnbaum, "A Study"; and "The Reading and Composing Behavior of Selected Fourth- and Seventh-Grade Students," *Research in the Teaching of English* 16 (1982): 241–61.

19. *Points of View: An Anthology of Short Stories,* ed. James Moffett and Kenneth R. McElheny (New York: New American Library), 19.

Reading as a Writing Strategy: Two Case Studies

Cynthia L. Selfe
Michigan Technological University

Any self-conscious writer can affirm that reading and writing are connected at some basic level in the act of composing. Evidence of such connections is not only intuitively credible, but easily observable. Nevertheless, most of the observations that have been made on the subject are too general to be of much help in identifying the specific reading strategies involved in writing. Only during the last decade have researchers and teachers begun to explore and accurately map the complex interactions between reading and writing that manifest themselves in the act of composing. Donald Murray, for example, suggests to us that reading may be a kind of generative writing strategy.[1] He notes that writers act as their own "first readers," scanning and rescanning their own prose to evaluate the content, form, and language of the material they produce. Other research, however, suggests that not all of our students are equally successful in using reading as a productive writing strategy.

This paper tells the story of two student writers: Jim, highly apprehensive about the process of composing, and David, not at all apprehensive about writing. A careful look at the composing processes of these two students indicates that Jim, the highly apprehensive writer, employs a much more limited range of writing and reading strategies and employs them less productively in his writing than does David, the confident writer.

Background

Before we can discuss the reading and writing strategies of Jim and David, we must understand the concept of writing apprehension. The term "writing apprehension" was coined by John Daly and Michael Miller to describe a generalized tendency to experience "some form of anxiety when faced with the task of encoding written messages."[2] Students with high writing apprehension generally select academic majors and occupations they perceive as having lower writing demands, score lower on measures of self-concept and self-confidence, and are evaluated differently by classroom teachers than are low writing apprehensives.[3] Although research in writing apprehension has been done to define the theoretical construct of writing apprehension and to establish the validity of the Writing Apprehension Test (WAT), no substantive research has yet been done to define the relationship between writing apprehension and the reading processes students employ as they compose.

Methodology

The cases I report in this paper were collected in 1980 at the University of Texas at Austin. For a study on the writing processes of high and low writing apprehensives, I selected four high and four low apprehensives from a sample of eighty-six students who had taken the WAT.

During this study, I asked each of the eight subjects to attend at least four hour-and-a-half sessions designed to document the complex processes of composing using several different methods of observation:

> Session 1: I asked the students to detail, in a role-playing scenario, the processes they used when they wrote a typical freshman composition. This role-playing activity allowed students to practice the technique of thinking aloud (also called "composing aloud") as they wrote, before they engaged in the remaining sessions.

> Sessions 2 and 3: The students were asked to compose aloud in response to two carefully designed assignments (persuasive aim, narrative mode) such as they might encounter in a freshman English class.[4] Subjects were not given a time limit for their composing efforts. These sessions were videotaped, coded for the writing and reading behaviors that occurred, and transcribed in script form.

> Session 4: In this final session, I showed the eight subjects selected segments of their composing-aloud videotapes and asked them to try to recall the mental processes that they employed in the featured situations.[5]

Although this original study was completed in 1980, it was not until three years later, when Bruce Petersen asked me to explore some relationships between reading and writing, that I reexamined the data, believing that if basic connections between reading and writing did exist, they would have to be manifested in the composing-aloud sessions I had videotaped earlier. I was right; such connections were there and so evident that they begged for interpretation. I selected two representative subjects, one high and one low writing apprehensive, and reviewed all the data associated with their performances in a new light—recording, counting, and analyzing the reading strategies they used, the reasons they used these strategies, and the timing of their activities. I also took another look at the interviews I had conducted with these students and found that they had articulated the reading-writing connection for me.[6]

Findings

In some obvious ways, both Jim and David exhibited similar patterns of writing and reading activities. They both, for example, frequently interrupted their composing efforts to reread or rescan portions of their own prose. However, a closer look at the two subjects indicated that— because they came to tasks of *writing* with different attitudes, experiences, and skills—each *read* his materials for different purposes and in different ways during the composing sessions. In fact, the subjects' *writing* and *reading* strategies were so closely related that their attitudes toward writing, their past experiences with writing, and their perceptions of their own writing competence must be understood before we can hope to understand their reading activities during the composing process.

Approaching the Writing Task: Attitudes, Experiences, and Skills

Like the other individuals identified as highly apprehensive about writing in my original study, Jim exhibited a distinct dislike of academic writing and the reading activities that he saw as part of such writing. As he noted to the investigator in an early interview:

> I don't like to write; hardly at all I don't like to write. . . . I really don't think I ever have as far as I can remember . . . I don't like to read; I think that's probably part of it. Probably part of it is that I'm hyperactive, I guess. . . . So, if I'm going to sit down and be still or something . . . I'd rather go to sleep than to sit still and write or read or something like that.

Jim avoided writing in an academic setting by choosing those classes that required minimal or no writing and by establishing elaborate rituals of procrastination that allowed him to put off writing as long as possible. He also avoided writing outside of school:

I: Do you write outside of class a lot? Letters? A diary?

J: No. I write a letter once a year, say. Every once in a while.

This attitude was common to the other highly apprehensive writers involved in the study as well. For instance, only one highly apprehensive writer in Jim's original group, a young woman who wrote regular letters to her family, reported engaging in *any* writing activities outside of school at all. She made a point of contrasting her family's friendly reception of her letters to her teachers' evaluative reception of her academic papers.

Jim, like his fellow apprehensives, traced his current apprehension to two sources: limited writing instruction in grade school and high school and negative evaluations of his papers by past teachers. In interviews, Jim reported doing very little writing in grade school and saw his high school writing instruction as less than complete:

I: Did you write a lot in high school?

J: I took one course in paragraph writing. I took a paragraph-writing course and an essay-writing course. And I think that was about all the real writing I did. . . . I can never remember having to write a two- or three-page paper in high school.

I: What did you learn in your essay class?

J: I don't remember . . . I must not listen. . . . I didn't like that class at all; matter of fact I hated that class. . . . I don't think I got a whole lot out of it. . . . See, I don't ever remember her telling us . . . I mean, anything about how to write. She didn't hardly ever write anything up on the board telling us stuff, not that I remember. I know I didn't take notes on anything. . . . I don't really think I know how [to write]. That's because I write like I talk. That's the only thing I know how to do. I don't ever remember being taught how to write, really.

In Jim's opinion, his lack of writing instruction in grade school and secondary school contributed to the negative evaluations he received on his papers from his college teachers. Because he had not mastered a number of writing skills that he knew to be important in producing successful academic prose, Jim *expected* to fail on the written assignments he handed in to college teachers. Unfortunately, because he avoided situations in which he could practice writing and rushed pell-mell through those writing assignments he was forced to undertake, his expectations of low evaluations were often fulfilled.

In contrast, David, one of the low writing apprehensives in the original study, enjoyed writing. He was attracted by the creativity and competence it allowed him, and although he agreed that composing could be "a chore," he liked the feeling of dealing successfully with the complex range of constraints a writing task usually involved. David, unlike Jim, was quite willing to involve himself in challenging writing situations both in and out of school. In school, he enjoyed his English classes and did not feel compelled to avoid courses in other disciplines that had heavy writing components. Like the other low writing apprehensives, David also reported doing a great deal of writing on his own time—keeping a journal, composing poetry, and maintaining a regular correspondence with friends and family.

In further contrast to Jim, David felt that his writing instruction in the past had been adequate and comprehensive, although he did mention that some of his teachers had concentrated too heavily on "spelling mistakes and grammatical errors." He reported doing explications, analysis papers, essay questions, research papers, persuasive papers, newspaper stories, yearbook articles, and poetry in high school and writing in a number of classes other than English:

> I had classes to write in . . . like my Shakespeare class . . . I think I had to write papers in about half of my classes, but not just English classes, in other classes too.

As a result of this past experience, David felt quite confident when undertaking most writing assignments:

> Well, I mean I'm no great writer or anything, but I do think of myself as a good writer. I mean I see the papers that some of the kids in my dorm hand in. At least I know what I want to say and how to organize it. . . . Spelling and stuff like that has never been hard for me. . . . I guess I'm an A or B student in English.

Because of their differing backgrounds, skill levels, and experiences, Jim and David approached writing tasks in two distinct ways. Jim's primary concern was with "getting it over with." Writing was so painful to him that he galloped through the composing process at breakneck pace, taking time for little or no planning and only minor revisions. From previous experience, Jim knew that his headlong rush through the writing process would ensure him a quick, if not high-quality, draft of his composition. Because of his apprehension, he found this method acceptable and even desirable; he was concerned less with *what* he had to say than with the fact that he was finishing "as soon as possible." He explained,

> It's not that I don't care: I care about the grade and stuff, but it's really that I don't like to do it [writing] at all. . . . I like to get it over with. Well, I can't say that because I put it off. Once I start I

> like to finish it, you know. I don't like to drag it out for . . . hours
> and stuff like that. Yes, I know the right way you have to take time.
> It's almost impossible not to. That's probably why I'll never be a
> good writer.

Jim also felt that he had a limited repertoire of writing skills to apply to
the assignments he was given in the experiment and was not at all
confident that he could produce successful papers.

David, on the other hand, approached assignments determinedly, if
not eagerly, with a strong sense of confidence in his ability to perform
successfully all those activities he expected would be involved. David
took more time to consider the assignment and his approach to it
before he began to write, and spent more time brainstorming and
listing ideas, focusing his topic, and outlining his essay before he began
drafting than did Jim. After completing an initial draft, David, unlike
Jim, made major revisions in the text he had created.

Reading as a Writing Strategy

The differing backgrounds, attitudes, experiences, and skills with which
Jim and David approached writing tasks predicted how effective they
were in using reading as a productive writing strategy. Specifically, the
two subjects differed in three ways:

1. First, before they began drafting, Jim and David differed in the
   amount of information they extracted from their reading of the
   assignments and the extent to which they used this information in
   their writing.

2. Second, as they wrote initial drafts of their papers, Jim and David
   differed in the reading strategies they brought to bear on the task.

3. Third, as they finished the first drafts of their papers, Jim and
   David differed in their willingness to use reading as a strategy for
   "re-seeing" their papers and identifying areas that needed major
   revision.

Preparing to Write: Reading for Rhetorical Information

Differences between Jim's and David's reading patterns became evident
soon after I handed them the assignment sheets and asked them to
begin composing. Jim, for example, spent one minute and forty-five
seconds reading the first assignment and fifty-seven seconds reading
the second assignment. Although he reported reading parts of both
assignments more than once, he scanned them in a cursory fashion and
admitted later that he only "glanced at them" to get a general idea of
what was required in the composing sessions.

In contrast, David was far less concerned with racing through the composing process and far more aware of the need to use reading skills to extract rhetorical information than was Jim; David spent three minutes and fifty-two seconds reading the first assignment and two minutes and fifteen seconds reading the second assignment before beginning any prewriting. Like the rest of the low writing apprehensives, David reported that he read the directions at least twice in their entirety:

> *I:* Can you remember how many times you read the two assignments?
>
> *D:* I'd say about four times. Sometimes I went back over them; I remember doing that about four times apiece.
>
> *I:* Did you read the whole assignment four times?
>
> *D:* What I'd do is I'd read the whole thing once or twice, and then I'd read parts of it.

But the difference in the time the two subjects spent on reading the assignments was less indicative of their reading effectiveness than were the specific strategies they exhibited as they read. In fact, the way the two students read the assignments laid the groundwork for the rest of their prewriting efforts and their essays as a whole. Jim, for example, did not seem to extract as much rhetorical information about purpose, audience, and organization from his readings of the assignment as did David. As he noted when I asked him about the audience he was supposed to address in the first assignment:

> *J:* I didn't think about them [the audience].
>
> *I:* At all?
>
> *J:* Not really, no.
>
> *I:* Do you usually?
>
> *J:* No.

It may be unfair to infer from these comments that Jim gained no sense at all of the audience he was to address from the assignments he read; however, it is certainly no exaggeration to report that he expressed very limited concern for audience in subsequent interviews and composing-aloud sessions.

Two explanations for Jim's distinctive reading strategies in the prewriting stage seem reasonable. First, given his protestations that he didn't "really know how to read" and that he "always hated reading," it seems likely that Jim may simply have lacked many of the reading skills necessary for extracting rhetorical information from the assignments. In

this sense, he may have been *incapable* of fulfilling the reading demands that the writing assignment placed upon him, a fact that may
have further increased his apprehension about the composing task.
Second, it was apparent that Jim considered a really close reading
detrimental to his effort to begin and end the writing process as quickly
and painlessly as possible. The more time he spent reading the assignment and identifying important rhetorical information, the more time
and effort he would have to spend on making his writing effective
within the rhetorical situation he identified. Jim, in his own way, sensed
a basic connection between his dislike of writing and his limited reading strategies:

> *I:* What did you say about reading and writing the other day?
>
> *J:* I guess . . . I don't know; I guess part of it . . . if I write some-
> thing, I've got to read it over; I'm not good at reading, I
> guess. . . . You know it just goes back to . . . if I'm going to sit
> there and just read or write, I'd rather be asleep or something.

David, on the other hand, proved more able and more inclined to
extract information about the audience, the aim of the communication
situation, and the organizational implications of the assignment than
did Jim. Moreover, David was more inclined than Jim to use the information he did gather to produce a successful composition. In one
interview, David described his reading strategy for the assignments:

> *I:* Why did you have to "go back over" the assignments? What
> were you looking for?
>
> *D:* Sometimes I wasn't exactly sure how . . . who the audience
> was and things like that . . . I was trying to find out which kind
> of . . . how I should say the things.
>
> *I:* You also referred back to the assignments several times while
> you were planning your essay. Do you know why you did this?
>
> *D:* I think it was because of the same reason. I was trying to
> figure out exactly what I was supposed to do . . . I think I
> wasn't sure who exactly I was talking to in both of those and
> how I should address them . . . and also what the circum-
> stances were.

Drafting: Accessibility of Reading Strategies

That Jim seemed to have few reading and writing strategies at his
disposal when compared to David was further demonstrated as the two
students composed the initial drafts of their assignments. Although

both interrupted their writing frequently to read short portions of their texts, they continued to engage in subtly different patterns of reading activities and to use different kinds of reading strategies. Figure 1, for example, makes it evident that Jim and David did not spend an equal amount of their drafting time engaged in the three major reading activities that I coded: reading a word or several words (Ra), reading a sentence or several sentences (Rb), or reading a larger portion of text (Rc).

	Ra (Reading a word or several words)		Rb (Reading a sentence or several sentences)		Rc (Reading large portions of text)	
	#1	#2	#1	#2	#1	#2
Jim	26	5	17	6	46	24
David	136	46	144	33	74	57

Note: All numbers represent units of five seconds (i.e., 57 represents 4 minutes 48 seconds or 0:4.48 [rounded down]).

Figure 1. Time spent on three reading activities

Jim, for instance, spent an average of 1.17 (one minute and seventeen seconds) reading a word or several words that he had written, 1.22 reading a sentence or several sentences that he had composed, and 2.55 reading large portions of his text. David, on the other hand, spent considerably more time engaged in *each* of these activities: an average of 7.30 reading one word or several words of his own prose, 7.20 reading a sentence or several sentences, and 5.40 reading larger portions of his text.

Even more significant than the amount of time devoted to scanning passages of various lengths, however, were the students' strategies for reading. Jim's primary motivation was to rush through the two short first drafts of his assignments, to "get it over with," in his words. The comments Jim made during his composing-aloud sessions and later interviews indicated that he did not use reading to discover and articulate his thoughts, to see how well the text that he had written conformed to the meaning he wanted to communicate, to evaluate the form and structure of his prose, or to assess the need for large-scale revision. Although Jim did interrupt his writing 39 times to reread one or several words (Ra) that he had written, he used these episodes for only two purposes: first, to retrieve specific words or phrases from his long-term memory (28 times), and, second, to confirm suspected

surface-level errors in spelling, grammar, and punctuation (11 times).
Examine, for instance, the following representative example from the
protocol of his second draft:

1:47.23 [Jim writes his first sentence.] *I come before you today to point
out an unfair rule that was* . . . [stops writing, taps head with
pencil, traces spiral binding of notebook on desk] *"that was,*
uh . . . is that 'instituted' or 'instigated'? Well, let's say [begins
writing again] *instigated* . . . I think that's it." [Continues writing]
last year. "Wait, ins-teh-gated, I think. Better look that up . . ."
[looks in dictionary, corrects spelling, and continues with the
next sentence].[7]

When he was "stuck," i.e., at a loss for an appropriate word or phrase,
Jim would take what another highly apprehensive writer called "a running jump" at the void. Perhaps even more descriptively, Jim called this
effort "fishing."

Like most of the other highly apprehensive writers studied, Jim also
applied these reading strategies to somewhat longer passages. At least
21 times during his two initial drafts, Jim interrupted his writing to
reread a sentence or two (Rb) when, in his words, he "lost track of
what I was going to say." This strategy, along with the information Jim
provided in later interviews, suggested that he was trying to stick to a
very specific story that he had decided very early in the predrafting
stage to relate. Jim reread sentences for much the same reason that he
reread words in the last example—as a strategy to retrieve a bit of
information momentarily lost to short-term memory. Jim also stopped
writing 7 times to reread sentences that he suspected of containing a
surface-level problem in spelling, grammar, or punctuation. It became
increasingly clear as the study progressed that Jim was not using reading
as a discovery strategy, one that would allow him to evaluate his attempts at capturing meaning and suggest new directions or alternative
forms for his paper. Rather, Jim was using minimal reading skills, at the
sentence level, to reduce the time he had to spend writing and to limit
his level of engagement in the writing task itself.

In interpreting these data, we can venture two guesses about why
Jim used a minimal number of reading strategies. The first explanation
has to do with his attitude toward writing and reading. Like the other
high writing apprehensives in the study, Jim habitually latched onto the
first narrative topic he could come up with at a very early point in his
composing, and refused to deviate from it in later stages. As a highly
apprehensive writer, Jim welcomed this strategy as an "express train"
through the maze of the composing process; he was not willing either
to spend the time necessary to discover new directions and try alternative methods of presenting the material, or to take risks in written

expression. Second, we might guess that, because he practiced reading only for limited purposes (e.g., retrieving a word, a thought, or a phrase, or correcting spelling, punctuation, or usage), Jim never took advantage of chances to develop more sophisticated reading strategies (for example, comparing intended meaning with actual text, exploring the effectiveness of material for a specific audience, discovering new directions, determining if the text's form followed its function, and assessing the need for or the effectiveness of larger revision efforts). Jim, therefore, was faced with a double dilemma. He did not use more sophisticated reading strategies—either he *could* not use them because he was unfamiliar with them, or he *would* not use them because they required more time—and, because he did not practice these strategies, he never learned to master them.

David, on the other hand, interrupted his writing more frequently than did Jim to read what he had written, and employed a much wider range of reading strategies. While Jim, for example, interrupted his writing only 39 times to read a word or phrase that he had written (Ra) and 21 times to read a sentence or two (Rb), David stopped to read single words or phrases (Ra) 125 times and a sentence or two (Rb) 137 times. More important, David used these short rereadings for a wider variety of purposes than did Jim. David read to retrieve words and phrases from his long-term memory (46 times); to recapture the narrative thread he had identified during his planning period (21 times); to evaluate parts of his text in terms of the rhetorical situation (19 times); to edit spelling, grammar, and punctuation (35 times); and to add, delete, or substitute words in his existing text (139 times).

A closer look at one particular cluster of reading activities—occurring as David composed the first draft of assignment 1—illustrates some of these different strategies:

4:35.00 [David begins writing the sixth sentence of his first draft] *Most of you probably aren't sure* . . . [stops writing, taps pen on desk] *"aren't sure* . . . ?" [Repeats and goes back to read the beginning of the sentence and get a running jump.] *"Most of you probably aren't sure what to expect from college* . . . " [stops and questions himself] "Is there a comma there?" [Rereads sentence once again and hesitantly adds comma.] *"Most of you probably aren't sure what to expect from college,* . . . " [continues to compose] *but probably suspect that it is different from high school. When I graduated from Austin High School* . . . [pauses briefly] *I didn't know the answer either. I still don't.* [Here David stops, suspecting that he has diverged from his original plan and the intent of the assignment—to offer useful advice based on his experience as a successful college freshman.]

4:35.55 "Hmm, doesn't sound like I can give them much help . . . I could
write another paper, 'How I Blew Off My Freshman Year' " [be-
gins to read first sentence again]. "*Most of you probably aren't
sure . . .* " [David's reading alerts him to the fact that he has
repeated 'probably' twice in one sentence, and he omits the first
occurrence. He then goes back to the first sentence to read again.]
"*Most of you aren't sure . . .* [he comments on the deletion he
has just made and continues reading] better . . . *what to expect
from college, but probably suspect that it is different from high
school. When I graduated from Austin High School I didn't know
the answer either. I still don't . . .* " [stops to evaluate and com-
ment]. "Hmm! I'm thinking now that these are seventeen-year-
olds and that they're not interested in me. They want to hear
about themselves and what *they're* worried about." [He then
deletes part of his first sentence and all of his second and third
sentences. He reads what is left.] "*Most of you aren't sure what
to expect from college, . . .* " [David substitutes a sentence that
addresses the students' concerns more directly] *you know it will
be different but you aren't certain what these changes will be.*

4:37.12 [At this point David seems satisfied with the passage, but scans it
one last time to make sure. He spots his comma splice and stops
to reread.] "*From college . . .* probably need a . . . uh . . . a . . .
semi-comma [*sic*] there [changes comma to semicolon and continues to read] *from college; you know it will . . .* [stops to
comment] . . . that ought to get it."

This example is representative of the number of purposes for which
David used reading. Reading, in fact, seemed to serve him as a multi-
purpose writing strategy, a catalyst that helped him make decisions
about the rhetorical effectiveness of his prose ("Hmm, doesn't sound
like I can give them much help"), his audience and their needs ("these
are seventeen-year-olds and . . . they're not interested in me"), the purpose of his paper (as when he deleted the sentences "I didn't know the
answer either. I still don't," because he wanted to assume the posture
of an expert), his stylistic concerns (as he deleted the careless repetition of "probably"), and the grammatical problems he recognized
("probably need a . . . semi-comma [*sic*] there"). In addition, David
seemed to be conscious of the importance of reading in his writing
process; as he noted in response to a question about why he went back
and read the preceding words or sentences several times, "I just sort of
go back to see what I've just said. And maybe, you know, that generates
more material for me when I do that."

In one sense, Jim's and David's reading strategies may not be as
different as we have suggested here. After all, when Jim read for surface-
level editing problems, although he did not articulate his strategies, he
may have been demonstrating a concern for audience that was similar

to, albeit much simpler than, the concerns expressed by David. And
when he read to retrieve words and phrases that would allow him to
recapture his narrative thread, he *may* have been discovering, on a
local level, what he was going to say next. Nevertheless, it became
increasingly evident as the study progressed that the two *were* employing very different reading strategies during the writing process. Jim,
unlike David, never used reading consciously and consistently to expand his involvement with the text, by exploring alternatives, assessing
the need for large-scale revision, or discovering new perspectives and
ideas. Rather, he used reading to locate only the most glaring surface
errors or to recover his original narrative topic—both strategies that
helped him limit his engagement with the writing task.

Postdrafting: Willingness to Revise

Just as Jim's and David's reading activities differed dramatically in the
predrafting and drafting stages, they continued to do so in the postdrafting stages. While both Jim and David took time to reread large
portions of their initial drafts after they had finished composing, each
used this kind of reading activity as a means toward a different end.

Jim ended each of the first drafts he composed during the experiment with a sigh of relief and a disparaging comment about his own
efforts. Without wasting much time, he then proceeded to reread the
draft he had composed, in its entirety, one time. Although Jim claimed
in an early interview that this activity led to a "revision" of his papers,
he later admitted that it was an automatic and often empty gesture.
Such reading, Jim realized, did not lead to "re-vision" of content, organization, or presentation, but to a minimal correction of grammatical
and spelling errors:

> At that point [when he rereads his first draft], I'm not looking to
> make big changes because if I go back and do that I'll start changing
> it [the paper]. And then I'll think, "Which one is better—the first
> time I wrote it or the second time?" Then I'd have to do it all over
> again, so I'd never get finished! So I figure the first time I get it
> down, I'm just going to leave it like that. You know, I'll correct the
> glaring misplaced words or some spelling, or something like that,
> but I'm not going to change the whole paper. I really just read and
> hope I don't see anything so bad that I have to write some more.

Jim followed the same approach, albeit with different results, in both
papers that he composed during the experiment. He spent three minutes and eight seconds (3.08) rereading his draft of the first assignment
and made no changes at all to his text. He spent two minutes (2.00)
rereading his draft of the second assignment. More important than the

time he spent on this activity, however, was the amount and type of revision that his reading efforts precipitated on the second assignment. As he reread, Jim stopped to add, delete, or substitute single words 4 times and to correct the spelling and punctuation of his text 8 times.

The data gathered in these case studies suggest two reasons for the distinctive reading pattern Jim exhibited in the postdrafting stage. First, of course, his impulse as a highly apprehensive writer was to finish the piece as quickly as possible. As a result of his anxiety, Jim was unwilling to dwell on the writing task, to linger over his prose as he searched carefully for areas that needed improvement. If Jim had truly read to "re-see" his work, to criticize honestly the meaning he had articulated, to adjust this meaning, or discover new meaning, he knew he would be letting himself in for more punishment, more writing, in the form of major changes. Perhaps even more than this general unwillingness to subject himself to the task of writing, however, Jim's lack of reading and writing skills may have kept him from revising his writing. He may have realized, quite realistically in this case, that he had limited revising, proofreading, and editing strategies to bring to bear on the problem areas he might identify as he read. As Jim said,

> I'm not sure I know *how* to revise my papers, if you know what I mean. That's probably one of my big problems, isn't it? I mean sometimes they don't sound just right, but then I'm not sure what to do about it. When you've gotten that far you're sunk, you know?

Even after the completion of this study, it is not clear whether Jim's apprehension or his lack of writing skills came first. It seems logical to assume that writers who lack a successful repertoire of skills or strategies for completing composing tasks will become apprehensive about writing, but it also seems credible that a generalized sense of writing apprehension would keep any individual from practicing and, therefore, mastering an effective set of writing and reading strategies. What we don't know is how, when, or why these conditions develop; whether the development of one is sequentially and/or causally related to the development of the other; or under what circumstances each of the conditions might be reversible.

David's reading activities during the postdrafting period stood in contrast to Jim's. David spent more time engaged in rereading portions of his completed first drafts. He spent six minutes and sixteen seconds (6.16) rereading the draft of his first assignment and four minutes and forty-eight seconds (4.48) rereading the draft of his second assignment. More important, however, David used rereading as a strategy for "re-seeing" his paper:

I: Why do you read your first draft after you've finished it? What are you looking for?

D: Well, I read it to see if it works. You know, I would make a major change if something doesn't work out, if it wasn't coming across just right, I have to deal with it. . . . I usually mark out whole sentences and sometimes paragraphs and rewrite them over.

I: But what exactly do you look for? What, for instance, would make you stop and change something?

D: Well, first, you know, I guess I'm looking for if it works with the audience. In the second one [assignment] like I said before I imagined myself talking to a bunch of really excited booster-type people in high school. . . . And then I look for if it [the paper] does what I want it to. . . . It's just kind of a hunch that I have that it's not right . . . or not what I wanted to say or should say according to the assignment. . . . Sometimes I just sit back and look at all the ideas I want to stress and all the ideas I have put down. And I always look for spelling and repetition . . . like it has seven *ise*s in four sentences or something like that, or the same sentence structure or else it will be really boring. If those things happen I have to make a major change.

David's activities during the postdrafting stage bear out his explanation of his rereading strategies. He rewrote a total of twelve sentences because he didn't think their content or form was appropriate for his audience and seven sentences because they didn't match his intended meaning. He also deleted two sentences because they "didn't fit" in his essay. Moreover, David added, deleted, and substituted twenty-three different words or phrases and corrected four marks of punctuation and five misspellings as a direct result of his rereading.

Conclusions

Because this paper presents a case study of only two subjects, engaged in composing aloud for only two freshman writing assignments (though typical ones), I will not presume to generalize too broadly from the findings I have reported here. I can, however, identify what I believe to be some fruitful areas of study for future investigators who want to complete investigations or experiments involving different methodologies, longer time spans, or larger samples. These suggestions, however, are made with two cautions in mind. First, I suspect that the results I have recorded may differ if different kinds of writing assignments are employed (a piece of expressive writing, for example, rather than a persuasive narrative to be used in a speech), if more composing sessions are analyzed, or if the study is carried out over a longer period of time. Second, in any such project using indirect methods of observation (protocol analysis, retrospective or concurrent interviews, role playing) to get at the cognitive processes involved in writing, we must also be continually wary about interpreting the data gathered. In looking back now, I see different information than I did when I originally analyzed my study of high and low apprehensives. The same data examined five years hence may well yield more new information. Unfortunately, until we can eavesdrop directly on the human brain at work, we will have to continue to use indirect and imperfect methods of guessing what goes on during the composing process.

I offer, then, three tentative conclusions drawn from the current study:

1. Not all students use reading in the same way as they compose. Individuals develop their own repertoires of reading strategies for use in writing tasks. Some individuals develop more successful repertoires than others.

2. Writers who are highly apprehensive about composing may be less facile in reading for useful rhetorical information in the predrafting stage and may have mastered fewer effective reading strategies to apply in the drafting and postdrafting stages of a writing task than have those with low apprehension.

3. Subjects who are highly apprehensive about writing may be less willing to spend the time necessary for a critical reading of their own texts during the composing process than are their less apprehensive counterparts.

These limited findings make it obvious that much remains to be done before we can confidently apply our research to pedagogical situations. We must begin to conduct further research on those questions derived from such early studies as this one. We do not yet know, for example, whether there exists a construct comparable to writing apprehension that involves reading. If we find that "reading apprehension" does exist, we must also conduct specific studies that help us define its exact relationship to writing apprehension. We might, for example, find that a certain level of reading apprehension is desirable in composing situations, that such apprehension is common in writers who worry about "making good" in the eyes of a reader. At the same time, we must try to find out more about the effects of past instruction or experiences with reading on subjects' anxiety about reading during composition. If past instruction does engender reading anxiety, how does it do so and to what extent?

If we are successful in isolating the sources of reading apprehension in the composing process, we must also search for effective ways of dealing with it. In the face of extreme apprehension, we may be able to teach writers to employ systematically a wider range of reading skills or to employ the skills they have already mastered more effectively. This instruction could also take the form of psychological techniques that help subjects control their fear of writing and/or reading.

Finally, we need to determine whether the reading patterns (or reading attitudes, or reading skills) of *skilled* and *unskilled* writers correspond in any way to those of *high* and *low* writing apprehensives, as this experiment suggests. If we find, in our research, that they do have much in common, we then have to work to determine which patterns (or attitudes) are due to lack of skill and which to anxiety. Such an analysis, in turn, can help us determine whether we can or should continue to study these phenomena in their separate manifestations.

With answers to these questions and others like them, we can begin to refine what we know about the connections between reading and writing. If the findings from this investigation are any indication, we may discover that our notion of reading and writing as two separate activities needs fundamental revision. Such a concept would have serious pedagogical and theoretical repercussions in all areas of English studies. It suggests, for example, that we, as a profession, may have created a false dichotomy between courses in composition and courses that involve the teaching of critical or close reading. We might discover, as some researchers have already begun to suggest, that *reading* drafts at various stages, using a range of different strategies, may be one of the essential processes involved in writing a successful composition.[8] Petersen and Burkland have already maintained, for instance, that the strategies they ask their students to employ when reading literature in their composition courses are critical in helping them become better writers.[9] If other studies document the same close connections between reading and writing suggested by this and other investigations,[10] we must realize that teaching students to become better writers may necessitate teaching them to become better readers.

Notes

1. Donald M. Murray, "Teaching the Other Self: The Writer's First Reader," *College Composition and Communication* 33 (1982): 140–47.

2. John A. Daly and Michael D. Miller, "The Development of a Measure of Writing Apprehension" (Paper presented at the annual meeting of the International Communications Association, Chicago, 1975); and John A. Daly and Michael D. Miller, "The Empirical Development of an Instrument to Measure Writing Apprehension," *Research in the Teaching of English* 9 (1975): 242–49.

3. John A. Daly and W. G. Shamo, "Writing Apprehension and Occupational Choice," *Journal of Occupational Research* 49 (1976): 55–56; John A. Daly, "The Effects of Writing Apprehension on Message Encoding," *Journalism Quarterly* 54 (1977): 566–72; and John A. Daly, "Writing Apprehension and Writing Competency," *Journal of Education Research* 72 (1978): 10–14.

4. Assignment 1 asked students to write a speech for an audience of seniors from their old high school in which they revealed the one piece of advice they wish they had been given before going off to college. The writers were asked to use an illustrative narrative from their own experience to persuade the audience to accept and profit from the advice. Assignment 2 asked subjects to write a speech for a policy-making board at the high school they had attended before coming to college. In the speech, the subjects were asked to tell of one practice at the school that was outmoded or unfair and to use an illustrative narrative from their own high school experience to persuade the board to change this practice.

5. For more detailed information on the methodology employed during this 1980 study, see Cynthia L. Selfe, "The Composing Processes of Four High and Four Low Writing Apprehensives: A Modified Case Study" (Ph.D. diss., University of Texas at Austin, 1981).

6. For more detailed results about the findings of this 1980 study, see Cynthia L. Selfe, "The Predrafting Processes of Four High- and Four Low-Apprehensive Writers," *Research in the Teaching of English* 18 (1984): 45–64. Also see Cynthia L. Selfe, "An Apprehensive Writer Composes," in *When a Writer Can't Write: Studies in Writer's Block and Other Composing Problems,* ed. Mike Rose (New York: Guilford Press, 1985).

7. Throughout this paper, material that subjects wrote as they composed aloud is italicized. Material that is both italicized and in quotation marks indicates that subjects are reading aloud what they have already written. Material in quotation marks but not italicized represents subjects' oral comments. Time is reported in hours, minutes, and seconds. Thus, material marked 1:47.23 represents activities that went on for 1 hour, 47 minutes, and 23 seconds into a particular composing-aloud session.

8. Elizabeth A. Flynn, "Peer Tutoring and Reading Activities" (Paper presented at the Conference on College Composition and Communication, San Francisco, 1982).

9. Bruce T. Petersen and Jill N. Burkland, "An Integrated Approach to Reading and Writing in the Research Paper: Theory and Practice" (Michigan Technological University, 1982, typescript).

10. See, for example, Bruce T. Petersen and Randy Freisinger, "An Investigation into the Universe of Discourse in Industrial and Academic Texts" (Michigan Technological University, 1981, typescript); and Nancy M. Grimm and Jill N. Burkland, "Directing Group Work" (Michigan Technological University, 1983, typescript).

The Writing/Reading Relationship: Becoming One's Own Best Reader

Richard Beach
University of Minnesota at Minneapolis–St. Paul

JoAnne Liebman-Kleine
University of Arkansas at Little Rock

Most composition teachers enjoin their students to think about their audience. They tell students to consider their reader's objections or adapt their style to suit the reader. Although this advice is valid, it doesn't go far enough. Simply thinking *about* a reader doesn't help students apply what they infer about their readers in order to assess and revise their writing. In addition to thinking *about* readers, they must also think *as* readers. They need to be able to adopt their readers' presumed perspectives, assessing their writing in terms of how their readers may react to or comprehend that writing. In other words, they must become their own best readers.

Of course, adopting readers' perspectives is a complicated process. Recent cognitive processing theory, however, sheds some light on how writers switch to readers' perspectives. In this chapter, we first propose a theoretical model of the process of adopting a reader's perspective. We then apply that model to the phenomenon of students' writing for the teacher as audience, and suggest some specific writing activities based on consideration of different types of audience attributes.

Schema Theory

Essential to our model is some understanding of the nature and function of cognitive schemata. Schemata are cognitive structures or scripts that help us organize information hierarchically. For example, we have a schema for "registering for a course at the university." In this schema, there are a series of categories defining the steps involved in registration, some steps being more important than others. These categories (picking up registration materials, selecting classes, filling out a registration form, getting an advisor's approval, reporting to the registration site, paying registration fees, etc.) help students store or organize new information about registering, and in turn are changed as students acquire new information. They therefore serve to link past and future perceptions of experiences. When students confront more elaborate registration procedures—perhaps at a larger school—they fall back on familiar schemata or modify existing schemata.

Schemata also provide links between writing and reading. Writers develop schemata about readers and how readers read, allowing them to imagine reader attributes and to use those attributes to assess their writing. Many writers have difficulty because when writing, unlike when speaking, they have no audience in front of them giving them feedback or clues about their responses. They must therefore use their audience schemata to create hypothetical rhetorical contexts. These audience schemata are drawn not only from previous writing experiences, but also from times when writers have been readers or listeners themselves.

A Model of the Adoption Process: Audience Attributes, Intended Effects, Assessment Criteria, and Rhetorical Strategies

Based on our discussion of schemata, we propose the following model of the rhetorical context. As we noted, writers have schemata about readers and about how they respond to texts. They also have schemata about writers and about how they use certain rhetorical strategies. There are, then, four components to the schematic knowledge writers use in becoming readers of their own writing—each of which is related cognitively to the other components of their knowledge. They are the schemata for audience attributes, intended effects, assessment criteria, and rhetorical strategies.

Writers use each of these components to make inferences about other components. For example, someone writing a letter to ask his mother to lend him some money knows that he is performing a particular *rhetorical strategy* or *speech act*—requesting a loan. He also knows that making such a request implies certain *reader attributes* that are particularly important to consider: that his mother has the money to lend, believes that the writer needs or deserves the money, and believes that the writer is sincere in making the request. In order to achieve his *intended effect,* the writer then uses these *audience attributes* to develop assessment criteria: the fact that the reader believes that the writer needs the money implies that the reasons for making the request must be both valid and relevant to these needs.

In other words, a writer assumes that a reader—his mother—will be reading his letter with these criteria in mind. Having defined these particular attributes and criteria as schemata, a writer, now reader, reviews his letter in terms of these schemata, focusing on the extent to which his reasons for the request are relevant and/or valid.

The following chart portrays the interrelationships among these four components:

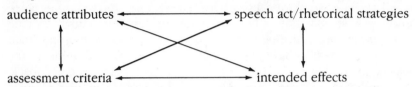

audience attributes ←————————————→ speech act/rhetorical strategies

assessment criteria ←————————————→ intended effects

Writers may initially adopt any one of these schemata. Ultimately, in assessing their writing, they will apply all of these components, moving from one component to the next by learned conditional reasoning: if I want to impress (intended effect) then I need to praise (speech act). If I praise, I need to be sincere (assessment criteria) and so on.

Perhaps the most important skill in this self-assessing process is the ability to infer audience attributes. Determining these attributes helps a writer select the appropriate assessment criteria (relevancy, sufficiency, significance, clarity, etc.), the appropriate effects (placate, convince, gain identification, etc.) or the appropriate rhetorical strategies (summarize, compare, provide background information, etc.).

How Do Writers Infer Audience Attributes?

In order to switch to an audience's schema, writers need to do much more than think about some global notion of "audience." Their audiences have so many different characteristics—some familiar, some not— that writers need to infer a number of specific audience attributes and use those attributes to assess their writing. For example, thinking specifically about what an audience may know about a subject helps a writer determine how much information to include. In contrast, in thinking about audience beliefs, writers assess their attempts to convince that audience in terms of the validity or relevancy of their arguments. Thus, different audience attributes imply different intended effects, assessment criteria, and rhetorical strategies.

In most cases, writers, even in writing to relatively familiar audiences, do not have empirical knowledge about their readers' knowledge, beliefs, attitudes, or needs. In order to make such inferences, they draw on knowledge of prototypical audience attributes gleaned through previous experiences with certain types of audiences. In writing a job application letter to a known, actual employer, for example, a writer is not only thinking about that particular employer, but also about employers in general. Knowing some particular audience attributes, for example that the employer knows little about the writer as a person but a lot about her previous position and company, may help an applicant highlight items relevant to convincing her audience of her qualifications. But this may not be enough. She may not know whether such items are sufficient, and so she may draw upon other knowledge. If she also knows other prototypical audience attributes, for example that employers typically want to know what employees can do for them, she may highlight other relevant items.

Clearly, many particular readers will be included in any general, prototypical audience category. In fact, it is helpful to consider these categories less as stereotypes for different types of people than as situations in which particular people function, viewing an audience as an intersection of prototypical and particular features.

Audience Attributes: Knowledge

What an audience knows about a subject is one important attribute that writers must consider and accommodate. Otherwise, readers will have difficulty comprehending the writing.

Recent reading research points to the importance of such prior knowledge in comprehending texts. For example, E. D. Hirsch, whose *Philosophy of Composition* argued that syntactic or stylistic features contribute to readability, has altered that position.[1] In an attempt to demonstrate empirically the validity of his earlier position, he gave two different versions of texts to groups matched according to reading ability. One version was written according to certain readability principles, and the other was not. He found that, in some of his experiments, comprehension scores were higher with the more readable version. He also found, however, that these results only held up when the topic was familiar to readers, for example the topic of "friendship." When the topic was unfamiliar to readers, for example "Hegel's Metaphysics," differences in the influence of a text's readability were less important.

The important influence of knowledge or "content schema" on comprehension has also been demonstrated by Richard Anderson and other researchers.[2] In one study, subjects from the United States and India, matched according to education, age, and profession, read two texts, one about a wedding in the United States, the other about a wedding in India. Even though the passages were equally "readable," the subjects did not comprehend them in the same way, because of differences in prior knowledge. As would be expected, the American readers did well with the description of the American wedding and less well with the description of the Indian wedding. Conversely, the Indian readers did well in reading about the Indian wedding and less well in reading about the American wedding.

Once writers have inferred their readers' knowledge, they can determine how much information should be included, according to the criteria of sufficiency of information. This assessment often requires a careful balancing act between too much and not enough information. For highly knowledgeable readers, too much elementary information can be irritating, actually detracting from comprehension. Conversely, for readers without knowledge, lack of information about unfamiliar concepts or phenomena also hinders comprehension.

In addition to determining the knowledge their readers bring to reading, writers must also consider how that knowledge changes during reading. Since as readers move through the text they acquire knowledge about its topic, the writer must continually infer how much knowledge readers have acquired in order to determine how and when to present new information. The writer then assesses the ordering or "staging" of information, determining what constitutes "given" or background information necessary for understanding new or unfamiliar information. Effective writers use information or experiences that are familiar to readers in order to introduce less familiar ideas.

Audience Attributes: Needs—Information or Actions

A writer also infers what readers need from the writing. Readers may need certain information or may need directions in order to do something, needs that direct readers' perspectives so that they attend to certain information and ignore other information. If a reader is reading a brochure describing a new phone, for example, and simply wants to know how to plug the phone in, he may be frustrated by the writer's failure to attend to that basic need. Therefore, many writers anticipate reader questions about a product or service and use those questions as subheads. Readers can then find those questions they need answered and ignore others.

Writers also determine what their audience needs to know in order to perform certain actions. For example, a writer telling readers how to construct a paper airplane envisions each step involved and anticipates the knowledge necessary for completing each step. Thus, anticipating readers' actions or behaviors, another reader attribute, helps writers infer reader knowledge and assess the sufficiency and relevance of the information provided.

In all of this, writers are assessing the relevance or significance of information relative to their reader needs. In assessing her directions for constructing the paper airplane, the writer determines that information about the history of paper airplanes isn't all that relevant to her audience's needs.

Audience Attributes: Beliefs

Another important attribute of an audience is its beliefs about the writer's topic or the writer. Again, writers can only make educated guesses about reader beliefs; but if they know their intended effects— to convince, to pacify, to gain sympathy, etc.—they can infer how their audience may react. For example, a writer reporting to a pollution control agency about its surveillance activities wants his audience to be sympathetic toward himself and his recommendations. Given this intended outcome, the writer begins the report by praising the agency's previous surveillance activities, inferring that readers might be pleased with the praise and thus develop a positive attitude toward what follows. Thus, by considering audience beliefs, the writer employs a strategy for accommodating those beliefs. Similarly, in arguing for a certain position, for example gun control, a writer may objectively restate the opposition's position in order to gain credibility with an audience. Having restated the opposition's position, he or she can then refute it.

Once writers ascertain their audience's beliefs or attempt to foster certain beliefs in that audience, they assess their writing according to the validity and objectivity of their assertions. For example, a writer is addressing an audience that favors school tuition vouchers allowing parents to send their children to the schools of their choice. She opposes the voucher system. In preparing her speech, she assesses the validity and objectivity of her arguments by anticipating her audience's counterarguments. If she knows that her audience believes that the public schools "don't work," she knows she needs to argue that the public schools do work with some empirical evidence to support her claim. Thus, anticipating audience beliefs assists a writer in assessing her own arguments.

Audience Attributes: Power and Status

Another important audience attribute is power or status. Audience status or power is particularly important to writers assessing their right to perform certain speech acts, such as requesting, informing, ordering, or criticizing, given their own and their audience's power. If the writer is an employee, for instance, and is writing a memo to her boss, she knows that she doesn't have the right to tell the boss what to do. Or, if he is a student, the writer knows he shouldn't write a paper that has nothing to do with an assignment.

In trying to establish their own power or status in the eyes of an audience, writers may directly state their own credentials or expertise, or may attempt to demonstrate their power or status through their ability to argue their case. The fact that a writer can cite facts and evidence to support her case implies her own status as an expert.

Concerns about power or status are particularly important when writers are requesting that an audience perform a task or are confronting them in some way. Writers must then decide on whether or not they should directly make demands or confront their audience, or opt for the more polite, mitigating form of requesting something or implying criticism.

Making Inferences about the Teacher as Audience

Our model suggests that students need to think about specific audience attributes in order to assess their own writing. In writing for their teachers, however, students often have difficulty inferring what those teachers know or believe about a topic. Teachers may not have the time or desire to inform students about their knowledge or beliefs about different topics.

Students also often don't have a clear sense of what their teachers want or need. Directions such as "Discuss Willy Loman as a tragic hero" don't provide students with strategies for writing a paper. Moreover, even if teachers don't assign such "Discuss X . . . ·" topics, they usually don't *need* anything from a student's writing. They don't need the writing to help them run a word processor or to make a decision, and they usually do not need students to inform them about their subject or help them solve a problem.

Thus, ironically, students often don't think carefully about their teacher as audience. To counter this, it may be necessary to build some audience analysis into assignments in order to encourage students to think about attributes of their teacher as audience. In a recent writing-methods class for English teachers, Richard Beach asked his students to write in their journals about their perceptions of him as their audience as well as about other intended audiences. For each of three papers—a memo to the teacher about their own needs and expectations, an auto-biographical narrative, and a curriculum unit—students were asked to make inferences about the teacher's and other audiences' knowledge, beliefs, needs, and status and to discuss how they used their inferences to assess their writing. In reading the students' audience analyses, we learned a lot about how students made inferences regarding their teacher and used these inferences to assess their writing.

The Memo Assignment

In the memo assignment, students were asked to provide some background information about their previous teaching experience, what they had tried in teaching writing, and what they would like to learn in the course. They were also asked to list some characteristics about Beach as audience, how these audience characteristics influenced their writing, and what they were trying to say or do in different sections of the memo.

In listing audience attributes, the students often mentioned the teacher's beliefs about them as "students," and how those beliefs would influence his response to their memos. They were therefore defining a rhetorical, interpersonal relationship starring themselves as "students" who want to impress and inform ("I wanted to please you, a discriminating reader") their teacher. They therefore assessed their memos in terms of making a positive impression ("I was conscious of wanting to say something and say it well").

Some students noted a problem with the memo assignment—that the memo would probably not result in any marked change in the course because the course syllabus was already fixed. Thus, although they knew they were providing the teacher with the information requested, they were not sure as to how the teacher would act on that information. As one student politely put it, "You need feedback to evaluate the class's understanding of the concepts discussed . . . you may or may not use the feedback to change what you do."

The students were therefore perceiving the teacher as someone reacting to their memo rather than acting as a result of reading the memo, and their main concern was simply with providing information rather than trying to influence the teacher's beliefs or change the course. As a result, many of the memos were somewhat bland. As one student noted, "The beginning part of the memo sounded like a résumé/job application." The memo assignment was not totally successful because it had no clear, pragmatic purpose. Without a clear sense of intended effects, students had difficulty defining audience attributes and assessment criteria, illustrating the interdependence of the four components of our model.

Autobiographical Incident Assignment

For the second paper, students were asked to write a personal narrative focusing on one event in their lives. The students knew that every member of the class would be receiving copies of these essays, and their audience analysis accordingly indicated that rather than the teacher as their primary audience, they were primarily concerned about the other students in the class as their audience.

In thinking about their peers, they were concerned about three phenomena. First, they were quite concerned about whether their readers would identify with the narrated event, so they selected experiences familiar to their peers. Their concern for the familiarity of the experience is reflected in comments such as, "This was an incident they could relate to and would find humorous," or "Many members of my audience are parents and so they could relate to my incident," or "Some of them probably have some experience coaching or watching more than an average amount of drama. That might make them more receptive to the setting for my embarrassing moment."

The students then used these inferences about audience knowledge to assess whether their writing provided sufficient background knowledge. Some students, however, had difficulty inferring their audience's prior experience and therefore found it "hard to determine how much my audience needed to know" or "how much information to include." Some students found that their peers' feedback on their drafts provided a clearer sense of audience knowledge, so that in revising their drafts they could add the appropriate background information.

Their second concern was with their desire to impress their peers with their writing ability: "Since I see my audience as intelligent, capable, and interesting people, I wanted to please them and appear capable and in control of my writing." Because they wanted to make a positive impression on a relatively unfamiliar audience, they were reluctant to "spill my guts" or "bare too much of my soul." They assumed that "being too personal" would undermine their attempts to produce "clear, controlled, clever writing."

This concern about self-revelation is related to a third concern, the fact that they were writing for English teachers. As one student noted, "I found myself constantly asking, What will they as English teachers think of this?" This concern led students to pay careful attention to language, on the assumption that their readers would be "very critical." As one student said, "I spent more time and effort reworking sentences and words." One student made a list of things to do—including "I'd better put in a literary allusion"—because he was very conscious that a teacher of English would be reading his paper.

These students, therefore, applied their inferences about audience knowledge to assessing sufficiency of information, degree of intimacy, and language clarity. It is interesting that publishing the writing shifted the focus of the audience analysis from the teacher to the students' peers. And, with that shift, some of their audience concerns shifted.

Curriculum Unit

For the final paper, students developed a curriculum unit on writing that they would use with their own students. For this paper, most of the students defined several different audiences: colleagues and/or students who would implement these activities, peers in the class, and the teacher.

Their audience analysis pointed to a major difference between this paper and the other two papers. Because they were developing activities that would actually be used by colleagues or by their own students, they were particularly concerned about what their audience would *do* with the activities—with audience actions. They therefore assessed the writing according to sufficiency or relevance of information for implementing the activities in the classroom. In thinking about their colleagues, they often inferred their colleagues' needs as teachers by thinking about their own experience. Thus one student noted, "I like to plan things in a detailed way. Therefore, I went through each stage of my activities and tried to anticipate everything I should be doing and the information my audience needed." Writers also focused on sufficiency; given the fact that their audience "already knew a lot about writing instruction, I didn't want to be too obvious."

Because they were writing something that would actually be used, the students were able to define clearly their purpose and audience. They were also able to assess their writing by envisioning an audience trying to implement their activities. Given this pragmatic goal, they were much less concerned about impressing the teacher. As one student noted, "Since we are developing this paper as a guide for teachers . . . there will be little attention to Dr. Beach as audience." This suggests that if writers can envision their audience using their writing to do something, they can use these anticipated actions to assess their own writing.

This informal study illustrates the way writers focus on different audience attributes depending on their writing's purpose, audience, and mode of discourse. In writing the memo, the teachers were primarily concerned about their teacher's knowledge, beliefs, needs, and expectations. In writing their autobiographical narratives, they were concerned about their fellow English teachers' perceptions of the significance of the episode and their expectations regarding style and clarity. In writing curriculum units, they were concerned primarily with the prior knowledge, needs, and reading ability of the students who would be doing the activities.

Activities for Teaching Audience Analysis

Obviously students need to learn to consider a range of different attributes, focusing on those attributes that are most relevant to their intended effects and rhetorical strategies. Students also need instruction on how to use these attributes to assess their writing. The following are some classroom activities designed to teach audience analysis. We've organized these activities according to different attributes. The following chart outlines these attributes, relevant criteria, and rhetorical/logical strategies:

Audience Attributes	*Relevant Criteria*	*Rhetorical/Logical Strategies*
knowledge	sufficiency familiarity	"given-new" (familiar to unfamiliar)
beliefs	validity objectivity	acknowledging reader beliefs, gaining identification
status or power	legitimacy formality of style	establishing credentials
needs: actions	relevance clarity	ordering of steps, analogies to familiar experiences
comprehension processes	clarity	readability strategies

Activities: Audience Knowledge

Analyzing Texts for Use of Prior Knowledge

   Purpose: to help students recognize writers' use of "given" or familiar prior knowledge in texts.
   Activity: Students read through texts and note instances when writers refer to what they assume is "given" or familiar knowledge in order to prepare a reader for new or unfamiliar knowledge. For example, in the

beginning of the Apple Writer IIe manual, the writers discuss the value of word processing. They include a series of vignettes about the familiar problems of having to revise texts on a typewriter. These vignettes prepare a reader for the less familiar information that follows regarding the uses of a word processor.

Students can next discuss the accuracy of a writer's estimation of their familiarity with the information provided. In some cases, a writer may underestimate or overestimate an audience's familiarity. Students could then discuss how a writer uses this "given" or familiar knowledge to prepare for new information.

Interviewing Peers to Estimate an Audience's Prior Knowledge

Purpose: to help students learn to make inferences about audience by interviewing peers.

Activity: Students form groups, each of which will write an advertising brochure for a school event, a city, a state, a tourist attraction, a park, etc., for another group of students. Before they begin writing, the groups interview each other to determine the audience-groups' knowledge of the event or place. Each group then determines its audience's amount and type of prior knowledge. For example, if a group is writing about the Wild Animal Park in San Diego, that group may discover that nobody in the other group knows about the park, but that they know where San Diego is and something about "open" zoos.

Using Estimates of Prior Knowledge to Assess Writing

Purpose: to help students switch to a reader's knowledge schema in order to assess their writing.

Activity: Once students have written their brochures, they go through their drafts to assess the sufficiency of information and make appropriate revisions, adding information as necessary. Each group then gives its brochure to another group. Students in each audience group go through their brochure and, using a "think-aloud" technique, indicate whether or not they understand certain bits of information, given their prior knowledge. The writers then can determine the degree to which they have accommodated their audience's prior knowledge.

Activities: Audience Beliefs

Debates Among Pairs: Switching to Opposite Perspectives

Purpose: to help students recognize beliefs counter to their own.

Activity: In this activity, student groups of six decide on debate topics stated in the form, "Be it resolved . . . " Each group then breaks into three pairs. One pair defends the resolution, one pair refutes the resolution, and the third pair serves as time-keepers and judges. After the first round of debating, the pairs switch sides and argue the opposite positions. The judges, rather than declaring "winners," assess the validity of the debaters' arguments and their use of evidence.

Letter Writing: Refuting Beliefs

Purpose: to help students assess the validity of their own beliefs.

Activity: Each student selects a person (a politician, civic leader, school authority, peer) who espouses a certain belief or position, and writes a letter to that person refuting that belief and espousing his or her own beliefs. Another student then assumes the role of the letter's audience and responds to a draft of the letter, presenting counterarguments. With these counterarguments in mind, the writers revise their letters and send them to their actual audiences.

Large-group Role-playing: Teacher Negotiation Session

Purpose: to help students infer and account for a range of competing beliefs in assessing their writing.

Activity: In this large-group role play of a teacher salary negotiation session, students assume a number of different roles: teacher negotiators, school board members, the superintendent, lawyers for the negotiating team, pro-teacher and anti-teacher parents, teachers, students, the local chamber of commerce, the local taxpayers' association, the local or state professional teachers' organization and the competing organization (NEA or AFT), the local newspaper editor and reporter, the local television news anchorperson and reporter, and whatever other groups a teacher may want to create. Each of these roles involves a different set of beliefs about teachers and teacher salaries.

The negotiating teams begin by announcing their bargaining positions. For example, the teachers may request a 16 percent salary increase, while the school board offers a 3 percent raise. In contrast to a verbal role play, all groups communicate using written memos; runners carry these memos to groups stationed throughout the classroom. The only participants who can converse orally are the newspaper and television reporters, who are free to roam around interviewing participants.

The various groups argue their positions for or against teacher salary increases in memos to the negotiating teams as well as to other groups. The taxpayers' association may argue, for example, that raises are too expensive, while the pro-teacher parents may argue that the raises are necessary to keep teachers from leaving their jobs. The superintendent may try to placate these competing groups with bland statements about the need to "maintain quality education."

At various points in the role-playing session the exchange of memos stops and participants read selected memos aloud. The newspaper and television reporters give reports on the progress of the negotiations. At the end of the session, students stand back and discuss the arguments and tactics employed in the role-playing. Students often observe that initially they must draw on prototypical assumptions about other groups' beliefs until they gain clearer ideas of other groups' actual beliefs from their memos. For example, in the beginning of the role play, no group may have any idea as to the newspaper editor's own beliefs about the negotiations. It is only after the editor has written some editorials that participants know the editor's stance. Then, in writing "letters to the editor," students have less difficulty assessing their own arguments once they know their audience's beliefs.

Students learn both that in trying to infer audience beliefs, writers must often rely on prototypical assumptions about people's beliefs— for example, that the chamber of commerce will oppose teacher raises— and that such assumptions are not always valid. For example, the chamber may favor salary increases in order to avoid a teacher strike that would tarnish the image of the town as a prosperous community. The memos can also reveal the status or power of each group, another important attribute for writers to assess, particularly in making a request, as noted earlier. For example, in the teacher negotiation role-playing session, the teachers' team could attempt simply to demand a 16 percent salary raise, or they could opt for the more mitigating form of requesting a 16 percent raise with supporting evidence justifying that raise.

Activities: Status or Power

Teacher Negotiation Role-playing Session: Establishing Status or Power through Writing

Purpose: to help students recognize that power or status is not a given, but can be established through writing.

Activity: One of the interesting things that occurs in the role-playing session is that students' perceptions of the status or power associated with different roles change as the role-playing progresses. Students begin with certain prototypical assumptions about their own and others' roles as teachers, parents, students, businesspeople, etc. As the role-playing progresses, however, students use their writing to shape other students' perceptions of their roles. For example, as the superintendent, a student may write highly assertive memos to all parties, attempting to dominate the session. Or, a student may convey a different posture for the superintendent, writing only bland pronouncements. When the students read their memos aloud, the memos themselves create a social world in which some students have more power or status than others. It is often the case that the television news reporter, depending on the role-player's ability, emerges as a powerful force because that reporter can often distort facts or dramatize conflicts.

Because the roles are constantly being redefined, students assess the memos according to the status or power implied by each memo's language. They must also interpret the memo writer's intentions or motives. Often the memos are used to threaten or intimidate simply as a negotiation tactic designed to help reach a settlement. In replying to the memos, students must then assess their own language according to the status or power implied by that language. If, for example, a member of the teacher negotiating team receives a memo from the head of the school board stating that her participation on the negotiations team may jeopardize her extracurricular coaching job, the teacher assesses the degree to which her own language should imply that she is or is not totally powerless in the situation. For example, the teacher may respond in an authoritative manner, mentioning the laws regarding threats to employees serving as labor negotiators.

Writing Letters to People in Positions of Authority

Purpose: to help students learn to assess their writing in terms of appropriate speech acts or style and the extent to which they foster audience identification with a problem.

Activity: In this activity, students write letters to people in "positions of authority," a category that could include parents, teachers, school administrators, politicians, business leaders, and other persons who shape policy influencing students. The students then address some actual problem resulting from these persons' policies. For example, a student may complain to a school principal about the lack of computers in a school.

In describing their problems and solutions, students assess the extent to which their audience will identify with their depiction of the problem. In Richard Nixon's Watergate speeches, for example, Nixon created identification between his television viewers and himself by appealing to a "silent majority" who appreciated "hard-working" Congresspeople who were not "wallowing in Watergate." Similarly, a student writing to complain about the lack of computers in her school may describe herself as someone who is interested in "fostering learning" and the principal as someone who is "also concerned with fostering learning."

In assessing these letters, students also assess the appropriateness of the types of speech acts they are employing—whether they are in a position to demand that something be done about a problem or only to request that something be done, and whether the formality or informality of their style is appropriate to their relationship with the audience.

Activity: Needs: Actions

Direction-giving Activities: Assuming an Audience's Perspective

Purpose: to help students learn to recognize that in order for an audience to do certain things, that audience needs certain knowledge.

Activity: In this direction-giving activity, students pair up, one member of the pair facing the front of the room while the other faces the back. A teacher then draws or puts up a figure at each end of the room. Each student in the pair must then write out directions for drawing the figure his or her partner cannot see. Students are encouraged to consider what their partners may already know in order to draw the figure. For example, a student might consider certain metaphors that would help someone envision the figure, such as "football," "eye," "fish," etc.

Students then monitor their partner's attempts to draw the figure, orally advising them until they successfully complete the drawing. The pairs then discuss the directions, noting which metaphors or references to prior knowledge were the most helpful in drawing the figure. The writers also discuss how they anticipated their audience's behaviors, for example by envisioning themselves drawing the figure. In all of this, students are learning to adopt their reader's perspective in assessing the sufficiency, relevance, and clarity of their directions.

Activities: Comprehension Processes

Studying Others' Writing for Organization and Formatting of Information

Purpose: to help students learn to assess how the organization and formatting of information assists readers in processing information.

Activity: Students analyze magazine ads, brochures, manuals, or reports according to their use of a number of strategies designed to

enhance readability, thinking through their own comprehension processes aloud and noting specific items that foster or impede readability.
Students may then discuss revisions that would improve readability.

It is often useful to look at different versions of the same text—an
initial version and a revision—noting the changes made. For example, I
have used the Apple Writer II manual and the much superior Apple
Writer IIe manual, the latter a model for a number of readability
strategies.

Following are some aspects of readability, in addition to vocabulary
and sentence length, students could use to analyze texts:

1. Forecasting: The writer summarizes subsequent information in a
   text so that readers apply the appropriate prior knowledge schema.
2. Subheads and underlining: A writer employs subheads or underlining to help readers forecast text content or highlight information most relevant to their own needs.
3. White space and typography: The writer visually formats information using ample white space and typographic elements so that
   readers can easily follow or locate information.
4. Illustrations or graphics: The writer uses illustrations or graphics
   to help readers visually comprehend the text.
5. Repetition of key words: The writer repeats certain crucial terms,
   often grammatical subjects of sentences.
6. The "scenario principle": The writer uses sentences in which
   human agents perform actions in defined contexts.

Peer Editing for Readability

Purpose: to help students apply their knowledge of readability strategies to their own writing and recognize how these strategies influence
a reader's comprehension.

Activity: Having gone through the analysis activity described above,
students then write their own text that will be published for other
students in a class, since publication often enhances concern about
readability. Students are encouraged to employ the strategies listed
above and to assess their texts in terms of readability.

As they are writing final drafts of their texts, students hold conferences with their peers and receive some line-by-line "telling" feedback
in which a reader thinks aloud about his or her own comprehension
processes. (It may be necessary for a teacher to demonstrate "telling"
feedback prior to such conferences.) Students then assess their texts
with their readers, mutually suggesting revisions to improve readability.

Summary

Based on our model of audience analysis, we have proposed activities designed to help students learn to infer audience attributes and use those attributes to assess their writing. These activities should help students learn to consider a range of different audience schemata, and learning to apply these schemata is one important step toward learning to become one's own best reader.

Notes

1. E. D. Hirsch, Jr., *The Philosophy of Composition* (Chicago: Univ. of Chicago Press, 1977) and "Cultural Literacy," *The American Scholar* 52 (1983): 157.

2. See Margaret Steffensen, Chitra Joas-Dev, and Richard C. Anderson, "A Cross-cultural Perspective on Reading Comprehension," *Reading Research Quarterly* 15 (1979): 10–29; and J. W. Pickert and Richard C. Anderson, "Taking Different Perspectives on a Story," *Journal of Educational Psychology* 69 (1977): 309–15.

Writing Plans as Strategies for Reading, Writing, and Revising

Barbey N. Dougherty

As writers and readers we have a mutual goal, that of constructing meaning. To accomplish this goal, we need structures to help build the texts we create—both as writers constructing written texts and as readers constructing interpretations of the texts writers have produced. These structures are provided by writing plans, which direct our reading, writing, and revising activities.

In expository texts, the form writing plans provide is particularly important because structure is not inherent in the information we present, but is something we impose upon it. There are eight conventional plans for structuring material: information, sequence, definition, collection, assertion and support, comparison and contrast, cause and effect, and response, the forms of which include problem-solution and analysis-evaluation.[1]

These plans exist as part of our culture and are acquired as a result of our experiences in reading and writing. Those of us, therefore, who have had more exposure to, and practice with, these plans will have a clearer grasp of these structures than others. In this paper, I argue that we can help our students become more effective readers *and* writers if we instruct them in the uses of writing plans.

Understanding Writing Plans

Writing plans are best understood as mental representations of various ways of approaching a topic. They consist of an image of parts related structurally and semantically. If we think of these plans as cognitive structures, as opposed to something in the text, we can explain a number of paradoxes in the writer-reader relationship. A cognitive view of writing plans explains, for example, why texts imperfectly realize writers' intended meanings and why various readers identify different plans of organization, disagree about a writer's primary purpose, and can identify a plan even when some of the component parts are missing. For another thing, a cognitive view explains how the texts we build when we read can be viewed as similar to the ones writers intend when they write.

As cognitive structures, these plans are like blueprints. Just as a blueprint describes the structural underpinnings of a building without yet realizing a particular building made of specific materials, so a writing plan sketches out the relationship of ideas with broad penstrokes without yet realizing any specific content.

As writers we use these plans as a way of exploring and thinking about a topic and as a strategy for revision, just as contractors use an architect's plan for implementing the architect's vision. Similarly, as readers we use the plans writers provide, or we create our own according to our purposes for reading, just as viewers of a building search for formal relationships as they analyze the building's harmony.

The plans I have identified bear some similarity to conventional methods of development (narration, description, exemplification, comparison and contrast, cause and effect, and problem and solution), but differ in one crucial way. The conventional methods of development describe only one kind of macrostructure—a hierarchical one where the methods of development give support to a more general idea. A familiar example is the kind of structure built in support of a thesis statement or topic sentence.

By contrast, the eight plans I describe reflect several kinds of text-level macrostructures. Descriptive and informative texts have parts that are only loosely related to a larger whole; sequential texts have parts that are related by time; comparison and contrast, cause and effect, and response texts have parts that are interconnected; while texts employing collection and assertion-support plans consist of parts that are hierarchically ordered.

Informative texts give more facts about something—the who, what, where, when, and why of a topic—while definition texts discuss something more precisely by putting it in a class of differentiating it from related items, by telling how it looks, how it works, or how it has developed. The macrostructure of these texts can be visualized as follows:

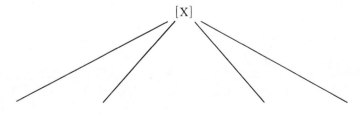

The generalizing statement [X] is usually inferred by the reader, and its optional nature is indicated in the diagram by brackets. In the illustration below, the generalizing statement is something like "These are some facts about Montessori":

> The Montessori method is an educational system developed for preschool children by Maria Montessori of Italy. It is designed to help children learn by themselves through structured activities. Special teaching materials are used to encourage children's natural desire to manipulate objects and discover on their own. These include geometric letters and shapes, devices with snaps, buttons, and zippers that teach children to perform everyday tasks, and materials designed to improve language skills and to introduce art, music, and sciences.

In these plans, individual parts work together loosely to describe or give information about the whole.

Sequential texts also have a loose structure, for component parts are related by time, one event following another like beads on a string. There is no generalizing statement. Ideas follow each other in sequence, for example:

> On January 30, 1933, Adolf Hitler came to power as Chancellor of Germany. On March 23, 1933, after the new general elections of March 5, Hitler made a policy statement in which he proposed to work for peaceful relations between Church and State. The Reichstag, in turn, approved the Enabling Act that transferred the duty of legislation from parliament to the cabinet for four years. Five days later, at the Fulda's Bishop conference, the Catholic Church withdrew its prohibition against Nazi party membership and called for loyalty and obedience to the new regime.

The text macrostructure can be visualized as follows:

Texts that explore relationships have a series of interconnected parts—a cause related to an effect, a problem to a solution, a comparison of one item to another, an analysis to an evaluation. The macrostructure can be visualized as follows:

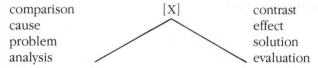

comparison   [X]   contrast
cause   effect
problem   solution
analysis   evaluation

A generalizing statement is usually inferred. If present, it enumerates the basis of comparison, or relates cause to effect, solution to problem, or evaluation to analysis. This kind of macrostructure is harder to use than the more loosely related macrostructures created by informative, sequential, or definition texts because the parts have to be connected, and there are vigorous rules for determining how to relate cause to effect, problem to solution, and comparison to contrast.

Texts that argue a point or explain a concept are hierarchical because the subsequent text supports the larger whole. The text produced can consist of a collection of parts equal in weight and making up a larger whole. These parts might be a collection of examples or reasons, a collection of parts dividing a whole (classification), or a collection of parts creating a larger whole (analysis). The macrostructure of these texts can be visualized as follows:

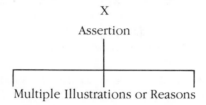

X
Assertion

Multiple Illustrations or Reasons

In a collection text, the parts illustrate or explain the whole (classification, exemplification) or they work together to define the whole (analysis). Or the text produced can consist of a detailed support of a single idea, in which case the macrostructure looks like this:

X
Assertion

Support

The support can consist of a narrative, a description focused to make a point, a preferred solution to a problem, a comparison weighted to favor one item, or a causal pattern traced to focus on positive or negative effects following from a certain course of action.

Using Plans to Build Texts

Knowing what the most-often-used writing plans are is one thing, but using them is something else. Instructing students in how to use plans can help them be more effective readers and writers.

Students need to understand that texts are built as a result of asking and then answering specific questions. As writers we use questions to probe a topic and explore relationships more fully for ourselves and our readers. As active readers we come to a text with our own questions, which in turn guide our interpretation. Sometimes we have different questions than did the writer, and so the texts we produce in response to a written text differ from the text the writer intended. For example, when I am deciding which of two movies to see on Friday night, I look at movie reviews using a comparison plan to direct my reading, asking first how X and Y are alike or different, and then evaluating those differences in terms of my needs. The writer may have produced his or her text using different questions, perhaps asking how plot, character, setting, camera angle, and editing work together to create an aesthetic whole. The writer has structured his or her text using collection, but I have structured mine using comparison and contrast. In either case, a plan has provided a structure directing the writer's production of the written text and my interpretation of that text.

The texts we build in response to the questions we pose vary according to our purposes for reading or for writing. In building a sequential text, we ask: When did X occur, or when does it occur, in relation to Y? We use these questions when we read to see how events are related to each other in time. When we write, we use these plans to report past events, give background information, help readers understand a process, or direct readers to perform a procedure.

In building an informative text, we ask the who, what, where, when, and why of a topic. When we read, we use these questions to direct our exploration of an unfamiliar area; and when we write, we answer these questions for the readers we imagine. Many newspaper, magazine, and encyclopedia articles are built by this plan.

When we use definition, we ask a series of questions in order to describe the distinctive features of the item we are exploring. What class of things does it belong to? How is it different from other things in its class? What are its features? What does it do? How does it operate? How has it developed? This is the plan of many introductory texts, in which the writer's main aim is to familiarize us with new concepts. It is also the plan we use when we are reading in unfamiliar areas.

When we use a collection plan, we explore the relationship of individual parts to a whole, and our questions vary, depending on whether we are classifying, explaining, arguing, or analyzing. When we classify, we ask: What are the types of X? How can each type be characterized? What makes it distinctive from those things to which it is related? When we explain a general idea, we ask: What examples can I give to support my point? When we argue we ask: What reasons can I give in support of my claim? And when we analyze we ask: What are the component parts of a larger whole? How can they be described, and how do they work together to make up the whole?

Familiar examples of texts built by collection are classification (there are four types of X), the five-paragraph essay in which three reasons support a claim, or the essay of exemplification where several examples illustrate a generalization. More complex examples are analytical pieces exploring the relationship of parts to a whole, for example papers analyzing art, music, and literature. Whether we are reading or writing, our inquiry is enhanced if we ask the right questions as we approach a topic.

In using assertion-support, we are concerned with what evidence or reasons we can give to support a claim. And to find our support, we use the conventional methods of development: narration, exemplification, comparison and contrast, cause and effect, problem-solution, and definition. As writers, we ask a variety of questions. What evidence can I find in my own experience or the experience of others to support my claim? How might I use comparison and contrast to show that one thing or one course of action is superior to another? How might I show that one course of action is the preferable solution to a problem? How might I argue for a state of affairs on the basis of the positive or negative consequences of following a course of action? Can I form a description to make my point more effectively, selecting those attributes that support my claim? Or how can I use an accepted value as a yardstick for arguing that the current state of affairs does not measure up to the end result desired?

These questions direct writers as they search for ways to support a claim for their readers. In turn, readers should ask the same kinds of questions when they want to discover how a writer has structured an argument or when they want to read other people's work in order to glean support for their own developing points of view. When they read critically, they go a step further, asking: How effectively has the writer supported his or her claim?

In using comparison and contrast, we ask: How are X and Y alike and how are they different? What are the more general bases for comparison underlying the specific details? Are there similarities where differences are most apparent and differences where similarities abound? And what can be made of these differences? Writers use comparison and contrast in order to define a concept for readers or to argue for something's superiority over something else, while readers use it to understand a concept or evaluate two or more things.

In using a cause and effect plan, we search for connections among actor, action, and goal. We can explore relationships among past events, asking: What is the relationship of X and Y? Of Y and Z? This kind of thinking is typical of historical analysis. Or we can explore the relationships among events occurring again and again. This kind of thinking is typical of thinking in the sciences, which seek explanations of recurring events. In geography, we analyze recurring relationships between geography and historical development in order to see the impact of geographical features on human history. Or we can predict what might happen next, asking: What will be the consequences of X? This kind of thinking is typical of economic forecasting. In ethical inquiry, we explore the consequences of a hypothetical instance, asking: What might happen if? For example, we might speculate about how we would identify the newly constituted individual if a brain transplant were possible.

Whatever the case, we will want to evaluate the sufficiency of our causal explanations. Rules for establishing sufficiency are well defined by methods of inquiry in various disciplines and have been nicely summarized by Jeanne Fahnestock and Marie Secor in *College Composition and Communication*.[2] In establishing sufficiency, we search for:

1. *a single difference.* This involves exploring parallel cases, one where an effect occurred, and one where it didn't, and then searching for a single factor to explain the difference. This is the strategy of controlled experiments.

2. *a common factor.* This involves a search for a common factor in an event which occurs again and again. This is how doctors hypothesized the cause of toxic shock syndrome.

3. *concomitant variation.* This involves exploring the relationships of two events to each other, for example the decline in SAT scores and the rise in the number of hours college-bound students watch TV, or the decline in SAT scores in relation to the increase in the number of students aspiring to go to college and taking the entrance exam.

4. *elimination.* This involves supporting a claim by eliminating other possible causes, until the most plausible one has been reached.

When you are writing, you will want to explore the sufficiency of your own explanations; and when you are reading, you will want to explore the sufficiency of the author's explanation.

Finally, in using a response pattern, we look for relationships between a problem and its solution or an evaluation and its analysis. When we are looking for a solution to a problem, we first ask: What is the problem? What are its causes and what are its effects? We then ask: What might we do to change the situation as we understand it? And does the change we envision address one of the causes of the problem? As we explore the solution to the problem, we need to apply the same rules for sufficiency we applied to causal thinking.

When we use analysis-evaluation, we ask two questions, the first directed to analyzing something, the second to evaluating it. After we analyze a topic, asking the same questions mentioned earlier—What are the parts of X? How can they be described? And how do they interrelate?—we evaluate by asking: How are my standards related to the topic as I have analyzed it?

Whether we are reading or writing, we ought to be concerned with the sufficiency of our explanations. That is, we need to ensure that our solutions fit the causes we have determined, and that our analyses fit our evaluations.

Using Plans to Achieve Your Purpose and to Interpret Others'

In addition to being useful as a tool for building texts, plans provide writers with ways of realizing their purpose and readers with methods of interpreting a writer's purpose.

As writers we use these plans as strategies for realizing our purpose at several levels. We choose our top-level plan according to our primary purpose for writing, and subplans help us realize subpurposes for writing. In conducting an experiment, for example, a scientist poses a question, sometimes stated as a hypothesis, and then designs and conducts an experiment in order to observe how accurate the hypothesis is. The text reporting the experiment illustrates how the scientist's purposes and the corresponding plans organize material from the top down. The top-level plan is response: The question is posed in the introduction, and the answer is given in the description of the results and the discussion of their implications. Each section in turn has its own subplans, realizing subpurposes. Frequently the question is developed by describing a problem and reviewing related research. The review of research can be developed by a sequential plan in which the history of the problem to date is examined, or by a comparison plan where past attempts to solve the problem are grouped and shown to be inadequate. The section describing materials and methods is frequently developed by description (of the materials necessary) and sequence (the steps in conducting the experiment), although the discussion might be organized by assertion-support with a subplan of contrastive analysis.

Thus the texts we produce as we write or read are layered. The structure might be visualized in a diagram resembling an upside-down tree: the trunk represents the purpose for writing, and the branches represent the way ideas are structured to achieve the top-level purpose. For example:

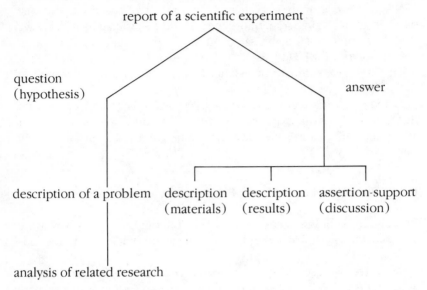

report of a scientific experiment

question
(hypothesis)

answer

description of a problem   description   description   assertion-support
                            (materials)   (results)   (discussion)

analysis of related research

When we write we select a top-level plan and revise according to our reasons for writing. When our primary purpose is to *inform* or *report,* we use a description, a sequence, or an unweighted comparison. When it is to *interpret, analyze,* or *classify,* we use a collection plan, dividing a whole into related parts. When our purpose is to *explain,* we may collect examples or illustrations, or use an assertion-support, cause-effect, or question-answer pattern.

As we shift to an evaluative, speculative, or argumentative stance, we choose other top-level plans. When we want to *recommend* or *evaluate,* we use a weighted comparison, analyze a topic and then evaluate it, or analyze a problem and offer a solution. When we *explore,* we can analyze a problem and call for a resolution. Or we can pose a question and respond by designing an experiment and reporting on it or by synthesizing the research findings of other scholars. Or we use cause and effect, posing a hypothetical "if" and exploring the consequences. When our purpose is to *predict,* we use a cause-effect pattern, predicting future consequences on the basis of current causes. And, finally, when our purpose is to *argue,* we use a collection plan, giving several reasons in support of our claim; or we use an assertion-support plan in which we make a claim and then use a single method of support, such as description, narration, exemplification, definition, comparison and contrast, cause-effect, or problem-solution.

Below are some purposes for writing with the corresponding options in choice of plan.

Purpose	*Plan*
to give information	description
	definition
	sequence
	unweighted comparison
to classify	a collection of items that separately make up a whole
to analyze	a collection of parts that interconnect to make up a whole
	an analysis of a problem, its causes, and series of possible solutions, one of which is favored
to explain	assertion-support
	a collection of examples or illustrations
	cause-effect
	question-answer
to argue	assertion-support
	a collection of supporting arguments
to explore	question-answer
	cause-effect (hypothetical "if")
	problem-solution
to predict	cause-effect
to recommend	analysis-evaluation
	problem-solution
	weighted comparison

When we read, we interpret a writer's purpose partly on the basis of what we perceive as the top-level plan.[3] When, for example, we identify the top-level plan as sequence or description we are likely to see the writer's purpose as informative, but when we identify the top-level plan as assertion-support we are likely to see it as argument.

Readers often identify a writer's purpose through explicit signals. Conversely, writers can assist their readers by making their intentions explicit. One such signal is the use of performative verbs like "argue," "explain," "recommend," "describe," or "define." Another is an explicit naming of the plan (the cause is . . . the effect is . . . ; the problem is . . . the solution is . . .). Predictions can also signal the plan of organization; for example, forms of "to be" and "to have" signal definition, and "is similar to" and "is different from" signal comparison and contrast; verbs like "causes," "leads to," and "results" indicate cause and effect. Parallel structure indicates a collection of parallel reasons or comparison and contrast, while various conjunctions indicate different plans:

sequence	first, next, finally
	before, during, after
assertion-support	for example, to explain
collection	first, second, third,
	moreover, furthermore, also,
	in addition
comparison-contrast	like, unlike, on the other
	hand, however, but
cause-effect	because, since, when, if,
	therefore, thus, so

In the example below, author Robert Deis clearly signals his organization as a collection of examples supporting his claim that snow is a vital element in the ecology of Maine. His plan is signaled by a lead paragraph that makes a general claim about snow, and then further signaled by separate paragraphs, each developing new benefits of snow. At the sentence level, the plan is signaled by conjunctions, repetition of key terms related to the benefits of snow, and parallel structure.

> Snow is one thing Maine usually has lots of during its long winters. Some people love it, some hate it, but few realize *how important a resource it is,* or appreciate *the critical role* it plays in the ecology of the Pine Tree State.
>
> That farmers know *one benefit* of snow is obvious from the fact that long ago it was dubbed a poor man's fertilizer. Eventually, scientists validated this bit of traditional wisdom by discovering that snow is indeed a source of nutrients for crops. . . .
>
> Most farmers *also* realize that a *good* thick layer of snow will insulate their fields and keep the ground water from freezing too

far down. The thinner the snow cover, the deeper the frost pene-
trates the soil. A winter with little snow forebodes a late planting in
the spring due to the increased time it takes the fields to thaw out.

That infamous season called mudtime is *also worse* when snow-
fall has been minimal. In spring the upper levels of the soil un-
freeze first, but the melt water is unable to drain down into the
frozen layers underneath. It stays on the surface until the lower
layers of snow thaw, creating a muddy headache for a farmer. . . .

To plants and animals living in Maine, snow is a *mixed blessing,*
but on the whole it is vastly more *beneficial* than harmful. It is true
that hunger-wasted deer sometimes can be immobilized, to become easy prey, by deep drifts. *But,* on the other hand, deep snow
slows down predators, such as feral dogs and coyotes, making it
more difficult to reach winter deer yards. Maine's white-tail *also*
can *benefit* as snow builds up and weights down on branches of
trees, bringing branches that would ordinarily be out of a deer's
reach within browsing level.

Snow is an especially important *asset* in the winter for many
small animals. It is one of nature's most efficient insulators due to
the countless dead air spaces that exist between the fallen flakes.
This is of vital importance to the many cold-blooded animals that
hibernate in the leaf mold or soil under the snow.

(Robert Deis, "Snow: Nature's Insulator," *Maine Audubon
Quarterly* 5, no. 2 (Winter 1981/82): 7, emphasis added)

The visual map below highlights the points in the collection above,
some of which are further subdivided.

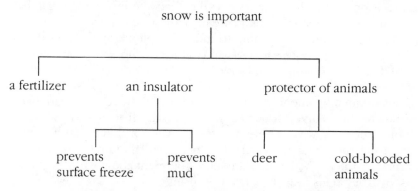

Although writers use explicit signals of their organization to invite
readers to share in their intended meaning, readers will at times ignore
these signals because their own interest and preoccupations override
the writer's signals. When one researcher, Linda Jones, gave a similar
passage on the single-tax theory to professors and to students, for
example, she discovered that they had different interpretations, despite
the fact both groups perceived an assertion-support pattern.[4] Professors
saw the text as argumentative, whereas students saw it as explanatory.

Jones accounted for the difference on the basis of prior knowledge and accustomed social role. Professors know that the single-tax theory was one of many possible justifications for taxation; so they read the text as an argument. Their identification of an argument was further reinforced by their usual role as critics of others' performances. On the other hand, students saw the text as explanatory because they were unaware of any controversy and because they usually read to acquire information. These differing interpretations underline the complexity of the writer-reader relationship and point to the need to develop a contractual understanding of the responsibilities of readers and writers.[5] Writers have a responsibility to be continuously aware of the needs and preoccupations of their readers, and readers have a responsibility to consider for whom and for what purposes a text has been written and to judge it accordingly.

Using Plans to Revise

Writing plans are useful in a third way: they provide a strategy for revision. Writers revise as they move through subsequent drafts, frequently moving from a loosely organized structure like those of information, sequence, or definition to one whose parts are interconnected or hierarchically ordered. Readers go through the same kind of revision as they reread a text. As they become increasingly familiar with a topic, the texts they build are increasingly complex.

The movement from simple to more complex structures has been documented by the research of Linda Flower, who shows, in "Writer-Based Prose: A Cognitive Basis for Problems in Writing," how effective writers literally transform their texts in the process of revision.[6] Initial drafts frequently follow what she identifies as a "survey" or "narrative" structure. In a survey structure, writers recall all they know about a topic—the who, what, where, when, and why. Or they recall items by reporting the order in which they occurred, building a sequential structure. Later, when writers are more confident about what they want to say, they transform their texts by using a different top-level plan, frequently replacing an informative, descriptive, or unweighted comparison plan with assertion-support, collection, or analysis-evaluation. In the process of working with their material they are able to see more clearly what it means to them and what its implications are.

I suspect readers go through a similar kind of revision as they read and reread a text, although I've seen no experimental confirmation of this. When I read a text for the first time, I construct a loose image of its parts, consisting of random facts and observations. But when I reread, I observe more carefully how the author has related ideas while at the same time making connections to what I already know. In the process, I build an increasingly complex image of the text, moving from an informative or sequential structure to a more complex structure like comparison, collection, or assertion-support. The text I finally build is a composite of what the writer intended and what I need because of my unique purposes for reading.

Implications for Teaching

The teaching implications that follow from my discussion of the uses of writing plans are several. We can help students write better and read more effectively if we give them specific strategies for building texts, making sure they are familiar with the conventional patterns of text building. We can provide examples of different kinds of texts, and we can provide them with the kinds of questions they need to ask to produce their own texts or to read the texts produced by others. We can help students achieve their purposes more clearly if we demonstrate how different plans help achieve different purposes, and we can help them interpret what others have written more fairly if they understand the relation of plan to purpose. Finally, we can help them build increasingly complex text structures if they understand the intimate relation between the plans they choose and the texts they build. As they become increasingly more confident in the content they are working with, they will have the courage to transform their texts by selecting a different plan for organizing and communicating what they know.

In sum, I believe that if we teach students about how to use writing plans to direct their inquiry as they read and write, we will help them become more effective in their reading and writing. In turn, others will judge their writing to be more successful. Research in composition and reading supports my claim. At the University of Michigan, for example, a survey of faculty revealed how highly they prize organization in expository texts.[7] The same preference is shown by faculty of the English Composition Board, who read placement essays given to entering college students. Students not yet ready for introductory composition are frequently identified by their inability to use conventional expository patterns. Moreover, reading research specialists, including Bonnie Meyer and Donna Alvermann,[8] have discovered that readers who identify and use the plans provided by the writer more fully understand the writer's purposes and the material being presented. In short, there is ample evidence to suggest that we do our students a favor when we make explicit the structures and uses of writing plans.

Notes

1. I am indebted for my description of writing plans to ideas developed by Bonnie Meyer in *Prose Analysis: Procedure, Purposes and Problems,* Research Report 11, Prose Learning Series, Department of Educational Psychology, Arizona State University, 1981, and Linda Jones in *Theme in English Expository Discourse* (Lake Bluff, Ill.: Jupiter Press, 1977), 138–50. I have adapted some of their ideas, but have created my own definitions, which differ in several respects from theirs. Two of the names—*collection* and *response*—I borrow from Bonnie Meyer, but my description of collection embraces a number of purposes for writing—classification, analysis, exposition, and argument. The eight plans I have identified do not give a complete linguistic description of all possible ways of organizing a text. I have chosen to discuss those I believe to be most useful as strategies of exploration and communication.

2. Jeanne Fahnestock and Marie Secor, "Teaching Argument: A Theory of Types," *College Composition and Communication* 34, no. 1 (Feb. 1983): 20–30.

3. Linda Jones develops a hierarchical model of text interpretation using tagmemics in *Theme in English Expository Discourse.* In chapter 5, "A Hierarchical Model of Theme," she shows how readers identify theme as they move from the performative interaction level through script, point, and concept. I use *writing plan* in the same way she uses *script.*

4. Jones, 47.

5. Robert Tierney and Jill Lazanksky, "The Rights and Responsibilities of Readers and Writers: A Contractual Agreement," Reading Education Report no. 15, January 1980, University of Illinois at Urbana-Champaign.

6. Linda Flower, "Writer-Based Prose: A Cognitive Basis for Problems in Writing," *College English* 41, no. 1 (Sept. 1979): 19–37.

7. Richard Bailey, "This Teaching Works," report to the faculty of Literature, Science and the Arts, University of Michigan, August 1981.

8. See Donna Alvermann, "Effects of Graphic Organizers, Textual Organization, and Reading Comprehension Level on Recall of Expository Prose," paper presented at the annual convention of the International Reading Association, New Orleans, April 1981; and Bonnie Meyer, "Research on Prose Comprehension: Applications for Composition Teachers," Research Report no. 2, Department of Educational Psychology, Arizona State University, 1979.

II Reading and Writing as Social Activities

Cognitive Stereoscopy and the Study of Language and Literature

David Bleich
Indiana University at Bloomington

The principle of cognitive stereoscopy is that knowledge comes when some other experience is perceived through at least two perspectives at once. The individual first integrates the two (or more) perspectives in the same way that two retinal images are integrated by the brain to produce three-dimensional visual "knowledge." In the case of conceptual knowledge, it can only emerge or be declared as such if another person says "I also know this." Knowledge thus requires a subjective integration and an intersubjective integration. How certain any item of knowledge is depends on how wide a community is needed for us to act on that knowledge, but there is no knowledge that does not require at least two people, each with at least two perspectives. Knowledge is always a re-cognition because it is a seeing through one perspective superimposed in another in such a way that the one perspective does not appear to be prior to the other. Because the perspectives are different, or heretofore unrelated in our minds, the new knowledge is sometimes described as the "aha" experience, or surprising and satisfying at once, as when we "get" a joke.

Piaget described this combination of perspectives as the internal reciprocal assimilation of schemata. He gives an example from his adult life. While driving in his car, he had occasion to use a handkerchief. When he was finished using it he needed to put it in a secure place and so he stuffed it in a crevice inside the car. Later it began to rain, and he needed something to keep his windshield only slightly open (the early car models had windshields which swung open from the bottom). His insight came when he remembered having stuffed the handkerchief in the crevice and "realized" that he could remove the handkerchief and stuff it into the crevice between the top of the windshield and the frame of the car. The schema of "stuffing the handkerchief" was assimilated to the schema of "holding the windshield open." The one schema was associated with the past need and the other with the present need. The two schemata were assimilated to one another to form the new schema. In this way, the new knowledge of how to keep the windshield slightly open can be described as the internal reciprocal assimilation of two schemata, or, in the terms I used above, the mutual superposition of two perspectives.

While this example suggests how reciprocal assimilation generally works in adult life, Piaget developed the idea through the study of how intelligence grows in infants. Each new phase of infantile mental capability, he showed, creates new "knowledge" by allowing the infant to combine the old schemata with the new situation to form a new schema of knowledge, which is then maintained until it encounters a new situation. Each new piece of knowledge thereby has a stereoscopic character: its pertinence to the present always has an allusion to the past.

My analysis of Helen Keller's acquisition of language suggested how cognitive stereoscopy is a principle in the infantile acquisition of language in general.[1] When she acquired language at about six and a half years old, Keller learned two *sets* of experiences and the principle of how each set depended on the other. Each set functioned through the sense of touch—the "touch words" which Anne Sullivan taught her and the "touch things" which she had theretofore known *only* through touch. When she learned that each of these categories was separate from the other, and that they were dependent on one another through *predication,* she acquired the two basic language capacities—the idea that "everything has a name" and the idea that when one predicates names on one another, we get new names—sentences—for new experiences. Because the elaborate mental groundwork had been laid in advance—before she became ill at the age of nineteen months—the two new ideas came fairly quickly under the strong influence of her teacher. The two categories are, in Piaget's terms, the two schemata of language, or the two perspectives on experience, which, when combined, produce the new category, "knowledge of language."

Naming and syntax both use predication. The sentence combines the "perspective" of the mutual predication of name and thing and the mutual predication of name and name. That is, two stereoscopies combine to form a new one in each new sentence. Name and thing are mutually predicated in the following way: the name of a thing changes if the thing is put to different uses, so that if a trunk is used as an endtable it may be called an "endtable." Conversely, if something is called by a different name it may become a different thing, as when a swinging stone was called a "pendulum" and thus was understood to be something else, even though it was the same swinging stone. In general, the principle is that names can change while the thing stays the same, and things can change while the name stays the same. In sentences, predication is also mutual, even though either the subject or the predicate may be privileged in any particular case. In the sentence "The boy is fat," the speech situation may be privileging the boy, as the predicate will be thought to be "about" the boy. But this same sentence could also be privileging "fat," as when it would be used to answer the question, "What is fat?" The sentence itself is only a juxtaposition of the two categories "boy" and "fat"; its use tells if and/or how to privilege one term. The stereoscopy is thus present in any use of language and is the ground on which a particular use of language may be called knowledge.

Now consider a name or sentence as a finished form, a unified item. As such it is in the more general category of "symbolic forms" (as described by Cassirer), which includes things like paintings and buildings, for example. A symbolic form is stereoscopic by virtue of its being both denotative and connotative at once, even though one of these perspectives is usually privileged over the other. The denotative meaning of the form is usually fixed (provisionally, in context), while the connotative is variable (in that same context). The line "miles to go before I sleep" has a fixed simple meaning, but we are not interested in this meaning when reading and studying the poem from which it came; we are interested in how much and what kind of variation we may make of the meaning within a collective activity of reading and commenting on the poem. Conversely, a mathematical formula may be elegant or cumbersome—or there may be elegant or cumbersome versions of the same principle. But if it is used to describe a moving train, for example, we are only interested in how accurately it will predict the motion and not in its qualities as a mathematical entity. A symbolic form cannot have only variable meaning or only fixed meaning; rather, both kinds of meaning must be present or available. For denotation to obtain, connotation must also be possible; for connotation to obtain, denotation must also be possible. Language creates stereoscopic knowledge by evoking both of these perspectival possibilities in each use.

Language and cognitive stereoscopy are not only the outcome of biological growth or even the intellectual growth of the individual. For language to emerge, there must be the enabling social and affective circumstance of the child's intimate relationship with the mother, or "mothering" figure. This relationship motivates and regulates the acquisition of language and cognitive stereoscopy, and subsequent relationships are needed for the continued function of these capabilities.

Since the child's birth, mother and child have been "separating" from one another; the child has become increasingly autonomous. The acquisition of language marks the major step in the onset of psychological autonomy—the feeling of, the experience of, and probably the knowledge of one's distinctness from others. This is the social sense of cognitive stereoscopy: the child sees him- or herself as detached from and attached to the mother at once—a part of the mother yet distinct from her. When language is acquired, the child can reconstitute subjectively the togetherness that preceded separation. The child knows he or she is a self just like the other self. The reconstitution is the knowledge of the relationship, the conscious sense of mutuality, which before had only been a syndrome of sensations and experiences. In this sense the primary motive for the acquisition of language and cognitive stereoscopy is affective and social. The sustaining relationship has been continued and at the same time transformed in a decisive way.

Self-awareness is a part of cognitive stereoscopy and becomes a subsequent means for its continuation and development. As far as we can tell, it is that sort of awareness that distinguishes human mental life from that of other species: it seems accurate to use "awareness" to describe animals' consciousness, and *self*-awareness to describe human consciousness. Self-awareness is the source of human foreknowledge of death, and is the ground from which ethical standards are derived. Cognitive stereoscopy, in its form as self-awareness, acts to stabilize and enhance social relationships throughout the cycle of human development. At the same time, cognitive stereoscopy and language, through their ability to create knowledge, perform a different sort of social adaptation—providing "names" that are commonly held and that can be used to improve the quality of collective life—scientific knowledge, for example, or knowledge on how to survive in the jungle.

When knowledge is called "objective," this means that it has been accepted by a collective: two or more people say they "know" the same thing. However, this objective knowledge should be more accurately described as intersubjective knowledge—knowledge that exists by virtue of the multiple perspectives that helped to validate it. If it is called intersubjective, rather than objective, it is more easily understood to be continuously available for change: it is not something independent of perspectives, but a creature of perspectives. The changing of social arrangements thus changes perspectives and thus changes knowledge.

Historically, the intersubjective government of the linguistic ability to objectify experiences has been suppressed in order to conserve the privileges of those having the economic advantage. A presumed independent standard of objectivity is used to back up highly centered political authority. Whereas if knowledge is understood to be stereoscopic, the knower, or observer, understands him- or herself to be "in" the picture, if knowledge is understood to be objective, or "two-dimensional," the knower or observer sees him- or herself out of the picture—the picture is seen as separate or apart. The standard of objectivity masks the implication of all people in any piece of knowledge, and permits that knowledge to be manipulated by those who have the means to do so.

I present the idea of cognitive stereoscopy along with its political and ethical dimensions within a present-day context of thought which has, in many quarters, cast serious doubt on the standard of objective knowledge already. The cultural climate is readier to assimilate this principle than it was, for example, a few centuries ago, when political and religious power was much more highly centralized than it is today.

Nevertheless, as Richard Ohmann has discussed in *English in America,* the teaching of language to young people in America is shaped by an ideology which promotes the instrumental use of language in the service of corporate interests and values.[2] In a later essay, "Use Definite, Specific, Concrete Language," Ohmann argues that most composition handbooks promote a "preferred style" which "focuses on a truncated present moment"; which "favors sensory news, from the surfaces of things"; which "obscures the social relations and the relations of people to nature that are embedded in all things"; which "foregrounds the writer's own perceptions" and thus greatly exaggerates their authority; and which urges the "denial of conflict" by picturing a world in which, for example, "the telephone has the same meaning for all classes of people." In general, he observes, these handbooks

> push the student writer always toward the language that most nearly reproduces the immediate experience and away from the language that might be used to understand it, transform it, and relate it to everything else. The authors privilege a kind of revising and expanding that leaves the words themselves unexamined and untransformed.[3]

The situation Ohmann describes is one in which language is itself objectified and idealized as if it were a material object. The individual writer is taught to use language as if it were outside oneself, as if one's partners in language use must understand the same meanings that one has oneself—or that one thinks one has. Rather than language becoming a source of debate and dispute, it is presented as a tool which should contribute to the interests of those whose livelihood depends on good memos and good reports. The intersubjective character of language on both a local and social scale is suppressed by the ideology which best promotes the welfare of the most privileged groups in society.

In most university departments of English, the subject is itself divided into a more privileged and less privileged component. Literature and reading now have greater weight than composition and writing. Those who teach in English departments are correspondingly divided into these two groups. While one could not say that the writing group is being "dominated" by the reading, we could reasonably say that there is no mutuality, no interaction between the two groups of ideas or groups of people. I take this to be a reflection of what Ohmann described: literature is the subject that was taught to the rich, to increase their cultivation; composition is the subject that has grown out of getting "literacy" into the minds of the previously poor, enslaved, or otherwise unprivileged. Thus, there is no unified subject of language, in which all people participate in similar ways. Rather there is one phase of language—literature—which is "better" than the other phase— writing. While small children do not experience a bifurcation of language in this way, education gradually teaches them to "see" two different subjects, each without commerce with the other, and each treated as almost autonomous. Therefore, while children normally have a stereoscopic sense of language—they see the unity in its various phases— they gradually "learn" not to see it, not to experience it, and to comply with the ideological values implicit in the artificial bifurcation of the subject as found in schools and colleges. Children are taught not to follow into social life what they achieve with language in infancy and early family life.

My conscious use of the principle of cognitive stereoscopy is therefore not, in my judgment, the application of a new method or technique, but the social extrapolation of the knowledge of language that all children acquire. My expectation of its success stems from the fact that people are *already* cognitively stereoscopic, though an educational training beholden to antisocial interests has inhibited the normal growth of this capability through the authoritarian classroom and the general suppression of interactive modes of teaching. The proposal that I will discuss presently grows out of a larger set of assignments and a larger conception of how a language course ought to function. But let me present an example first, and then discuss some of its implications for the teaching of reading and writing as a unified subject and for the restructuring of the classroom toward this end.

Traditionally, in either literature or composition courses, essays are assigned one by one. Usually, they are marked for errors, commented upon by the instructor, and then given a grade. Each essay is viewed as a unit that is supposed to reflect incremental "improvement" in the overall quality of the writing, without any special notice being taken of the topic or the writer's interest in it. To develop a stereoscopic sense of language in students, almost all of these procedures are changed, including the correcting of technical errors and the overall grading. I would like to focus now on one particular change—the abandonment of the "unit-by-unit" convention and the use, instead, of a series of assignments, with a strong accent on the double essay assignment. The assignment series, or longitudinal approach, asks students to write essays and then study the features of the writing style they already have. Emphasis is placed on studying the essays comparatively—this essay versus that one, last semester versus this semester, essays about one's life-experience versus essays about one's literary experience. Various contexts for comparison are proposed, and students use the dialectic technique to identify as many aspects of their style as can be done in a year. This regular habit of comparing essays perspectivally makes use of the already-present capacity to "triangulate" in conceptual thought, gradually enabling students to see any single aspect of their work in terms of two or more perspectives at once. It is this activity of thinking about one's language from two perspectives at once that I would like to discuss in some detail.

My examples, however, are not from students' work but from teachers'. The general situation, nevertheless, was socially structured like most classrooms, with an "authoritative" leader—me—and a group of serious people there to try and test my proposals. The differences between this situation and most classrooms was that there were no grades or other types of formal, binding evaluation by the group leader, and that my essays were part of the collection of work, and thus came under the same scrutiny as everyone else's. The specific occasion was a workshop of secondary school teachers participating in the Northern Kentucky Response Project, which aimed to familiarize the participants with ideas and techniques for studying literature through response essays. The workshop topic—"the authority of the English teacher"— was to provide an opening perspective, a subject for which the knowledge coming out of our discussions would be a predicate. The group, either in consensus or individually, or both, formulates new predications—"the English teacher's authority is such-and-such," for example—which are then reviewed by the group. We are seeking pertinent formulations of this "knowledge" rather than binding edicts. We

are seeking to *re-name,* or re-symbolize, what we then understood to
be "the English teacher's authority." Here, then, is the first pair of
essays, by Ms. J. The second question was not given until the first essay
was completed.

> *Q1:* Retell Hemingway's "Hills Like White Elephants" as fully and
> as accurately as you can.
>
> *A1:* The man and the woman who are the main characters are
> having drinks at a bar. They talk. Their sentences are short. He
> speaks of surgery. Their sentences are ambiguous; they speak of
> times gone by. Their conversation is light, yet the tone of the story
> revealed in the dialogue is dark. Deep undercurrents run through
> the spate of words. There must be an abortion, he says curcum-
> vently [*sic*]. Her depression frames the listlessness of her replies.
>
>   The woman would prefer to drift. She wishes life to continue as
> it exists—or perhaps even to return to a time when this shadow
> had not yet covered the equatorial sun. The man's desire to urge
> her out of inertia is coupled with his own accustomed blandness.
> Together they gaze into the future and see it far removed, as though
> viewed through the wrong end of a telescope.
>
>   There is a vitality in the story, but it beats slowly and softly,
> muffled beneath the shallow surface, like the baby's heart beneath
> that of the woman who wants to be "amusing."
>
> *Q2:* Discuss what you think Hemingway was trying to do in writing
> "Hills Like White Elephants."
>
> *A2:* Hemingway was showing off in "Hills Like White Elephants."
> He was performing his particular type of literary pirouette with
> verve and style. Take the very bones of a story, a skeletal frame,
> and hang on it a few shreds of incident—this is how the dance
> begins. Then take ten paces, twenty paces, thirty or more back and
> fire from the hip, whizzing dialogue, like bullets, through the
> narrative's skull. When the death dance ends, the reader's brain has
> also been pierced, and Hemingway, like a sweating Nureyev, waits
> in the wings for the applause.

To articulate the stereoscopic knowledge suggested by this essay
pair, I am reporting the collectively observed similarity between the
two essays, and a basic difference. The similarity is Ms. J's identification
with Hemingway. In the first essay, this identification takes the form of
her actually trying to imitate Hemingway's succinct style, the short
sentences and the literary accent, as shown, for example, in the "frame"
metaphor of the last sentence of the first paragraph. In the second
essay, the gun duel imagery and the dance metaphor show her participation in what she sees as violent behavior by the author. In presenting
these metaphors, Ms. J becomes an "author" in order to present what
she thinks Hemingway is doing.

The difference between the two essays is that the first stresses the soft vitality of the story, while the second emphasizes the ostentatious violence of the author. The first mentions the "muffled" heartbeat beneath the story's "shallow surface," while the second brings out the story's "bones" and "skeleton" and "skull" juxtaposed to the "pierced" reader's brain. Needless to say, these differences are open to an indefinite number of readings if we only hold them out as an independent pair. The public purpose of the group, however, views the pair with specific interest in the question of authority. From this standpoint, ideas of passive and active, actor and spectator, peace and violence become aspects of Ms. J's sense of pedagogical authority.

We intuit first of all, without trying to put the two essays together in a neat or bounded predication (because they display both similarity and difference), that the pair suggests a certain emotional dynamics related to Ms. J's ideas of authority. We also see that her sense of the teacher's authority is probably connected with her sense of the author in the actual reading experience, while her sense of what it is to read is implicated in how she will present readings to those over whom she has authority. Furthermore, her essays show a "taking" of authority relative to the peer group to whom these essays are presented. Compared to other essays, hers are more of a performance, a dance, and perhaps a "showing-off." Yet, viewing the first essay by itself, we would not draw this last conclusion, and we would be contemplating only the quieter experience she gives in that essay. On the other hand, viewing the second essay by itself would make it hard to guess that there is that quiet dimension to Ms. J's reading experience, that the taking in of the story is not only a penetration of the brain but also the quiet contemplation of intimations of the past and future, of muffled, unspoken, and distorted feelings.

When we do put the essays together as a predication of mutually dependent thoughts, that is, when we consider that this variety of thoughts and feelings is part of the mind of one individual, we see that in a general way, but on only this occasion and at this moment, Ms. J's options have a certain accent, a certain range, that does not *go* anywhere but that emphasizes certain things over others, certain values, choices, and wishes which play a large role and which could be understood as preferred by her at this time. For example, her perception of the "violent" behavior of the author is predicated on her perception of the quiet character of the story. This suggests a certain predicative relationship between the feeling of authority and its exercise. However, we do not say that the feeling governs the exercise, but rather, because the predication is unified and internally reciprocal, we take it as a *single* strategy of self-presentation. Predicated on that is the public issue with which the group is concerned—the teacher's authority; that is, this latter issue is then predicated on the thought represented by the *pair* of essays. We then have a provisional hypothesis regarding the continuity between Ms. J's reading experience, her record/report of it to this group, and her *prima facie* orientation as an authority figure in the classroom.

The total process involves Ms. J's subjective predications—the two essays understood as predicated on *one another*—and the inter-subjective predication between the group topic and the pair of essays. Both predicative processes are needed for even these first essays to acquire any public meaning and value. In dealing with any language initiatives—essays in this instance—the developing of knowledge depends on the assumption of cognitive stereoscopy in the individual, and on the necessary subsequent exercise of intersubjective negotiation by the group to which that individual belongs. The cognitive closure permitted by this latter step then becomes a provisional subject for subsequent predications by this group. The recursive process is then continuously stereoscopic and is the agency of collective growth in the study of language and literature.

Here is a second pair of responses to this exercise, by Mr. R, which bring out a somewhat different orientation toward the authority issue:

> *A1:* A man and a woman are sitting in the bar of a railroad station somewhere in Spain, waiting for a train. They are discussing a "simple operation" the woman is to have. The man assures her that there is nothing to it—just "letting a little air in." The couple go back and forth throughout the entire story discussing whether or not the woman should have the operation. Although it seems like the man would rather she have the operation and the woman would rather not, it also seems that neither wants to impose his/her will on the other. The man wants it "just like it used to be." The woman wants the man to be happy. She "doesn't care about herself." The discussion is really tedious and repetitious—very much like it might be in real life. The story never makes clear what the "it"—the operation—really is, although I've heard people say that it was an abortion. The couple have several drinks while they are waiting—beers, then 2 specialties, Anis del Toro—which tastes like licorice—then more beers. The man goes to check on the train and has one more anis. That's basically the story. One detail that sticks in my mind is the curtain over the door—stringed beads "to keep the flies out."
>
> To recap the action, the couple sits down and the man orders "dos cervezas." Then the woman asks about the "Anis del Toro" and the man orders two. He assures her that the operation is simple. She asks, "Will everything be as before?" He says, "Certainly, it's just a simple airing—I want it to be just the two of us."

The woman says that she doesn't care about herself. She just wants to please him. The man assures her that she doesn't *have* to have the operation. It's her decision. That pattern is repeated over and over again.

A2: I haven't the slightest idea. But since I'm an English teacher, I can't say that so I'll make an educated guess. I'm going to believe those who say the operation is an abortion. Regardless, it's obviously *not* just a simple operation. Hemingway is showing the tension through the tedium of the conversation. Neither the man nor the woman is voicing his/her real concerns. The man wants her to have the operation but doesn't want to seem to be pressuring her. The woman is afraid of the operation, and perhaps she would like to have the baby, but she doesn't want to risk offending or losing the man. But none of this is what they say. Instead they talk around the issue, trying to reassure themselves and each other—but accomplishing nothing. The world itself is disinterested—operating on schedule, serving drinks, keeping out the flies. The couple seeks diversion in their drinks, but really finds none. Around them are "hills like white elephants." Perhaps resembling a woman's pregnant belly. For not understanding the story, I think that's pretty good. But not for all the world would I have guessed that the operation was an abortion. Nothing in the story gives me that impression, although when I consider the subject, it all fits together.

Where Ms. J's work showed concerns with the power and performance values of authority, Mr. R's is oriented around competence and duty. Yet in his case too neither essay by itself is enough to lead us to this conclusion. For example, an unusual feature of the first essay is that Mr. R, unlike any other reader in this group, tries to "recap" the story in his second paragraph; but looking only at the essay it is not possible to say why he does this. Also, we note that in the first paragraph Mr. R interrupts his retelling to comment on the story in that it "never makes clear what the 'it'—the operation—really is." It is difficult for us to place a value on this comment. However, in view of the second sentence of the second essay, beginning "But since I'm an English teacher . . . " and introducing a note of self-evaluation, we begin to think of what Mr. R did in the first essay as evidence of his thinking that this assignment is testing his competence as an accurate reader. In other words, when Mr. R notes that the term "abortion" is not used, he is not making an affirmative point about the style of the work, but is rather apologizing for his own uncertainty about what is happening in the story. Similarly, the "recap" is a going-over-it-to-get-it-right rather than an attempt to vary his perspective.

If the second essay were considered alone, it might be possible to read Mr. R's self-reference ironically, and then see the whole essay as making the point about "tension through the tedium of the conversation"; we would assume that the end of this essay says that what the actual operation was was not important to the point about "tedium." But the two features of the first essay mentioned above argue against the ironic reading of the second: one would have to read an ironic voice into the *pair* of essays and this does not seem likely (though it is certainly possible).

What most determines how to understand these essays is Mr. R's presence and deportment in the group. We all see and "know" him firsthand. Because of many other comments he made before and during the discussion of these essays, there is no doubt that we are to read the essays "straight"; that is, because of our public knowledge of Mr. R, there is no need even to ask "what he meant." He volunteered his own sense of duty as an English teacher and his own sense of what competence means in this job. In this context, his reading of the title image in the second essay should be understood as reflecting both naiveté and conservatism; naiveté in his not using the idiomatic meaning of "white elephant" to see an unwanted pregnancy, conservatism in his reluctance to entertain the abortion reading immediately. These latter values reflect his sense that the teacher's authority has to do with competence and duty. Mr. R sees authority in a soldierly sort of way, and he explained to us his strong regard for behavioral discipline in the classroom. Thus a recursive use of the principle of stereoscopy leads, as it did with Ms. J, from reading to values, and yields, when discussion closes, a comprehensive sense of cognitive activity which governs reading, language use, and language choice.

The action of the whole process should be described as the predication of the present language action on the preceding one. As with Ms. J, we can discern an emotional release in the second essay based on the material of the first. The act of writing the first essays raised certain intrapsychic issues in both writers, and they "answered" their first essays in their second ones with more obviously personal and emotional initiatives. Mr. R in particular reflected at least twice on his own thinking—in the second sentence of the second essay, and toward the end, where he wrote, "For not understanding the story, I think that's pretty good." In writing single essays, most people do not disclose the *development* of their thought; in fact, students are taught to keep the derivation of their thesis out of a "final" essay, and to present only arguments and reasons on the same issue. Giving such single thoughts, however, actually falsifies the complexity and social pertinence of the thought since it gives the erroneous impression that all essay-writers have only one "point" to make and are in fact more dogmatic than they really are. They are taught to suppress the natural dialectic of the thought process, which usually comes up with a whole range of "maybe" thoughts—which are always equated with "opinion" and "subjectivity"—in favor of writing down the certain thought, or the seemingly certain thought. In a sense, students are taught *not to have opinions* by being taught to write mainly about facts, certainties, and, as Ohmann observes, surfaces.

I believe that in both pairs of essays above, we have seen thoughts that suggest the *derivation* of the thought process itself—that is, thoughts imply basic inward contradictions of feeling, value, and knowledge. I stress that the essays themselves do not clearly demonstrate such contradictions; but the essays *as understood and discussed by the group to which they were contributed* do show the kind of complexity I described above. Here then we come to a peculiarity characteristic of using the principle of cognitive stereoscopy self-consciously, namely, that we require a full carrying-out of the recursive process—from private writing to group discussion—before any sense of the derivation of thought can be perceived and believed. For all practical purposes, knowledge of the stereoscopic shape of any one person's thought comes *only* retrospectively and collectively, which means that even when this knowledge is accepted and agreed upon by author and group, it is of only limited use—and perhaps none at all—in predicting either language initiatives or language responses by a particular person. It is of definite use, however, as a systematic means of establishing a subject for the predicate to be developed in subsequent group initiatives. It is of use, that is, as a contribution to the strength and intellectual purpose of the group. The individual in question is always growing and changing, and the stereoscopic process takes account of the continuousness of growth and change. Furthermore, this process also shows the senses in which growth and change are not arbitrary, even though they are unpredictable. Just as an individual grows, the value of authority is under continuous revision, even though pedagogical institutions tend to stabilize values. In any event, the self-conscious use of the principle of cognitive stereoscopy brings out the subjective and intersubjective terms of the dialectic between the collective needs for change and revision and for stability.

It is a traditional epistemological principle to separate questions of fact and value. With the two questions I posed for this exercise, I also tried to make this separation—one question asking the respondent to "retell" the story, another to give a judgment of what the author was "trying" to do. The resulting essays suggest, however, that regardless of the questions asked a stable separation of fact and value cannot be maintained: they too are reciprocally predicated. The retellings cannot be understood except as the expression of values, while the judgments make no sense except as predicated on (relative) facts. We are thus led to the thought that both fact and value represent two genres of cognitive initiative: is it a fact or a judgment that Hemingway's writing of the story is a "performance"? Is it a fact or a judgment that both figures in the story wanted things to "be as before"? (Mr. R's first essay first says that the man wanted things as before, and then says that the woman wanted it that way.) If these questions are not explored in a collective framework we must stop our reflection on the lame academic conclusion of "ambiguity." Under collective scrutiny, it is possible to say how Ms. J took the fact of performance and, to coin a word, *envalued* it. Similarly, Mr. R's value of competence and accuracy (we may retrospectively say) led him to "recap" the story so that he mentions the *fact* of the story that *both* figures are concerned about things between them being "as before." There is no better circumstance than the presence of a group of classroom size (with the accompanying multiplicity of perspectives) for enabling us to discern how fact and value operate as two forms of cognitive initiative with language for any given person.

The political interest in not following through on the implications of cognitive stereoscopy—that is, the interest in dividing the childhood sense of the unity of language experience—is the preservation of the authoritarian classroom: the privileged leader and the underprivileged collection of individuals. This structure requires that knowledge be something *given and received.* The authority is conserved when the giver judges if what he or she gives has been adequately received. Because the receiver has no authority to judge either him- or herself or the giver it can only be that knowledge moves in one direction, and this motion is the total of pedagogical action.

The principle of cognitive stereoscopy implies that even though there is a significant difference in age and experience between teacher and students there is no difference in the way language choices are made in the mind of each. Put another way, the observed differences in language use are due *only* to age and experience, and once these are accounted for the fundamental mutuality in all language interchanges may be disclosed and self-consciously appropriated in the collective negotiation of knowledge. This means that there cannot be an area of classroom functioning in which the language mutuality is rejected. If there is, as when a grade is given for the total performance, any gestures toward mutuality which precede this grade are already voided by the

students' anticipation of the "final" judgment. If the "given and received" model of knowledge is to give way to a more collective model,
there cannot be an inherent structural principle of exemption. Even in
the extreme case of the mother and infant, where the authority of the
one is much greater than that of the other, the authority is exercised
only in the cause of physical safety. The actual use of language is truly
mutual, according to the normal interests of both infant and mother.
Normal children appear pugnacious and "fresh" only because of the
parents' surprise at how well the principle of mutuality has "taken." By
the time the child is school age, he or she is well on the way to
suppressing this mutuality with adults, in favor of various forms of
compliance that are demanded by the sociopolitical values of the
society at large. In college, the most successful students are those who
have fully mastered the language of compliance and the principle of
knowledge-to-be-received.

In connection with this concern, the essay-pair procedure is also an
address to the literature/composition bifurcation in the profession of
English. I call special attention to the fact that Ms. J and Mr. R were not
asked to write response-statements in the extended manner I have
outlined elsewhere. The questions are probably quite familiar to high
school students, for whom, I am told, they are standard examination
questions that call for answers ritually learned in class. These teachers,
however, knew that (1) they would not be graded, and (2) they were
supposed to speculate in answering the second question. I therefore
tried to use the teachers' relative emancipation from classroom coer-
cions to provide the emotional space I usually create through the collection of response statements. Because the teachers did use this space as
I had hoped, their essays were highly negotiable—that is, discussable
in terms far beyond the mere adequacy of the answer to the question.
In being thus eligible for a richer analysis, they are the kind of language
initiative that discloses the underlying relatedness of reading and writing, and then, in public, of speaking and hearing.

Group negotiation isolates first the apparent perception of the text,
and then the translation of the perception into language (the retelling),
which in turn is viewed as a language contribution to the group. We
may in fact read each of the second responses as a translation of each
first response, each pair subsequently being translated into public
understanding. Every judgment made along this path by both Ms. J and
Mr. R and by the others must be carefully articulated. Often, when a
second and third party "resays" what he or she thinks we (I) have said,
it is quite a surprise at first, only to seem more and more accurate as
we allow it a certain authority. There is this continuing attention to the

minutiae of language, to the small, incremental, usually invisible steps
by which we arrive at what we finally say. The enabling principle of this
process is cognitive stereoscopy, insofar as it warns us to *presuppose*
(expect) perspectives other than the one we think animated what we
said; at the same time we are expecting (presupposing) others to perceive our consciously rejected implications. But our expectations do
not reduce the surprise at the new views of our language; they only
reduce the tendency to reject these views without careful discussion.

My description of cognitive stereoscopy and its role in language use
aims, in part, to show how the use and distribution of authority is
implicated in the way we use language. The imbalance of authority
between literature and composition teachers reflects a value regarding
language that I want to change, namely, that some forms of language
are independently more important than other forms (and, therefore,
that the people who use those forms are more important). I think there
is no longer any reason to believe that any one manifestation of language "belongs" more to English than any other. Once the various uses
of language are understood as mutually implicated, it will be obvious
that the various users are similarly mutually implicated, and a more
productive attitude toward the development of knowledge will obtain.

Notes

1. David Bleich, *Subjective Criticism* (Baltimore, Md.: Johns Hopkins Univ.
Press, 1978), ch. 2.
2. Richard Ohmann, *English in America: A Radical View of the Profession*
(New York: Oxford Univ. Press, 1976).
3. Richard Ohmann, "Use Definite, Specific, Concrete Language," *College
English* 41 (Dec. 1979): 396.

Social Foundations of Reading and Writing

Deborah Brandt
University of Wisconsin–Madison

One of the common ways that writing and reading are distinguished from speaking and listening is along social lines. We speak and listen together and—for the most part—write and read alone. From Virginia Woolf's famous room of one's own to recent interest in the interiority of textual space, writing and reading are generally conceived of as private, solitary episodes with language. It is not surprising that the rise of literacy is often treated as the cognitive counterpart of private property in accounts of the development of bourgeois cultures. On an individual level, both learning to write and learning to read are sometimes described as learning to withdraw from the supportive cues and collaborative effort of conversational meaning-making and instead to sustain what Barry Kroll has called "the autonomous production of texts,"[1] to be weaned away from interpretive dependence on situational context and learn to make meaning solely out of the semantic resources and logical relationships of written language.

This tendency to view writer and reader in closed engagement with language is reinforced in the decidedly cognitive bent of much current research in composition, where interest centers on the processes and structures of a writer's mental plans or on the study of written texts as records of cognitive activity. On the reading side—I think particularly of much contemporary literary theory—it is assumed that the reader's primary engagement is with the text. Readers transact with the text, resist the text, or rewrite the text, but in any case the mental experience of reading is often described as a matter of going off alone with language. And this going off alone with language seems to be in marked contrast to the ways that speakers and hearers normally understand each other in the here-and-now of everyday cooperative conversation.

But what is really going on when people write and read? Do the physical and temporal separation of writer and reader alter their attitudes toward language and meaning? Is understanding accomplished any differently through written discourse than it is through oral discourse?

In the following pages I will examine the writing processes of two writers in order to suggest that meaning-making in composition proceeds along very similar routes to those of meaning-making in oral interactions. Although similarities to oral meaning-making can be traced in many aspects of the writing act, I will concentrate on one: why writers interrupt their writing and begin to read what they have written.

Many studies of composing and revising processes have shown that writers read as they write as a way to evaluate how well a text realizes an intention or as a way to edit for error or mistranscription.[2] This research in general reveals that good writers pause to read or scan frequently and purposefully while poor writers do not. In one study Margaret Atwell found that reading during writing enabled writers to adhere to global text plans. If denied access to their evolving texts, even good writers experienced some difficulty with text organization and coherence.[3] Recently attention has also been given to the generative nature of reading during writing. In an extremely interesting formulation Nancy Shanklin has suggested that a writer, like Louise Rosenblatt's reader, enters into a "transactional" relationship with his or her developing text.[4] During the process the text activates relevant schemata—that is, anticipatory knowledge structures—in the writer's mind that promote the generation of further text.

All of these studies hold in common that reading during writing serves some sort of important orienting function during composing. Quite simply, reading during writing keeps writers from "getting lost," from "losing their place." And I would like to suggest that this place that writers seek when they read is the here and now that is being shared publicly with the (eventual) reader of the text. Like a speaker who must attend to the intersubjective context of an unfolding dialogue in order to participate appropriately and successfully, a writer too must monitor what Ragnar Rommetveit calls "the temporarily shared social world"[5] that the language of any text activates. It is only through this shared or shareable world that a writer can make things known to others.

To begin to see how reading during composing involves a constant monitoring of the here-and-now, I provide below excerpts from some think-aloud protocols of a college-aged writer named Mark. The excerpts demonstrate that the writer paused to read or scan as a way to gauge what a reader would likely be bringing to bear at any point in the text. And what a reader would likely be bringing to bear had a great deal to do with what the writer could do or mean.

The first excerpt is a typical example of one of the most common reasons Mark stopped to read during writing: to monitor the topic of his discourse, to see what was in current, shared focus. Such monitoring occurred most often after he had been sidetracked by lower-level concerns. Here Mark works on a paper about an interview with a French-born poet:[6]

> *The inner thoughts were not* . . . expressible . . . *easily expressible "outside the skin" of French language and he eventually returned to his native tongue as his sole medium* . . . I'm still uncomfortable with this word but we can deal with these things later . . . *for creative expression* . . . [Scans] . . . So already we're not talking about Professor Snyder . . . we're talking about the writing of . . . which is fine, which is fine . . .

Monitoring the focus of discourse sometimes allowed Mark to slip something into the text that he had been holding back, much like a conversationalist who must wait for the appropriate moment to get a word in among competing participants.

Another purpose that reading served for Mark during composing was to test for ambiguity or multiple reference. Reading allowed him to anticipate and consider possible alternative interpretations that the language of his text invited:

> *The average Britisher is likely to have access to a fund of knowledge which he will probably be able to read, because in a historical sense* . . . *an* historical sense? . . . *reading is a social activity* . . . that doesn't mean reading in groups . . . that is, rather the structure of society is one that permits, encourages reading . . . [Reads] . . . the average Britisher is likely to have access to a fund of knowledge he will probably be able to read because reading is a social ac— . . . that's not a good way of putting it . . . reading is a so-cially . . . that sounds strange . . . a socially accepted activity . . . if it wasn't accepted it would be an Orwellian society . . . I think social is the wrong word.

Mark monitored his text not only for the focus of discourse and for the possibility of multiple reference but also for what he could assume—or what he hoped—a reader could infer by virtue of previous text. In the following passage, as he prepares to make a major transition in an analytical essay, Mark broadly rescans his text. The point he wants to make hinges on a reader's successful recovery of earlier information and a mutual awareness between writer and reader of the broader implications of that information. In scanning the text Mark essentially poses the questions, "Where are we?"

> I've shown that there's a great deal of individual interpretation
> involved . . . uh . . . I'm now trying to talk about the general char-
> acteristics . . . yes, most of the arguments against a literacy study
> have been hinted at already . . . okay . . . the common factors of
> literacy . . . the valid relationships . . . we've already shown what
> these assumptions are . . . it's all circumstantial . . .

It is interesting to note that Mark's concern with the success of his
argument is not directed at the logic or reasonableness of his ideas. His
concern is with gauging the conditions of mutual awareness—what
Rommetveit calls "commonality with respect to interpretation"[7]—
through which his ideas, here and now, can appear logical to others.

Mark's concerns during his reading and scanning bear remarkable
similarities to the processes by which people make sense for and of
each other in everyday interaction. In an essay called "Making Sense:
Natural Language and Shared Knowledge in Understanding," sociolinguist Rolf Kjolseth demonstrates that in order to share meaning with
others we must establish a shared context or setting through which that
meaning can be understood.[8] To constitute meaning we also must
constitute the conditions by which that meaning can be realized. And
we constitute or activate these settings largely through our language.
Language in use is simultaneously a manifestation and facilitator of the
setting in which it occurs; to use language is at the same time to reflect
and establish, constitute and perpetuate, a shareable social reality
through which understanding can be accomplished.

This process of using language to constitute intersubjective settings
for understanding is made possible, Kjolseth points out, because
members of a social group share commonsense interpretive knowledge
that each participant brings to bear and can expect others to bring to
bear during an encounter. These "grounds" of interpretive knowledge,
as Kjolseth calls them, serve as a constraint and a resource during
meaning-making. Through this nonpublic, impalpable knowledge-at-
hand we are able to make sense of and *through* the public surfaces of
discourse. Although these grounds of interpretive knowledge encom-
pass a wide range of culturally-endowed beliefs, facts, scripts, and the
like, they also include a more particular, dynamic kind of shared
knowledge: the knowledge shared by a "we" by virtue of our mutual
participation in a particular encounter. Kjolseth names this knowledge
"emergent knowledge":

> A "we" knows this knowledge and can lay claim to it, and sanction
> its relevance. "We" are its witnesses and representatives. And thus
> our "weness" is sedimented in this emergent knowledge and each
> use of the emergent ground exemplifies this "we."[9]

The transcripts cited earlier attest to the extent to which the writer was involved in monitoring the ground of emergent knowledge that his text was establishing.

Kjolseth's model of making sense of social interaction has striking resemblances to some psycholinguistic explanations of the reading process. According to these views, reading is primarily a process of matching up information coming from a text with what Frank Smith calls "the theory of the world in our head."[10] In other words, readers bring to a text stores of prior knowledge about the world and about the nature of discourse that allow them to fill in the inferences and make the predictions necessary for comprehension. Anthony Sanford and Simon Garrod describe the process as establishing the "domain of reference" to which a text apparently belongs: in a quite literal as well as metaphorical sense, readers must determine where a text is coming from.[11] Such competency is what allows a reader to "make sense," for instance, of the following two sentences:

> The policeman held up his hand and stopped the car.
> The goalie held up his hand and stopped the ball.

Comprehending these two sentences involves more than syntactic and semantic processing; readers must invoke knowledge of "scenarios," that is, knowledge about settings, episodes, social roles—Kjolseth's knowledge-at-hand—in order to read successfully.

But like the static, generalized knowledge in Kjolseth's versions of background, scenarios are necessary but not sufficient to accomplish comprehension in an unfolding discourse. Scenarios provide "implicit focus," a store of relevant knowledge to be called upon. But readers also must keep track of incoming information from the text. Such information constitutes "explicit focus," which is similar to Kjolseth's emergent ground of knowledge. Comprehension occurs as a result of the high transactive merger of implicit and explicit focus. Implicit focus prepares for and amplifies information in explicit focus; at the same time, information in explicit focus—especially that which is new or unexpected in a text—modifies the scenario in implicit focus. That is how "the theory in our head" is enriched, enlarged, and altered by encounters with texts.

Contexts for Reading and Writing

Kjolseth's explanation of the way understanding is accomplished in everyday life begins to break down the distinctions between the contexts of speaking and listening and the contexts of writing and reading.

Although oral interactions generally occur in a shared physical setting while written interactions do not, *both* kinds of interactions require all participants to establish, through an orchestration of language and shared knowledge, a publicly accomplished here and now by which meaning can be constituted. The actual context of any language act is the socially forged conditions of mutual awareness through which private understandings can be realized. Hence the context of any language act is established and sustained by a "we."

To view writers as being in a state of "weness" when they compose is to say more than that writers write with an audience in mind. It is to say that writers are participants in the public events of their own texts and that the unfoldings of those events bear upon writers' unfolding options for making things known. Reading during writing reinforces attention to the public here-and-now reality through which a writer is attempting to share meaning. It is only by keeping in touch with this shared reality, by not getting lost, that a writer comes to mean.

When we begin to treat writers as in some important sense not alone when they write, we can begin to account for many aspects of the phenomenon of writing, especially the sense of discovery we experience in writing, the sense we have of a text developing its own intentions, or the sense we have of not knowing what we mean until we write it. We can only mean what we can share. When our private understandings meet the air of public discourse, they take on public meanings with which we, as participants in that discourse, must then contend.

Viewing writers as being—indeed, as needing to be—in a state of weness when they compose also can account for the breakdowns that occur in the writing processes when authors fail to attend to the here and now in which they are participants. Such a breakdown is demonstrated in the following excerpt of a think-aloud protocol of another college-aged writer named Paul, whose overwhelmingly local concerns during composing prevent him from engaging consistently in the "event" of his developing text. In the excerpt below, Paul writes about the importance of sending and receiving personal letters, rereading as he goes:

> *I get* . . . um . . . not I get . . . oh, why not? . . . a feeling . . . *a feeling* . . . *I really can't describe when I* receive . . . *receive* . . . personal letters . . . *personal letters from my* friends . . . *friends* . . . um . . . *Again, if the letters were viewed extraneously, one would find that there would be little meaning* . . . there would be little meaning to him? . . . *to him* . . . to one . . . to him . . . [Reads] . . . Again, if these letters were viewed extraneously one would find that there would be little meaning to him . . . however

... semicolon ... however ... comma ... no ... *on the other hand* ... comma ... I ... I ... Again if these letters were viewed extraneously one would find there would be little meaning.

Although Paul repeatedly read his text during composing, it usually was in order to search for surface errors, or it served as a kind of incantatory distraction whenever he became "stuck." Rarely did Paul read as a full participant in the world of his text, and so rarely did he have access to the resources for meaning that this world was offering. In Kjolseth's terms this writer was unable to attend either to the emergent ground of his discourse—what he shared here and now with others—or to the transcendent ground of his discourse—what might be potentially relevant and shareable with others. It is in the transcendent, anticipatory, potential ground of a developing text that a writer can generate new, surprising, and sustaining meaning. And, Kjolseth thinks, it is the ability to attend to this transcendent ground in a discourse that lies at the heart of communicative competence:

> Communicative competence depends upon transcendent knowledge. . . . Should a member for whatever reason persist in disattending to the interaction's transcendent ground, his participation will be incomplete, inappropriate, and threaten (in a dyad, destroy) the accomplishment.[12]

Paul's tendency to concentrate on the word-by-word progression of his text could be likened to a reader's decision to start paying attention to the number of *s*'s on this page. The consequences for such a reader would be the same as they were for Paul: meaning-making would break down; the reader would soon become lost.

Writing and Reading in the Classroom

These brief glimpses into the short-circuiting of Paul's composing process provide renewed evidence of the need to make writing strategies a central concern in writing instruction. Although much attention has been given to strategies of planning before composing and revising after composing, more can be done to encourage students to pause to scan and read during writing and to develop ways to make that reading profitable. "Free-reading," the equivalent of free-writing, allowing students to turn off the critic and proofreader, can encourage them to engage with the "transcendent" world coming into view before their reading eyes. Students can learn that their best "source" for whatever they write is always their own evolving text, as it offers possibilities for making and remaking meaning.

Beyond the development of socially based writing strategies must be raised the issue of the social context that surrounds any writing or reading assignment. While writers and readers wrestle with the here and now of a text, they do so, of course, within a wider social context that constrains their language use. Some of the most compelling evidence of the impact of classroom context on students' writing comes from James Britton's study of the school-sponsored writing of 500 English adolescents, *The Development of Writing Abilities (11–18)*.[13] His analysis showed that 87 percent of the writing he collected was written in what he called a "transactional" mode, conveying "low-level" information (i.e., factual, not analytical) and, in audience function, addressed to "teacher-as-examiner." Although the lack of expressive and speculative writings among the samples was widely bemoaned, Britton's investigation is an oddly cheerful testament to students' natural abilities as language users to adopt discourse appropriate to a social situation. The situation of many classrooms—where questions are asked to test knowledge rather than to constitute it and where teachers are evaluators of students' writing rather than readers of it—predicts just the kind of written discourse Britton's research team discovered.

The inescapable fact that whatever writing is done in a composition class will embody the goings-on in the class suggests certain responsibilities and opportunities in designing a course in terms of the "context of situation" it provides to its writer-participants, a context that ideally will invite a wider range of expression than mere demonstration of knowledge. Courses and assignments should be viewed in terms of the potentials for meaning-making that students can find in them—not only in terms of content (ideas, topics, information) but in social and linguistic terms as well. Ideally a writing class should undertake common pursuits, form social relationships, establish channels of communication, agree upon terms, develop a common history—create, in other words, a public context through which to make known private experience. The aim should be to have the class resemble as much as possible the kind of environment that written discourse normally gets made in, to provide members of the class with access to the same coherent range of clues, constraints, and resources that "real" writers rely upon during the process of composing.

With that aim in mind, I present below three tenets for designing writing courses and assignments. None of these suggestions is new; they have been made by countless others. I offer them here in the light of the opportunities they offer for establishing a basis of "weness" in the writing classroom.

The course should be thematic. By pursuing one theme, a series of related questions, throughout a semester, a class can develop a set of concepts, a common vocabulary and common "indexical expressions,"[14] a body of shared experience, a collective frame of mind, to serve as a semantic reservoir for each writing assignment. Such continuity contributes to nearly every conceivable aspect of composing, from the dilemma of what to write about to related decisions about how to refer to something in a text, or about what parts of a text need to be elaborated for a reader and what parts can be presumed to be understood without explicit mention. A thematic approach also provides opportunities to use writing epistemically, as a way for a group to explore complex problems, conflicting viewpoints, and changes in understanding that occur with the acquisition of new knowledge.[15]

One class I taught, for example, took as its theme the nature of writing itself, considering how writing (both the process and the product) functioned in our immediate lives, at school, and in occupations of the students' interest. We took up related issues such as the so-called literacy crisis and the impact of technology on the production and dissemination of writing. As this "thick soup" of reading, talking, and writing developed over the semester, students increasingly worked more independently on issues of individual interest within the broad topic.[16]

Writing assignments should grow out of the activities of the group. Writing is always written and read in relation to some pursuit, and it is in that relationship that much of the meaning of a written text will lie. This is obvious in pragmatic, utilitarian discourse: a television repair manual is meaningful in relation to televisions and the activity of repair. And it is equally true of academic discourse, which is meaningful in relation to the values and traditions of a discipline as well as to the questions, understandings, and methods of inquiry that occupy that discipline at any moment of its history. In large measure learning to write is learning to exploit the relationship of discourse to enterprise. Unfortunately, in composition classrooms, where writing papers becomes the main enterprise, this relationship is often skewed or even lost. Thus, a student might be asked to engage in the activity of comparing and contrasting or the activity of narrating solely in order to write a paper. Rather, the aim should be to contextualize writing assignments within the activity of inquiry that the class pursues as a group. Comparing and contrasting might be used as useful methods of investigation, not as a theme for a paper. Written reporting likewise could be used to bring into the class relevant information that the group needs to proceed in its work.

The class should serve as the primary audience for the writing. The necessity of having students share their writing is entailed in the other two conditions I have just mentioned. Information needs to be exchanged; different viewpoints need to be aired and incorporated. Also, having a wide, authentic audience responding to their writing helps students turn their attention away from the examiner-teacher as audience and toward a more sustained consideration of the needs and expectations of readers.

These three broad tenets are offered as essential ingredients for enriching the contexts in which writing and reading occur. Such a concentration on the environment of the writing classroom offers an alternative to conventional and even to newer approaches to "modeling" in the composition classroom. Unlike prose modeling, in which students imitate formal products, or even process modeling, in which emphasis is put on taking students through the "forms" of planning, drafting, and revising, a contextual approach attempts to *model circumstances* that invite, promote, and guide the production of written discourse.

Social Considerations in Writing and Reading Research

To view writing as an event that occurs within a public context, a context of a "we," can bring a new and much-needed perspective to composition research by reuniting the study of writing processes with the texts that those processes bring forth. What writers do when they write cannot be understood in isolation from the dynamic, moment-by-moment contexts in which they write. All composing strategies—from planning to revising—are in important ways socially-based, contributing in some way to the social reality that a writer is in the process of accomplishing. Labels such as "rhetorical context" or "task environment" must be taken out of the undifferentiated backgrounds of writing models and centrally integrated into explanations of writing processes.

Such a social perspective on the processes of textual meaning-making is equally relevant, of course, to the study of reading. Readers accomplish contexts for understanding in the same manner as writers. Indeed, any writer's success in coming to mean during composing depends upon an assumption that a reader also will read in a state of "weness." As Ragnar Rommetveit observes, "Meaning is attained only by transcendence of the individual mind; solitary reading becomes comprehensible only when conceived of as embedded in a genuinely social game."[17]

This mutual reliance on what Rommetveit has labeled "the architecture of intersubjectivity" forms the social foundations of reading and writing. Much work remains to be done to uncover and articulate the game by which writers and readers accomplish understanding.

Notes

1. Barry Kroll, "Speaking-Writing Relationships in the Growth of Writing Abilities," in Patricia L. Stock, ed., *Fforum: Essays on Theory and Practice in the Teaching of Writing* (Upper Montclair, N. J.: Boynton/Cook, 1983).

2. Sondra Perl, "The Composing Processes of Unskilled College Writers," *Research in the Teaching of English* 13 (1979): 317-36; Sharon Pianko, "A Description of the Composition Processes of College Freshman Writers," *Research in the Teaching of English* 13 (1979): 5-22; and Lillian Bridwell, "Revising Strategies in Twelfth Grade Students' Transactional Writing," *Research in the Teaching of English* 14 (1980): 192-222.

3. Margaret Atwell, "The Evolution of Text: The Interrelationship of Reading and Writing in the Composing Process" (Ph.D. diss., Indiana University, 1980).

4. Nancy Shanklin, "Relating Reading and Writing: Developing a Transactional Theory of the Writing Process" (Ph.D. diss., Indiana University, 1980).

5. Ragnar Rommetveit, *On Message Structure: A Framework for the Study of Language and Communication* (New York: Wiley, 1974).

6. Italicized in the transcript are the words the writer records. All excerpts presented here are taken from a series of oral protocols collected from two students enrolled in an introductory composition course in the summer of 1982. The students thought aloud as they composed papers and assignments in conjunction with the course. A total of nine protocols were collected. As no time limits were set, some taping sessions extended over several days. The aim of the protocol study was to trace contextual influences on composing processes. For a fuller description of the study and its results see Deborah Brandt, "Writer, Context, and Text" (Ph.D. diss., Indiana University, 1983).

7. Rommetveit, *On Message Structure.*

8. Rolf Kjolseth, "Making Sense: Natural Language and Shared Knowledge in Understanding," in Joshua A. Fishman, ed., *Advances in the Sociology of Language,* vol. 1 (Hague: Mouton, 1971).

9. Kjolseth, p. 65.

10. Frank Smith, *Understanding Reading: A Psycholinguistic Analysis of Reading and Learning to Read,* 2nd ed. (New York: Holt, 1978), 57.

11. Anthony J. Sanford and Simon C. Garrod, *Understanding Written Language: Explorations in Comprehension Beyond the Sentence* (New York: Wiley, 1981).

12. Kjolseth, pp. 70-71.

13. James Britton, Tony Burgess, Nancy Martin, Alex McLeod, and Harold Rosen, *The Development of Writing Abilities (11-18),* Schools Council Research Studies (London: Macmillan Education, 1975).

14. The term "indexical expression" comes from work in ethnomethodology that studies how members of a social group accomplish understanding in everyday interaction. Members develop labels for commonly shared experiences so that when a label is used members can "fill in" the full resonance of its meaning by recovering the context of the original experience. "Watergate" is

such an expression. As Aaron Cicourel explains, "Descriptive vocabularies are indexes of earlier (and present) experiences and thus reflect elements of the original context so as to permit the retrieval of information that would locate the activities in a broader horizon of meaning than contained in treating each lexical item as a dictionary entry" (*Cognitive Sociology: Language and Meaning in Social Interaction* [New York: Free Press, 1974], 87).

15. Kenneth Dowst, "The Epistemic Approach: Writing, Knowing, and Learning," in Timothy R. Donovan and Ben W. McClelland, eds., *Eight Approaches to Teaching Composition* (Urbana, Ill.: National Council of Teachers of English, 1980); and William E. Coles, Jr., *The Plural I: The Teaching of Writing* (New York: Holt, 1978).

16. For a fuller description of the course and sample assignments, see Brandt, "Writer, Context, and Text."

17. Rommetveit, p. 86.

Speech Acts and the Reader-Writer Transaction

Dorothy Augustine
Chapman College

W. Ross Winterowd
University of Southern California

In the first chapter in *Speech Acts: An Essay in the Philosophy of Language,* John Searle marks the distinctions and relationships among (1) talking, (2) characterizing talk, and (3) explaining talk.[1] We are *talking* (or writing prepared talk) now, for instance, and our ability to do this underlies the possibility of writers' and readers' *characterizing* this kind of talk as rhetoric or written discourse or composition. Furthermore, our characterizing statement may be *explained* by rules that experienced writers and readers know or can invent, in this case, rules governing sentences, introductory paragraphs, contextual frames, cohesion, and the like.

Needless to say, rhetoricians do a lot of talking in order to explain what they characterize as discourse. Only recently, however, has this talk focused on these characterizing statements themselves. We have started to examine conventional characterizations of rhetoric or composition, such as those found in textbooks from Aristotle to Peter Elbow, in terms of questions like "What happens when writers write?" or "Do paragraphs produced in the real world resemble those prescribed by textbook rules?"[2] Sooner or later, these analyses of writing will generate evidence sufficient to counter the convention and to offer characterizing propositions about the nature of composing that can be explained with rules or models that are simple, general, and testable.

That rhetoric, specifically composition, involves an implicit dialogue is one proposition of this kind, for it characterizes written discourse as a transaction between writer and reader, a transaction relying on the writer's and reader's tacit knowledge of the regularities of conversation. All of us whose native language is English, for example, conform to certain "rules" of turn-taking in conversation, and we adhere to what the philosopher H. P. Grice describes as "the cooperative principle."[3] These tacit rules or regularities have only recently been discovered as underlying the surface forms and even the content of conversation. Unlike Molière's Monsieur Jourdain, however, none of us is surprised that we have been speaking according to these rules or regularities all our lives. We recognize them as "intuitively valid," as linguists like to say. Furthermore, such linguistic or philosophic discoveries help explain why researchers in rhetoric have shifted from attempts to characterize the written word (the "facts") to attempts to characterize the generation of texts (the underlying rules which regulate the "facts").[4]

Of course, composition is unlike conversation in obvious ways. It is prepared or rehearsed, unlike most conversation; it is more formal in its vocabulary and syntax; and, perhaps most obvious, it appears one-sided, a monologue. Nevertheless, successful composition may be described as *implicit* dialogue if for no other reason than that the concept of "reader" requires writers to pay attention to regularities of behavior which involve a partner in the discourse, a "silent" partner, to be sure, but one who is equal and, ideally, equally competent in the linguistic business at hand.

Sophisticated writers, for example, are hardly surprised by the statement that they have invented a reader. Everyone understands that writers' workshops are valuable and good editors are sought after precisely because writers need to test the possible and probable "responses" they have projected (consciously or unconsciously) to their theses, proofs, points of view, etc. One may, therefore, consider the hypothetical responses projected by writers as a correlate to the conversational "cues"—silent and spoken—that speakers constantly receive from listeners in live dialogic situations: Speakers "know" whether they should continue to speak, stop to explain a point, back up, or skip ahead because of the listeners' verbal and nonverbal signals. These signals can be as blunt as a listener's interrupting a speaker with a request for information or clarification, or as subtle as a listener's dilated pupils, interpreted by the speaker as silent affirmation of what is being said.[5] There are no immediate cues of that kind, however, in the writer-reader transaction, and this may be the most fundamental reason for the writer to invent the reader, to project the hypothetical responses that will indicate whether the reader is "going along" with the claim, argument, proposal, or other *illocutionary act* initiating the discourse or any of its parts. If the writer projects a *perlocutionary* response that challenges or questions an initiating illocution, then that response must be addressed in the compositional forms and content of proof, qualification, concession, background, refutation, etc., and the resulting discourse will assume the features of the language game we call rhetoric.[6] A simple illustration in speech-act format can clarify this notion:

> Illocution: (I *assert* to you that) The Equal Rights Amendment is misunderstood by a majority of voters.
>
> Perlocution: (I *challenge* you to) Prove it!

Rhetorical discourse, in Chaim Perelman's words, will manifest the writer's facility for generating the reader's "adherence to the theses" offered for his or her assent.[7] Implicit in Perelman's description of rhetoric's function is the presupposition that someone "out there" will object to "the thesis." As far back as Aristotle (rhetoric is "the faculty for observing . . . the available means of persuasion," *Rhetoric*), theoreticians have described the function of rhetoric and the work of the rhetor without paying too much attention to the *causes* of either—the hypothetical responses of an imagined audience, responses on the order of "Prove it!" or "Says who?" or "So what?"

At this point, a bridge from one aspect of the tradition, invention, may help to relate the above to a more familiar concept. Invention, most of us feel, is the first of the rhetorical arts, because when a writer provides form without the substance of a topic, we find it abhorrent to our ideal of rhetoric's function. But topics—the methods and procedures for discovering issues, lines of agreement, or problems, or for assessing values or beliefs—should be understood as more than prescriptive inducements to substantive "thought." By employing the topic of definition, for example, writers would presuppose or project a reader's asking, "What do you mean by *that?*" when a "that" has just been introduced into the discourse. Likewise, we would rely on cause and effect when we hypothesize that a reader will question the relationship between what we claim to be antecedent and what consequent. Whatever topic we use, consciously or unconsciously, felicitously or not, we attempt to address and satisfy what we project as the probable response to our overall or localized illocution in the discourse, our *advice, argument, assertion, claim, proposal, request, warning,* or other speech act underlying the surface structure of what we are communicating to the reader. We do that, for the most part, because of our competence as speakers and listeners in everyday "language games" with their intrinsic rules for generating form, style, and even content. The "logic" of invention, seen in this light, is hardly a set of rules imposed from without. It is already there, in the structure of human dialogue as a coherent series of inter-influences.

   This short illustration is not meant to reappropriate the tradition by redefining its parts, but to demonstrate how the "how" of classical thought may be distinguished from the "why" of current research in composition.[8] What has come to be known as the current-traditionalist school refers more or less to the positivist philosophy that reality is external and fixed, and that language functions as a container for and carrier of meaning. The epistemic philosophy of the new rhetoric, on the other hand, understands meaning to emerge from rhetorical situations, each with its own rules of evidence, etc.[9] In this view of reality, language acts as a kind of chemical reagent, a device for detecting and identifying each situation and the particular set of rules attending it, as well as the agency for our definitions and evaluations of the world.

Intention and Super-intention

The implications for rhetorical theory of research in philosophy and linguistics are rich. But chief among them, we believe, is this: that every declarative sentence that we read or hear, write or speak, may be represented as the subordinate clause (what we will call the "propositional intention") of an underlying main clause. The dominant or main clause of the sentence (what we will call the "rhetorical intention") is identified by illocutions on the order of "I *advise, (assert, claim, 'joke,' warn)* you to [that] . . . ."[10] For example, the first sentence of this paragraph must be considered the subordinate clause of an underlying or deep-structure sentence represented roughly as "We *state* to you that 'the implications for rhetorical theory of research in philosophy and linguistics are rich.'" The main clause, identified by a performative verb and therefore indicative of a speech act, together with the subordinate clause, forms what we will call the "super-intention." We can illustrate these relationships by means of the familiar tree diagram.

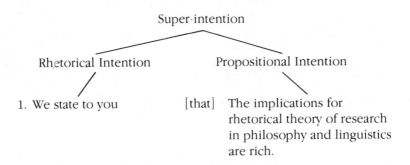

Super-intention

Rhetorical Intention   Propositional Intention

1. We state to you [that] The implications for
            rhetorical theory of research
            in philosophy and linguistics
            are rich.

Propositional intentions, then, account for most of the surface structures of what we read or hear in discourse. "Rhetorical intentions," indicative of and accounting for the *purpose* of introducing the proposition(s) of the subordinate clause are, for the most part, "understood" in composition (as well as in conversation), much as is the deep-structure "you" of the imperative. The problem is that rhetorical intentions are more highly subject to misinterpretation by readers than by listeners, for there are no live cues to rely on in facing a page of print. This is one of the reasons composition is a much more complicated language game than the spoken word and its (usually immediate) response.

A less apparent handicap for writers is the fact that rhetorical intentions are represented by the performative values of the underlying dominant clause, and there are many performative verbs with their own accompanying semantic environments. Referring to our first sentence again, for example, a reader may have interpreted the rhetorical intention to be governed by an underlying performative like *claim* rather than *state*. That would be a perfectly reasonable "reading" of the rhetorical intention, for in the first sentence of the first paragraph of a major division of an essay, rhetorical intentions are more properly realized in performatives, like the verb *claim,* suggesting "proofs," and the accompanying semantic "uptake" of readers *expecting* clarification of terms and points of view that *claim* would require (and that *state* would not require, or at least not as strongly as *claim* would). One would not expect as full a discussion to follow a statement as would follow a claim; the meanings of the two illocutions realized as intentions justify different perlocutions or responses on the part of the reader. Other possible rhetorical intentions for the same proposition as it appears above in the surface structure may be explicitly realized in performatives like *propose, offer, argue, maintain, inform, instruct, pronounce, declare,* or even *advise.* All of these performatives could represent the intention governing that particular proposition (though we would expect a majority of readers to vote for *claim*). Indeed, the competent reader may have held all the possible verbs in suspension—in a rhetorical juggling act—until through further reading one "meaning" was confirmed (and the others disconfirmed) by the content, style, and form of what followed. No competent reader, however, would have interpreted the same proposition to be governed by a rhetorical intention informed by a performative like *deny, warn,* or *inquire.*

To illustrate this point of the reader-writer transaction further, we can factor out what we take to be the dominant clauses or the performative values or the rhetorical intentions or the purposes of any stretch of discourse, as follows:

Super-intention

Rhetorical Intention	Propositional Intention
I *declare* to you that	. . . government of the people, by the people, for the people, shall not perish from the earth.
I *insist* to you that	My Mistress' eyes are nothing like the sun.
I *instruct* you that	(You) Lift receiver, deposit coin, listen for dial tone.
I *question* that	It is a truth universally acknowledged, that a single man in possession of a good fortune, must be in want of a wife.
I *vow* to you that	I am not a crook.
I *tell* you that	(You should) Call me Ishmael.

Though we do not expect a perfect match between the rhetorical intentions we have assigned and those that the reader might, the point is
that we could all agree that the above is a *possible* and reasonable list of
rhetorical intentions which make purposeful sense of the list of corresponding propositions. Naturally, one could interpret a "vow" as a
"lie," but that fact serves only to reinforce our point: underlying performative values will govern the purpose of discourse, whether those
values are intended by the writer-speaker or responded to by the
reader-listener. Where gross discrepancies occur between writers'
underlying intentions and readers' responses, we have the "misunderstanding" that I. A. Richards valiantly tried to account for in his analyses
of the surface meanings of discourse.

Such a deep-structure analysis is easily tested and validated in terms
of the real-world responses we hear every day to declarative sentences.
A possible response to

2. Prices slumped,

for example, might be rendered in ordinary conversation as "Are you
serious?" The deep structure of that response may be represented as

3. Do you ((claim) (joke)) to me that "prices slumped"?

And we mark such responses as the surface structure of 3 as coherent precisely because we understand that the listener is searching not only for the semantic or propositional intention of the speaker, but also, and more important, for the speaker's rhetorical intention or purpose in relating the proposition. The listener, in fact, is making an attempt to reconstruct the performative verb of the underlying dominant clause. He or she must understand the super-intention, the whole of the discourse, before he or she can make sense of any of its parts.

What we are saying is simply this: Writers can make their intentions explicit by supplying the deep-structure performative verbs that account for their rhetorical purposes; if readers have understood the writer's intentions, then they can reconstruct and make explicit the deep-structure performative(s) of the main clause(s).

Notice the ambiguities in the following speech acts and how they might be resolved:

4. S: Two dollars on Sea Biscuit!
   H: Are you *betting* or *bidding* on Sea Biscuit?
5. S: I shall return.
   H: Are you *promising* or *threatening* me that you'll come back?
6. S: You should learn Greek.
   H: Are you *suggesting* that I learn Greek or *ordering* me to?

And for anyone who has taught freshman English, a classic example of a misunderstanding will come to mind:

7. Swift: We should breed, fatten, and slaughter the poor of Ireland.
   Freshman: Are you *advocating* the proposal that we should breed, fatten, and slaughter the poor of Ireland?

The fact that we do not normally pose such responses as those in 3–7 proves that as readers and listeners we are superbly efficient, most of the time, in constructing and reconstructing rhetorical intentions.

Of course, in the semantic environment of satire, as in 7, the competence allowing for a deep-structure "analysis" is essential, because understanding the *propositional* intention alone, that is, what appears in the surface structures of the essay, is insufficient for comprehending Swift's *purpose* in his proposal.[11] The naive reader may understand perfectly the semantic import of the surface structures of the entire essay or their reduction to a "thesis," but will misconstrue Swift's *rhetorical intention* in communicating that proposition if his or her competence in language games does not allow the necessary "deep-structure analysis" of possible performative verbs in the main, underlying clause. Such a reading demonstrates the difference between what Searle calls "brute facts" and "institutional facts." His famous football analogy bears repeating here:

> Imagine a group of highly trained observers describing an American football game in statements only of brute facts . . . Within certain areas a good deal could be said, and using statistical techniques certain "laws" could even be formulated. For example, we can imagine that after a time our observer would discover the law of periodical clustering: at statistically regular intervals organisms in like-colored shirts cluster together in a roughly circular fashion (the huddle). Furthermore, at equally regular intervals, circular clustering is followed by linear clustering . . . and linear clustering is followed by . . . linear interpenetration. . . . But no matter how much data of this sort we imagine our observers to collect and no matter how many inductive generalizations we imagine them to make from the data, they still have not described American football. What is missing from their description? What is missing are all those concepts which are backed by constitutive rules, concepts such as touchdown, offside, game, points, first down, time out, etc., and consequently what is missing are all the true statements one can make about a football game. The missing statements are precisely what describe the phenomenon on the field *as a game of football*. . . .
>
> No one, I guess, would try to offer a description of football in terms of brute facts, and yet, curiously enough, people have tried to offer semantic analyses of language armed with only a conceptual structure of brute facts and ignoring the semantic rules that underlie the brute regularities. . . .[12]

Satire, like the underlying rules of football, may be understood as an institutional (semantic) fact, and Swift's essay, like men in colored jerseys running about on a striped field, may be understood as a collection of brute facts or regularities. Competence in understanding football and satire is the ability of the players and observers to rely on constitutive rules explaining why the participants behave in such and such a way. In understanding "A Modest Proposal," readers rely on the regularities of linguistic behavior not available for observation, a repertoire of skills one of which is the ability to refer to *possible* performatives and probable rhetorical intentions that will make sense of Swift's surface structures. The naif graduates into sophistication not because he finally reads "A Modest Proposal" more closely (the familiar pedagogical admonition to reconcile, in effect, more brute facts), but because he reconstructs Swift's underlying, tacit, illocutionary *denial* of what is on the page, a rhetorical reading. The transaction between reader and writer, to be sure, depends upon their sharing the same institutional fact, governed and explained by constitutive rules. Even more profound, however, is their ability to agree on the performative value(s) or rhetorical intention(s) communicating and interpreting the institutional fact(s) they share. "A Modest Proposal" affords an extreme example of how the "constitutive rules" of the speech-act transaction between writer and reader account for the "institutional fact" of ridicule by wit and satire.

Though this essay is not meant to treat models of instruction or the English curriculum in a practical way, we cannot resist touching on an object lesson here. A naive interpretation of Swift's essay can be traced to a thin repertoire of rhetorical skills, to the reader's limited experience of rhetorical intentions. Young adults in the twentieth century have been primarily educated, perhaps as have no other previous generations, in the "scientific" style and to writing, themselves, in the expository mode. Neither does more than attempt "to inform," only one of the three aims of discourse, "to persuade" and "to please" being considered irrelevant to the "plain, dispassionate style" of certitude in reporting and describing objective phenomena. If rhetoric is reduced to explanation, rhetorical intentions can only be realized and interpreted as statements of clarification made bearable by brevity and sincerity.[13] The linguistic, psychological, and cultural effects of such education can only be guessed at, but one likely result fits neatly into our case for constructing and reconstructing rhetorical intentions in written discourse. If student writer-readers are educated to exercise and expect only those rhetorical intentions on the order of "I *inform*," "I *instruct*," or, at the most, "I *advise*," then of course they do exactly that. Underlying rhetorical intentions on the order of "I *deny*," "I *joke*," or "I *criticize*," all possible indicators of Swift's propositions in "A Modest Proposal," lie outside the student's culturally acquired constitutive rules of composition. Notice that the naive reader will participate in the speech act initiated by Swift. The misunderstanding, however, occurs because the performatives appropriate to satire, or even to persuasion or argument, are missing from the reader's experiential inventory of those that govern writers' purposes and readers' expectations in discourse.

To summarize this section: In any speech act consummated by the reader's appropriate perlocution, where the exchange of intention and response is coherent or felicitous, an underlying, implicit performative clause is understood by the participants to carry the rhetorical intention or purpose of the discourse. (Needless to say, the performative clause may appear in the surface structure: "I promise that I'll return" versus "I'll return.") As the rhetorical constituent of the super-intention, the main, performative clause will govern both the writer's and the reader's attitudes toward the subject matter of the discourse, represented by the propositional content (predication and reference) in the subordinate clause. The preceding sentence, for example, is subordinate in the deep structure to the main clause "We claim that." *We claim that* "as the rhetorical component of the super-intention . . ." We do not *question, deny, criticize, suggest,* or *admit* the proposition. We do not, in fact, allow for any other performative value to govern the purpose of our proposition, though up to this point we have not stated any claims in the literal or surface features of this essay. The reader will nevertheless have understood or reconstructed our *purpose* by having responded to the *claim* implicit in the previous paragraphs. Perhaps that response or perlocution is on the order of "So what?" or "Prove it!" The next section is meant to continue the implicit dialogue here by addressing what we project to be potential to our implicit claim.

Intention and Response

Consider the following two two-sentence speech acts (for the time being, we will substitute the more general terms *intention* and *response* for the more specialized terminology of speech-act theory):

8. a. Intention: I *admit (christen, condemn, confess, congratulate, declare, pronounce, sentence, will, . . .)* ([to] you) that "x."

   b. Response: I *affirm (agree, assent, concede, grant, regret, . . .)* ([to] you) that "x."

9. a. Intention: I *assert (claim, insist, propose, request, suggest, . . .)* ([to] you) that "x."

   b. Response: I *challenge, (deny, doubt, object, question, refute, . . .)* ([to] you) that "x."

Both responses are coherent with their intentions. But 8b is coherent with 8a only, whereas both 8b and 9b are coherent with 9a. In the real world, in other words, with necessary conditions of felicity[14] and cooperativeness having been met, one kind of illocution may elicit a perlocutionary challenge, denial, doubt, etc., while another may not. This is an interesting anomaly, and while the phenomenon has been characterized and explained in the philosophers' taxonomies of performative values, it has not been discussed by theorists interested in the "constitutive rules" of rhetorical discourse. In exploring this anomaly, we hope to show how the sources of composition and the reader-writer transaction depend on a special kind of speech act explicitly realized by a special class of performative verbs in the initiating illocution and a challenge or denial (or what is projected as a challenge or denial) in the perlocution.

The philosophers' analysis of 8a and 9a clarifies and defines the conditions that must be in force in order that admissions and assertions be valid or true or taken to be valid or true of a state of affairs. Searle's taxonomy classifies a speech act informed by verbs like *admit* as "declaratives," and those informed by verbs like *assert* as "representatives."[15] We could, for instance, distill from any real-world utterance on the order of 8a the abstraction, *I declare to you that a certain state of affairs exists;* from 9a the abstraction, *I declare to you that a certain state of affairs exists "as such."* And, as Searle's analysis has already shown, the semantic environments of each class of performatives invest the "I" and the "you" of the main clause with certain social and epistemic privileges and constraints; conditions of felicity and cooperativeness are givens in 9 as well as in 8 in order that the speech acts be consummated by appropriate and coherent perlocutions or perlocutionary effects. One performative like *admit* is *promise,* for example, and to make a promise involves a complex understanding of underlying rules that must be adhered to by the participants in the speech act in order that the promise be consummated. Clark and Clark outline these underlying rules or conditions of felicity:

> Imagine that Alan says to Ben "I promise you that I will go home tomorrow." The rules Alan must adhere to are these:
>
> 1. *Propositional content rule.* The propositional content "I will go home tomorrow" must predicate a future act of Alan (which it does).
> 2. *Preparatory rule.* Alan must believe that Ben would prefer Alan's going home tomorrow; and Alan must also believe that it is not obvious to Alan or Ben that Alan would go home tomorrow in the normal course of events.
> 3. *Sincerity rule.* Alan intends to go home tomorrow.
> 4. *Essential rule.* By uttering this sentence, Alan undertakes an obligation to go home tomorrow.
>
> If any one of these rules is not fulfilled, Alan could be said to be making an "infelicitous" promise. Hence these rules are often called the *felicity conditions* of a promise.[16]

The same conditions would hold true for *admit* and all the other performatives in 8a, with adjustments, of course, for the semantic restrictions of the verb. For example, *admit* would predicate a past action by the speaker, not a future one, as with *promise,* and so on.

But felicity conditions having been met, an audience does not have the option to challenge an illocution or intention informed by a verb like *promise* or *admit*. Verbs like *admit* must belong to a subclass of performatives that are explicitly *arhetorical*, that is, a speech act initiated by a performative like *admit* is composed of one illocution and one perlocution, of one "conversational turn" each by the participants. The evidence for this rule is illustrated in 10, with unacceptable perlocutions marked with asterisks:

10. a. (I admit that) I was smoking behind the barn.

    b. Well, I hope you'll never do that kind of thing again.
       I'm glad you had the courage to say so.
       Welcome to the club!
       In that case, you're forgiven.

    c. *You can't prove that.
       *Are you certain of what you're saying?
       *Who cares?
       *I don't believe you.

Rhetoric begins, as Kenneth Burke has shown us, with the human option to say *no,* and one cannot respond to an *admission* with a perlocutionary *denial* or *challenge.* In arhetorical language games, all of the constituents of the illocution will be recognized as valid by the audience: the authority of the speaker to make such an utterance (ethos); the real-world truth of the proposition (logos); and the influence of both on the audience (pathos) all obtaining in the responses in 10b. Such an illocutionary act will not be challenged by any perlocution on the order of "Prove it" (logos), or "So what" (pathos), or "Says who" (ethos), all indicative of the responses in 10c. As J. L. Austin remarks on a smaller category of illocutions, informed by what we think of now as the "classical" performatives such as those in 8a, the saying is the doing. One may as well challenge a lunar eclipse as to respond to 8a or 10a, respectively, with any of the alternatives in 9b or 10c.

Suppose, though, that felicity conditions are violated, resulting in a defective speech act. The "scenes" may be described briefly by positing some perlocutionary effects in which the negative *may* obtain. We can use a well-worn illocution in the example.

11. a. Illocution: I pronounce you man and wife.
       Perlocution: But you can't marry us. You're not a priest.

    b. Illocution: I pronounce you man and wife.
       Perlocution: Nice try, but you've got the wrong couple.
                    We're the parents of the groom.

c. Illocution: I pronounce you man and wife.
Perlocution: But we want to be confirmed.

In 11a, the response is to ethos, in that the audience believes the speaker not to have the authority invoked by the pronouncement. In 11b, the response is to pathos, in that the audience understand themselves to be outside the act of the utterance; it is inappropriate or irrelevant to their real-world concerns or situation. In 11c, the response is to logos, in that the proposition of performing a marriage is inappropriate, inconsistent, or incoherent in the "scenic" state of affairs. Notice the traditionally rhetorical contexts (that is, challenges to ethos, pathos, and logos) in which defective arhetorical speech acts may be seen to "violate reality." But notice also that, the sincerity of the exchanges notwithstanding, the speech acts represented in 11 describe a burlesque of reality principles, the foundation of a farcical scene by Shakespeare or Woody Allen perhaps, a violation of expectations built upon a violation of the constitutive rules of arhetorical speech acts.

When an illocution carries the rhetorical value of a performative like *assert,* however, the constitutive rules describe a different kind of language game, for any or all three of the constituents may be denied, questioned, challenged, objected to, refuted, etc., without violating the preparatory rules of felicity or cooperativeness. Suppose, for example, that the proposition in 10a, "I was smoking behind the barn," is preceded by the rhetorical intention indicated by a performative like *suggest,* a clearly rhetorical performative:

12. a. (I suggest that) I ((was) (may have been)) smoking behind the barn.

All of the possible perlocutions in 10b are also possible as responses to 12a. But the following perlocutions, unacceptable challenges to authority, truth, or relevance in 10, are permitted as responses to a suggestion:

12. b. You can't prove that.
Are you certain of what you're saying?
Who cares?
I don't believe you.

If the response to an intention informed by an arhetorical performative verb is one of negation or challenge, then either some principle of reality or some condition for felicity must have been violated, as in 10c or 11. If a "negative" perlocution obtains (or is projected) to an intention informed by a rhetorical performative, as in 9b or 12b, the initiating intention-response pair will extend to what we characterize as dialogue, discourse, or composition. The person initiating the speech act will attempt to address the challenges to his or her authority to offer such a proposition, the truth of the proposition, or the real-world relevance of the proposition to the audience. Performatives like *assert,* therefore, may be thought of as belonging to the subclass *rhetorical,* with the semantic power of initiating a potential series of turn-takings. We can take a well-publicized illocution this time to illustrate the point.

> 13. a. Linus Pauling: (I *assert (claim, . . .)* that) Megadoses of vita-
>   min C will help to prevent disease.
>   b. Audience: I *deny (question, . . .)* that you have the author-
>   ity to make any claim about nutrition and
>   health.

In 13b, the audience directs the response to the credentials of the writer, the ethical constituent of the illocution. In 13c, the response is directed at the truth or validity of the state of affairs as represented by Pauling, that is, to the logical constituent of his claim:

> c. Audience: I *deny (question, . . .)* that megadoses of vitamin
>   C can prevent disease.

In 13d, the response is directed toward the relevance of the claim to the real-world concerns or situation (pathos) of the audience:

> d. Audience: I *deny* that your claim is meaningful for me (be-
>   cause I am allergic to ascorbic acid).

Of course, the audience may affirm as well as deny, accept as well as question any or all of the constituents of the illocution. In that case, however, rhetoric does not follow; the exchange begins and ends in a two-sentence language game of one turn each for the participants. There is no ensuing "art of the probable," no attempt to "remedy misunderstandings," no need to depend upon the constitutive rules of argument or persuasion in order to present evidence for one's case.

But, quite simply, a significant condition attached to rhetorical in-tention(s) realized as underlying performative clauses on the order of 9a is the writer's presupposition that a challenge or a negative *may* direct the reader's response. It is this potential response that teases the concept of rhetoric from the universe of discourse.

One "rule" governing rhetoric is this: the writer must hedge his or her rhetorical bet by addressing and resolving the denials or challenges to any or all of the constituents of a super-intention informed by a verb such as *assert.* In doing so, the writer will compose more than subject matter and will at least attempt to bring together or reconcile the differing views or presuppositions regarding the materials of the discourse—his or her authority to speak on the subject, the relevance of the subject to the reader, and the real-world "truth" of his or her proposition(s). If the writer is successful, he or she will have established a new meaning for any proposition, any "x"; he or she will have communicated "news." The following represents the underlying model of the reader-writer transaction in successful discourse.

Writer: I *assert* to you that "x."
Reader: I *deny* that ("x" is a true representation of reality).
        (I have any stake in "x").
        (you have the authority to assert "x").
Writer: I *offer* (n "proofs" that "x" is true).
        (n "proofs" that "x" is relevant to you).
        (n "proofs" that I am a credible source).
Reader: I *require* (q "proofs" for the truth of "x").
        (. . .)

And so on. Not so surprisingly, one could reduce any finished piece of rhetoric to the abstract turn-taking described above. The evidence generated to address potential negative responses to the writer's intention(s) will mark the form of discourse as representative of the ego-sharing involved in all language games. If subject matter is transformed into subject in the process of composing, that is exactly what is involved.

One way of looking at the topics of invention or prescriptions for style and arrangement is that they are implicit codifications of probable negative responses by audiences to writers' intentions. Indeed, in arhetorical situations, represented in 8 and 10, considerations such as style or arrangement are beside the point. A speaker or writer whose intention is to make an admission, confession, pronouncement, promise, etc., need only learn or have available for imitation a certain linguistic "ritual." The performative values of verbs like *admit* carry with them prescribed forms and styles signified by the writer's (or speaker's) reliance on ritualized language (e.g., the priest reading from a prepared text in performing a ceremony; legislators employing legal consultants to check on the wording of a newly written bill). This attention to the ritual of the speech act marks the behavior of the participants as outside the probable. It is either "correct" or it isn't. As a matter of fact, in some arhetorical situations, any deviation from the "text" nullifies the speech act. A verdict of guilty may be overturned on a "linguistic" technicality as well as an evidential one: the defendant was not "formally" charged; a witness was not properly interrogated.

Formal or stylistic latitude, at any rate, is very narrow in the speech acts identifying civil, religious, or social speech acts realized as contracts.

One may even entertain the notion here that some academic "styles," especially in the sciences, tacitly militate against the reader's option to say no; rigidly prescribed form in an essay is, in a sense, indicative of a contract, an arhetorical speech act initiated by performatives like *declare, inform,* or *pronounce,* in which, preparatory conditions having been satisfied, a negative response is ruled out. Scientific papers do not "argue"; for the most part, their authors "declare" that such and such is the case because a certain process was overlaid on a certain set of givens, a theoretical or practical ritual that the investigators report on. That writers in the humanities should allow that model of research and communication to influence their own practice is understandable in a "scientific age," but it has taken a terrible toll. The inordinate amount of time and attention given to form and style in composition courses based on current-traditionalist notions of rhetoric would seem to bring about the arhetorical situation in which students "expect" no response, except perhaps that of assent, in their reading and their own writing. Is it any wonder that despite the recent renaissance in emphasizing invention, heuristics, problem solving, and other aids for investing students' writing with substance, point of view, purpose, *meaning,* their essays may still lack the excitement of their "real-life" talent for dialogue and debate?

In the next section, then, we intend to show how and why the theory laid out above can significantly affect the teaching and learning of writing.

Implications for Teaching

Rhetorical situations are marked by debate over propositions, exchange of views and evidence, and influence over decision making, with persuading the audience toward a particular action or idea as the final cause. This is so whether or not an audience apart from the writer is addressed or conceived. The phenomenon of writers' "changing their minds," or their theses, in the process of composing is, after all, a familiar one to accomplished writers, and this firsthand knowledge, if nothing more, strongly suggests that underlying the surface structures of written discourse we may "discover" the rules for rhetorical competence.

We have posited that these rules may be made explicit by referring to concepts describing spoken dialogue and specifically to speech-act theory and the intention-response model of philosophy and linguistics.

A preliminary analysis of rhetorical intentions made tenable the idea that the successful reader-writer transaction depends upon both participants' constructing and reconstructing the same (or a semantically equivalent) performative verb in the main, deep-structure clause of the declarative sentence serving as a statement of thesis or topic. Furthermore, we demonstrated that rhetorical intentions are marked by a special subclass of performative verbs, performatives with the semantic potential to elicit responses which are coherent with the rhetorical or propositional intentions but which, nevertheless, may deny or challenge any or all of the constituents of the super-intention. If a challenge to the authority of the writer, the truth of the proposition, or the relevance of either to the reader does ensue (and the writer must suppose that any or all may), then an underlying, extended, and implicit series of speech acts describes the form and content of the resulting discourse.

Given that summary, we would like to make two practical observations.

First, if our case is valid, it represents in the abstract what every competent writer and reader knows intuitively. (To paraphrase a truism of linguistic research, none of us knows consciously the "rules" of composition, but we all read and write as though we did.) That is, our attempt to raise the rules of composition to formal representation should not be interpreted as a vague prescription for classroom practice, but as a descriptive model of rhetorical competence in writers and readers. Teaching speech-act theory to naive writers in the hope that they will translate its maxims and terminology into their practical struggles with the written word would seem to be as vain an endeavor as teaching them grammar in the hope that their editing problems will disappear. The point is that, just as competent speakers know the rules for putting the parts of speech together, though they may not be able to define "noun" or to give an example of one, competent writers and readers know the rules for successful transactions in discourse, though they may not be able to define "rhetorical intentions" or be consciously aware of responding to them. Humans acquire linguistic competence through exposure to models—mostly imperfect. We do not subsequently "imitate" the models so much as creatively adapt them to our own purposes in, as Chomsky puts it, manipulating the world.

The proper "use" of our theory, it seems to us, is as an aid to the teacher's formal understanding of the discipline more than as an immediate editing tool for the student. Until very recently in composition research, we have been more or less concerned with the interaction of underlying systems of linguistic behavior—the teacher's and the student's—with little attention to the systems themselves.[17] This essay, as we stated at the start, is one more attempt in a growing body of research in rhetoric to realign our thinking about composition and its processes. Like some others who have looked at received "characterizing statements" of rhetoric and found them to misrepresent our realities, we have implicitly questioned some tenets of the tradition by explicitly offering a novel characterization of the system itself.

Second, we have to admit at the same time that many, if not most, of our students cannot yet claim rhetorical competence. And so we have to address a potential response from the reader: Who cares about theoretical adjustments to the tradition when I have students who consistently compose two-sentence paragraphs and cannot formulate a recognizable thesis? We admit that our answer must disappoint any immediate expectations of practical payoffs—for in order to rely on the constitutive rules for rhetoric, writers and readers need the time to "acquire" rule-governed behavior rather than just "learn" formulae.[18] A history of reading "just for fun" is the necessary condition for reconstructing, say, Swift's rhetorical intention in "A Modest Proposal." Experience in writing "just for the hell of it" is prerequisite to formulating and constructing super-intentions. Competent writers and readers have long, and wide, apprenticeships. Paradoxically, they come to our classes as students with little need for "instruction." Since they have already internalized the rules, they need learn only to perfect their game.

For those students lacking such an apprenticeship, we can only point to the wrongheadedness of much of the English curriculum in perpetuating incompetence, a wrongheadedness stemming from attitudes toward reading and writing that, according to Clinton S. Burhans,[19] depend on myth and unexamined assumptions about language and literacy. In previous sections, we touched on the counterproductiveness of college-level courses in writing taught solely in terms of exposition, and of their emphasis on form and style. We would argue that if a "learned" form makes the meaning in a piece of writing rather than the writer making the meaning in the process of rhetorical give-and-take, that writer must always be judged as "naive." As for reading, it is safe to say that naive writers at any level of instruction need exposure to all the modes of discourse, all the divisions of rhetoric's implicit dialogue, critical essays as well as fiction, argumentation as well as biography, so that form and style can be understood to develop in any piece of writing as a function of underlying speech acts, not as ends in themselves. As teachers of composition, we can rephrase T. S. Eliot's profound quip about the difference between mature and immature poets to read "Competent writers steal; naive writers copy." Competent writers will rely on the whole range of possible intention-response environments for meaning they have been exposed to in their reading, and they will do a sophisticated mental cut-and-paste job in adapting those possible "models" of implicit dialogue to their own writing.[20] Our prescription, then, must be stated as a goal: adjustment of the curriculum to present characterizations of literacy—what it is that writers-and-readers do.

The major division of speech acts between rhetorical and arhetorical describes a novel concept, and we believe a valid one, of the transaction between writer and reader. It has allowed us to characterize rhetoric as a corollary to recent, valid descriptions of language. Understood as such, rhetoric is rich in possibilities for research that may qualify either the characterizing statement or the explanation we gave for it in the preceding pages. Our concept, moreover, while it marks much of the tradition as intuitively sound, also indicts much practice regarding convention as pedagogically shortsighted and even counterproductive to the means and ends of a society in which dialogue rather than dicta is preferred.

Notes

1. John Searle, *Speech Acts: An Essay in the Philosophy of Language* (London and New York: Cambridge Univ. Press, 1969).

2. Linda Flower and John R. Hayes provide protocol analyses of writers thinking aloud in the process of composing, showing that writers are guided by creative goal-setting rather than by "learned" rules ("A Cognitive Process Theory of Writing," *College Composition and Communication* 32 [Dec. 1981]: 365–87). "Studies That Challenge Traditional Paragraph Prescriptions" is the heading for seven entries in a recently published annotated bibliography by Marian Price, "Recent Work in Paragraph Analysis: A Bibliography," *Rhetoric Society Quarterly* 12 (Spring 1982): 127–31.

3. See H. P. Grice, "Logic and Conversation," in *Syntax and Semantics, Vol. 3: Speech Acts,* ed. P. Cole and J. L. Morgan (New York: Seminar Press, 1975). Simply put, in adhering to the cooperative principle, speakers are informative, truthful, relevant, and clear, "and listeners interpret what [speakers] say on the assumption that they are trying to live up to these ideals." Herbert H. Clark and Eve V. Clark, *Psychology and Language* (New York: Harcourt Brace Jovanovich, 1977), 122.

4. "Rhetoric," in other words, "can be viewed as an inherent system which is 'discoverable,' rather than as a set of rules imposed from without." Dorothy Augustine, "Geometries and Words: Linguistics and Philosophy: A Model of the Composing Process," *College English* 43 (Mar. 1981): 221–31.

5. The anthropologist Edward Hall has reported on an extended experiment meant to explore why any two conversants were seen to move in close physical synchrony when they were studied on slow-motion film:

[Finally] two people in conversation were wired to electroence-
phalographs to see if there was any comparability in brain waves.
Two cameras were set up so that one focused on the speakers, the
other on the EEG recording pens. When two people talked, the
recording pens moved as though driven by a single brain. When
one of the individuals was called out of the conversation by a third
person, the pens no longer moved together. . . . The only thing
that destroyed synchrony was if one of the people was called out of
the conversation by a third party. Synchrony stopped, and a new
chain was set up with the new interlocutor.

(*Beyond Culture* [Garden City, N.Y.: Anchor, 1977], 73.)

6. Any speech act is composed of illocution and perlocution, or intention
and response; for example, *Illocution*: I advise you to stop smoking; *Perlocution*: I answer that your advice is unrealistic. The examples are abstractions, for
normally we speak to each other "indirectly": "Why don't you stop smoking,
for heaven's sake?" "It isn't that easy."

In speech-act theory, an illocution initiates a purposive exchange of in-
tention(s) and response(s). An illocution is always a "performative sentence,"
indicated by the main verb's being one of the class of true, linguistic verbs that
includes *advise, answer, appoint, ask, assert, authorize, beg, bequeath, beseech,
caution, cede, claim, close (a meeting), command, condemn, counsel, dare,
declare, demand, deny, empower, enquire, entreat, excommunicate, grant,
implore, inform, instruct, order, pledge, pronounce, propose, request, require,
say, sentence, vow, warn, write.* Perlocutions may also be thought of as performative sentences, though of course the semantic environment requires that
the main verbs include those performatives in the subclass of "response performatives," such as *answer, cede, challenge, enquire, deny, require,* etc.

7. Chaim Perelman and L. Olbrechts-Tyteca, *The New Rhetoric: A Treatise
on Argumentation,* trans. John Wilkinson and Purcell Weaver (Notre Dame,
Ind.: Univ. of Notre Dame Press, 1969). The naive writer has no such facility for
inventing readers or for projecting their probable or potential responses to
what is being said in the composition. Mina Shaughnessy reports, for example,
that the basic writers with whom she worked had trouble locating their own
intentions, let alone projecting responses—their own as well as others'. "Without [the] conviction that he has 'something to mean,' the writer cannot *carry
on the kind of conversation with himself that leads to writing*" (italics added).
And the point is not simply that student-writers like Shaughnessy's lack rhetorical purposes, for the problems of basic writers, she reminds us, are the
problems of all writers writ large: "Without these dialogues [with oneself],
thoughts run dry and judgment falters." (*Errors and Expectations* [New York:
Oxford Univ. Press, 1977], 81–82.)

8. A recent collection of essays treating the subject is *The Rhetorical Tradition and Modern Writing,* ed. James J. Murphy (New York: Modern Language
Association, 1982).

9. Patricia Bizzell maintains that successful writing-across-the-curriculum
programs are informed by epistemic notions of rhetoric ("Cognition, Convention, and Certainty," *PRE/TEXT* 3 [1982]). The paradox appears that had writing
across the curriculum been introduced before the new rhetoric's emergence,
there might not have been a common mechanism to account for success or

failure; everyone would have had access to the causes only through his or her discipline's "objective" definition of rhetoric and its function.

10. This analysis of deep-structure intentions is adapted from John Robert Ross, "On Declarative Sentences," in *Readings in Transformational Grammar,* ed. R. A. Jacobs and P. S. Rosenbaum (Waltham, Mass.: Ginn, 1970), 222–72.

11. A full discussion of the underlying intention in Swift's "A Modest Proposal" is given in W. Ross Winterowd, "The Rhetoric of Beneficence, Authority, Ethical Commitment, and the Negative," *Philosophy and Rhetoric* 9 (Spring 1976): 65–83.

12. Searle, 52–53.

13. In *Literacy and the Survival of Humanism,* Richard Lanham attacks the C-B-S (clarity, brevity, sincerity) "model" of writing on the same grounds, though with a different aim. (New Haven, Conn.: Yale Univ. Press, 1983.)

14. Felicity conditions, discussed below, are those presuppositions about the speaker, the listener, and the proposition "which an illocutionary act must fulfill if it is to be successful and non-defective." John Lyons, *Semantics Two* (London and New York: Cambridge Univ. Press, 1977), 733.

15. John R. Searle, "A Taxonomy of Illocutionary Acts," in *Minnesota Studies in the Philosophy of Language,* ed. K. Gunderson (Minneapolis: Univ. of Minnesota Press, 1975), 344-69.

16. Clark and Clark, 242.

17. This situation has been given much attention in sociolinguistic studies of standard versus nonstandard dialects in the schools. See, for example, William Labov, *The Study of Nonstandard English* (Champaign, Ill.: The National Council of Teachers of English, 1970), 39-42.

18. Stephen Krashen advises that we should think of literacy as a "second dialect," and that the teaching of writing can profit from the pedagogy of second language learning. More specific to our concern here, Krashen distinguishes between "acquiring" or internalizing the rules of a second language through social interaction—and thereby achieving full competence—and "learning" a second language—consciously recalling and intellectually applying the rules of its grammar so that one is "understood" by competent speakers, but is also identified by them as "speaking with an accent" or "making mistakes." The critical age for acquiring a second language or dialect is, depending on the researcher, as early as six but no later than adolescence.

19. Clinton S. Burhans, "The Teaching of Writing and the Knowledge Gap," *College English* 45 (Nov. 1983): 639-56.

20. Finally, one more note on the theory. Below is a tentative classification of performatives distinguishing between those that are rhetorically weighted (entailing a potential negative response in the perlocution) and those that are arhetorical (entailing only an affirmative in the perlocution). Again, some discrepancies may occur between our designations and the reader's; we stress that our classification is a possible and reasonable ordering of the more familiar performatives.

Arhetorical Performatives	*Rhetorical Performatives*
answer	advise
appoint	assert
ask	beg

authorize	beseech
bequeath	caution
cede	claim
close (a meeting)	counsel
command	entreat
condemn	implore
confess	offer
dare	propose
declare	request
demand	require
grant	[?] tell
inform	warn
instruct	write
order	. . .
pledge	
promise	
pronounce	
[?] say	
sentence	
vow	
. . .	

Further subclassifications are possible. For instance, all arhetorical verbs warrant the authority of the "I" in the main clause (as judge, priest, teacher, etc.) to perform the speech act, but so do some in the rhetorical class. *Advise, counsel,* and *warn* are ethically charged, and evidence of the writer's authority to perform those services for the reader is needed to make those speech acts rhetorically felicitous. This observation may lead us to expect a disproportionate reliance by the writer on ethical proofs in essays of advice, counsel, or warning. Also, the assumption taken from cognitive psychology that personal narrative is the first stage among those leading to rhetorical competence is given a theoretical boost by the appearance of verbs like *confess, declare, inform, instruct, pledge, pronounce,* or *vow* in the arhetorical column, none of them admitting a complexity of underlying rules by the writer's needing to project a response. Intentions, after all, must be practiced before possible and potential responses can be projected. These observations, indicative of future studies, may allow us to make coherent both rigorous analysis and our best intuitions.

III Using the Writing of Others

Writing Based on Reading

Marilyn S. Sternglass
City College of the City University of New York

Recent interest in integrating instruction in reading and writing has focused primarily on the similarities in the processes, both reading and writing now being recognized as constructive processes. In the past, there has always been tacit acceptance that writers construct new meanings in the process of writing, but now it is also understood that readers are creating new meanings as they interact with texts, meanings that did not exist independently before either in the mind of the author or of the reader. Such an approach to reading-writing relationships is currently referred to as a transactional approach. But although increasing attention has been paid to the effects of a transactional model of reading and writing on a reader, less attention has been paid to how the writing process itself is constrained when writers draw on outside textual materials as primary sources of information for their new texts and what the effect of this constraint is on their readers.

Two issues that impinge directly on the writer-reader relationship in such a context are the level of prior knowledge assumed of the reader and the level of inference that can reasonably be expected of a reader attempting to make sense of a new text. On the issue of prior knowledge, Robert de Beaugrande has pointed out that previous experience is crucial in the processing of a text because its continuity and coherence can only derive from a combination of presented knowledge and prior knowledge.[1] He says that without such interaction, processing would require that an unmanageable number of alternatives be considered. This interaction between the information presented in the text and the information possessed by the reader has been recognized as important for some time now in discussions of reading comprehension.[2] Levels of inference might best be considered in terms of a model of cognitive operations developed by Andrew Wilkinson and his associates.[3] On this model, there are four operations associated with inference: explaining, inferring, assessing, and deducing. When we speak of inference on the part of a reader, we are concerned with the way that the reader overcomes possible discontinuities in a text by engaging in one or more of these operations. The reader's task is to derive a relational meaning either from information explicitly stated in the text or implicitly inferable from a combination of the information available in the text and the reader's prior or world knowledge.

Writers thus use these cognitive operations to facilitate the processing of text for their readers. Examples of these operations include the following:

Explaining: "The role of women is rapidly undergoing a major change. This could be because women are starting to enter the job market more abundantly than they have in past years."

Inferring: "Liv Ullmann had to forget her past society and way of life and convert to a Hollywood movie-star image."

Assessing: "Apparently, a domestic job, such as that of the housewife, is not satisfying enough for the future woman."

Deducing: "There is no written obligation on the husband or wife to meet her family's needs, but since they have intimate feelings for these particular relatives, they loan them the money, with no questions asked."

Writers are thus conscious of their responsibility to help readers build appropriate connections as they respond to their texts; sometimes, however, writers make unwarranted assumptions about their readers' level of prior knowledge.

The new factor in the interrelationship between reader and writer that must be considered when students are being *taught* to use outside texts as information sources for their writing activities is the effect of having both the writers and the readers familiar with the *same* source texts. In this type of interaction, since the writer assumes that the reader, typically the teacher or a classmate, is familiar with the source, the writer may not realize the importance of specifying enough of the supporting evidence within the text to permit the text to function as a comprehensible entity for a reader who may be unfamiliar with the source material. The opening paragraphs of the following student paper illustrate these assumptions as the writer fails to identify fully the individuals whose lives she is describing:

> When a person strives for their main objective in life, they are often forced to lose their family ties, innocence, and sense of identity. People must always sacrifice a part of their past in order to attain something new.

> Upon entering the world to make a life for yourself, you seem to lose your family ties. Such as what Richard Rodriguez says "I can remember occasions when I entered a room and my parents were speaking to one another in Spanish; seeing me, they shifted into their more formalized English. Hearing them speak to me in English troubled me. The bonds their voices once secured were loosened by the new tongue."
>
> You can sense how Liv Ullmann has sacrificed her family ties when she says "One of them is for Linn, but she is going home to her grandmother and cousins and a white Christmas in Norway." Liv Ullmann must stay in Hollywood for Christmas instead of spending it with her family. Thus, she is sacrificing time spent with her family to accommodate her career.

This excerpt illustrates several of the issues arising when readers are assumed to be familiar with the same source texts as the writer. First, the backgrounds of the people being discussed are not identified. Second, the writer demonstrates undue dependence on directly quoted material from the source texts and does not even recognize when references within the quotations will be completely incomprehensible to readers unfamiliar with the source texts as, for example, in the reference of "one of them is for Linn," where readers could not possibly know that "them" refers to Christmas trees that Ms. Ullmann has received as gifts. So, although the writer uses the cognitive operations of explaining and deducing in the last two sentences of the sample cited, she does not overcome the difficulty imposed by the classroom setting of assumed familiarity with the source materials. This is the type of constraint that must be specifically pointed out to students so that they can learn to adjust their writing to appropriate levels of explicitness for different levels of prior knowledge on the part of their readers.

Another possible danger is that student writers may assume that readers know everything that they as writers know, and that they can leave out crucial evidence or "jump around" in the course of presenting a position because the reader possesses the information necessary to follow the argument without seeing the evidence presented logically, in the form of a causal chain of underlying relationships. In the following writing sample, an unreasonable amount of inference is required by the readers to create the causal chain. There is an abrupt shift in topic between sentences 2 and 3 in the paragraph, requiring readers to draw on their world knowledge on a new topic for which they have not been prepared by anything in the text. The main ideas of the first two sentences could reasonably lead to a relational statement dealing with the effect of smaller family sizes on the husband-wife relationship. But it is very difficult to construct a relational or superordinate statement relating this concept to the economic conditions of the country (as is required for the third sentence) unless readers are prepared by some transitional statement indicating the significance of the relationship between family structure and economic conditions.

> If the usage of Birth Control increases there will be fewer ties between a husband and wife.

> > (Required inference: The wife will have fewer children and thus she may desire to go to work.)

> The wife will feel like she does not have to stay home as often, and the husband will be forced with doing the daily chores.

> > (Required inference: New topic raised concerning economic conditions of country and not related to content of previous sentences.)

> The cost of living will force more people to work and there will be less home life.

> > (Required inference: As a consequence of both parents' having to work, no one will be available to take care of the children.)

> The children will spend most of their time in a daycare center or with a babysitter.

Roger C. Schank has noted that the amount of inference required to represent the meaning of a paragraph will be precisely as much as will allow for the creation of a causal chain between the conceptualizations.[4]

This creation of a causal chain is linked to the notion of macropropositions as explicated by Teun A. van Dijk.[5] According to this theory, readers construct relationships between sentences as they work their way through texts. Macrostructures are created by combining information from two or more units of information within sentences of a text. They exist on a more global level than sentences as units of meaning. What happens in the process of reading is that information must be reduced. In a cognitive process model, smaller or less important elements of information are deleted and replaced by larger units that link information from several sentences together. Readers trying to make sense of complex pieces of discourse tentatively construct macropropositions as they work their way through the text and then replace the macropropositions with new ones as their hypotheses are confirmed or refuted by the rest of the discourse. Some of these macropropositions will be derived from relationships explicit within the text, but others will have to be inferred by readers as they create the links of the causal chain. If student writers have been able to assume a perfect shared-knowledge base with readers, they may feel less constrained to provide the essential information underlying the causal chain in the text.

Two problems can thus arise in the context of sources shared between readers and writers. One, the case of the writer assuming too much of the reader, has already been discussed. The other is students' feeling compelled to spell out every bit of information in excruciating detail. Unfortunately, it is this second pattern that has dominated the teaching of composition until very recently. I am referring, obviously, to the five-stage design of composition organization requiring writers to produce a macrostructure statement, in the guise of a thesis statement, that will dominate and control the writing of the paper. The role of inference is virtually eliminated as the writer tells the reader what he or she will say, says it, and virtually challenges the reader to discover a way of finding this reading episode interesting or personally motivating (perhaps a particularly challenging task because it has been neither interesting nor motivating for the writer either). In this fashion, the writer sets up the explicit thesis statement to reduce the processing operations required by the reader, and initiates a series of expectations about what will be found in the remainder of the paper. From the following student example, I would be willing to wager, every reader of this article could predict accurately the exact topics of the paragraphs following this introduction.

> When a person strives for their main objective in life, they are often forced to lose their family ties, innocence, and sense of identity. People must often sacrifice a part of their past in order to attain something new.

Any reader who didn't predict "losing family ties, losing innocence, and losing identity" as the three topics that will follow hasn't spent a day in the composition classroom in the last twenty years. The point here is that the utter predictability of the forthcoming composition markedly diminishes its interest value for a potential reader. I don't wish to argue here that it is not helpful to be able to predict the direction of a paper and perhaps even some of its development, but when everything is revealed at the outset, the motivation to continue reading is sharply reduced.

What has to be considered is how to make student writers sensitive to the appropriate amount of explicit information to be presented within two possible contexts for their writing. In the first context, they can assume shared knowledge with their readers and then determine how much implicit knowledge can be expected. In the second context, when writers draw on outside sources not familiar to the reader, they must learn to present their text at the appropriate level of explicitness, a level clearly different from the shared-knowledge context. Obviously, in the first situation, writers must understand what world knowledge it is reasonable to expect their readers to have. Reasonable expectations permit the writer to take advantage of what the reader knows so that he or she will not bore the reader with "commonsense" pieces of information. In the following student writing sample, the writer directs the reader's attention to the common-knowledge notion that dating normally only occurs between two persons at one time and the presence of a third person makes the situation "unnatural." Without this world knowledge background, never stated explicitly in the text, the reader could make no sense of this passage. The writer, however, is confident that this assumption is common and knows that readers can be expected to supply the information through inference and thus connect the causal chain of the argument.

> The power of "human nature" has not been taken into consideration by Skinner and Kinkade, which makes the ideas discussed in *Walden Two* and *Twin Oaks* very unrealistic when applied to the real society. By "human nature" I mean those feelings and emotions that we all possess, which inevitably govern our actions and attitudes in certain situations.
>
> In the society described in *Walden Two*, people are ruled more by intellect than by feelings. The type of society created by Skinner is a utopian system which sounds quite desirable on paper, but totally impractical in reality. *Twin Oaks* practices this way of life in their system of dating. It is suggested if two people care for the same person, spending time together as a trio eases problems of jealousy and rivalry. Of course, on paper, this sounds very quaint and desirable, but obviously does not apply to realistic standards. Human nature inevitably intervenes, and those involved will find it difficult, if not impossible, to carry out this foreign behavior.

Through phrases like "does not apply to realistic standards" and "foreign behavior," the writer attracts a reader assumed to share this knowledge of and attitude toward dating customs.

In the case of the writer's drawing on sources unfamiliar to the reader, a different set of assumptions and relationships must be constructed. The amount of information provided to the reader must be adequate to establish a context for the reader, and should also, ideally, relate the new information to something already known by the reader. In addition, the writer must consider that the reader may have a different value system and that such a difference may have to be accounted for in the text that is being created. In the student excerpt cited below, the writer establishes a historical perspective from which his reader can then examine his views on the changing American family:

Throughout American history the family has had its ups and downs, and has pulled through each of these as strong or stronger than before. It has gone through a drastic change in the 20th century which caused a shift from the joint family, which includes mother, father, children, grandchildren, aunts, and uncles, to the nuclear family, which includes only the mother, father, and children. This change was brought about mainly by the industrial revolution. It forced people to move away from the farms into the cities where room was scarce and joint family living was nearly impossible. But now at a time when divorce rates and illegitimacy rates keep rising, forming millions of one parent households, can the nuclear family still remain the most important institution in American society without any serious change? One possibility is communal life. This alternative living style gives the partners freedom to express themselves much more openly than in a single partner relationship. Another alternate plan could be the complete termination of family life. Finally, the nuclear family could remain the same with only a few minor changes.

In another paper on the same topic, the changing American family structure, the student writer clearly favors the perpetuation of the traditional role of the mother of the family. But because she realizes that she must at least acknowledge that her readers may have a different perspective, she feels constrained to indicate that there are alternative views. She therefore positions her own perspective as the clinching argument in each paragraph, hoping thereby to influence her readers' views:

The next issue is who raises the children. Is it mother, dad, sitter, or daycare? In the past mother was the key role in the family. Today it's a combination of mother, father, and sitters. For many families the above combination is effective. The children develop a relationship with many children and learn other styles of living. The children learn the concept of give and take at an early age. They become a more flexible type of child. The previous points do not lead to a very family oriented situation. A mother should be home with the child during the day teaching manners and discipline and the father should be the support system when he is home. The parents should work as a team and always agree on discipline and strive to be consistent. It helps to have family conferences so the children have input also.

As I have already pointed out, the level of explicitness is also related to the issue of inference. Readers can infer information from texts because they already possess notions of the world and context within which the specific text appears. The most current way of looking at inference is from a schema-theoretic point of view. Understandings or representations of the way the world is organized have been called schemata by Frederick Bartlett.[6] For Bartlett, a schema is an integrated, organized representation of past behavior and experience that guides an individual in reconstructing previously encountered material. In other words, in the reader-writer relationship, the information incoming from the text will be related by the reader to some organized representation of past experience. An example of that prior experience could be the world knowledge of dating customs cited earlier. If there is new information in the text being processed by the reader, that new information may be added to the existing structure in memory, it may alter the structure, or it may reconstruct it entirely. Thus, writers arguing controversial questions often find it desirable to open with an aspect of the issue that might bring agreement between the writer and the reader so that when the new and potentially more controversial evidence is introduced it might be seen as an attempt to alter an existing structure rather than replace it entirely. The student discussion of family structures previously cited illustrates an attempt to alter a structure with the transitional sentence "The previous points do not lead to a very family oriented situation" serving as the switchover point.

Van Dijk has proposed the notion of a frame that organizes knowledge about certain properties of objects, courses of events, and actions that typically belong together. Knowledge that is part of the frame, i.e., the reader's world knowledge, therefore need not be explicitly stated in the text. From this perspective, all the events surrounding a dating experience could be said to belong in a frame. Such a frame would consist not only of the knowledge that dating is done in pairs, but that certain kinds of activities customarily occur on a date, certain hours of the day are more likely to be dating time, and the members of the pair generally agree tacitly on the financing of the date in advance. As these general characteristics indicate, over time the specifics within these categories may differ radically as the mores of the society change. There is thus the potential for confusion if the writers of one generation assume a frame of reference for readers of another generation whose customs may be substantially different. In general, however, frames are very useful and permit writers to make reasonable assumptions about the world knowledge of their readers in relation to the topic being dealt with.

Inferences, then, can draw from two sources. One is the prior knowledge of the reader, based on his or her worldly experience, i.e., from schemata or frames; and the other is prior knowledge based on the reader's experience with the specific texts being used by the writer as sources of information. Particularly in the latter case the writer needs to be sensitive about the explicitness of information presented. Naturally, the amount of world knowledge that could be assumed for any group of readers for any particular text would also have to be carefully assessed.

If the writer can assume that the reader knows the source material, he or she must search for a way to add something new to the topic. Tasks, then, requiring the student to draw on outside reading materials must be designed so that each writer can formulate a unique contribution. Among the forms that such a contribution could take would be analysis that links ideas or experiences together in a new way, or that encourages the writer to integrate his or her own background into the source material and reinterpret either his or her experience or the experiences depicted in the sources in a new way. From this unique perspective, the writer has an opportunity to introduce something original to the reader even if the reader is already familiar with the sources. If the writer does not reshape the source material in some such fashion, the text produced may be efficient, that is, easily read, but not very effective.

Beaugrande has proposed the category of "design criteria" as one standard of textuality. The three design criteria that he postulates are efficiency, effectiveness, and appropriateness.

> The EFFICIENCY of a text results from its utilization in communication with the *greatest returns for the least effort,* so that PRO-CESSING EASE is promoted. The EFFECTIVENESS of the text depends upon its *intensity of impact* on text receivers, promoting PROCESSING DEPTH, and upon its *contribution toward the producer's goal,* constituting the RELEVANCE of text materials to *steps in a plan.* The APPROPRIATENESS of a text depends on the *proportionality between the demands of a communicative situation and the degree to which standards of textuality are upheld.*[7] (Emphasis in original)

In other words, Beaugrande is pointing out that the information presented in a piece of writing must serve the *intentions* of the writer. The efficiency of the text, i.e., the level of explicitness, the amount of inference required, and the effort of the reader in processing the information, should have an effect upon the reader that serves the writer's purpose. The efficiency level should allow the reader to process the information with little effort but not with so little effort that the reader is bored, that is, not engaged with the topic at all. The danger with setting the efficiency level too high is that the reader may say, "I already know this," or, even worse, "Who cares?" Effectiveness must complement efficiency in order for the paper to have an impact on the reader that will create conditions for attaining the writer's goal. Thus, the writer must balance the needs of the reader with his or her own intention.

Examples of student writing illustrate how some of these concepts function. In the next writing sample, the student develops an insight based on two essays about two individuals' lives. The writer points out that the two individuals were manipulated into situations in which they felt obligated to perform in ways others expected of them. That insight is developed with specific examples from the texts. For readers familiar with the source texts, the piece of writing is very efficient to read, but also very boring. There is no attempt to relate the generalization either to the author's experience or to the reader's. There is no new information in this writing, no real intention on the part of the writer to involve or interest the reader. What we see here is a far too typical example of perfunctory writing, a demonstration of knowledge rather than a discovery of knowledge or any new insight. On Beaugrande's scale, this would be an ineffective piece of writing.

> In the essays, both Ullmann [Liv Ullmann, *Changing*] and Rodriguez [Richard Rodriguez, "On Becoming a Chicano"] were indirectly manipulated into situations they did not choose to be in. Both felt obligated to perform in the way that was expected of them instead of making their own decisions and doing what they really wanted. At the end of a long day, Liv Ullmann did not feel she could relax and take a break, much as she may have liked to. Instead, she felt obligated to give an interview to the Swedish journalist so that it would not be reported that she had become "stuck up." It even reached the point where she didn't dare doze on the plane for fear the *Times* reporter would view her with her mouth open. It seems that Miss Ullmann had reached a stifling situation; her decisions were governed by the people around her. In the same way, Richard Rodriguez was forced into doing things he really didn't want to. For example, he felt that he must forsake his Chicano culture and language because all that he had known before was not considered relevant by others. Rodriguez felt that he was only technically the person he once considered himself to be—a Chicano. Long ago he had given up being a Chicano because of the cultural consequences and pressures he had had to face.

In the next student writing sample, the writer draws an implication from the experiences of the two people she has been reading about. From the descriptions of these individuals' breaking away from their families, the writer recognizes that the families have also been changed, and have learned to function without the individuals' participation. She then recognizes that a similar change has occurred between herself and her family, that each has begun to exist more independently, and that just as the family excludes her from their shared experiences, so is she excluding them from her new life as a college student. This new insight becomes the focus of the reader's attention even if the reader is familiar with the source texts, because it generalizes beyond the discrete experiences of these individuals and develops a new insight that the reader can examine from his or her own perspective. Thus the source texts are combined with the writer's personal experience to draw the reader's attention to a wider topic.

> Along with a loss of innocence people are often forced to break away from their families. Family ties usually decrease if one leaves home to pursue a career. Rodriguez noticed "uncles would laugh good-naturedly, but I detected scorn in their voices. For my grandmother, the least assimilated of my relatives, the changes in her grandson since entering school were especially troubling." He also reminisced of a family gathering in which he slipped away to read almost unconscious of the family reunion outside. For Ullmann her ambition included leaving her home and country, spending lonely holidays with people she barely knew. *As in both cases the family learns to function without them.* Ullmann recalls "Call Linn in Norway. She says she is busy watching television, so I could be brief." This came to me during Thanksgiving at home. Although the whole family shared in conversation I felt subtly excluded since I was no longer a part of all their recent events discussed and my family wasn't a part in my recent experiences. (Emphasis added)

The next step in development for this writer would be to reflect on her new insight and use it as a take-off point in her writing to explore her own feelings about this change in her family relationship. She would then find that the experiences she has read about (Rodriguez's and Ullmann's) would be available to her for purposes of comparison or contrast in regard to her own experiences. But she would have transformed a general task to one that is now personally meaningful for her. The likelihood is that her intrinsic interest in the topic would also spark greater engagement on the part of her readers and that a true transaction could now take place between writer and reader. Thus, outside source texts have the potential to play an important role in stimulating the thought processes of student writers and lead them to discover new insights which can then be shared with readers.

In summary, writers must consider the prior knowledge of their readers, both from world knowledge and familiarity with particular source texts, as they construct their own new texts. Readers must be presented with a level of explicitness that will allow them to create a causal chain through reasonable inferences. But they must not be presented with a level of explicitness that will bore them and thwart the intention of the writer. Only by introducing new information to the reader and arousing the reader's interest can the writer complement the efficiency of the text with the criterion of effectiveness, and only by stimulating an appropriate response on the part of the reader can writing serve the purpose of its writer.

Notes

1. Robert de Beaugrande, *Text, Discourse and Process* (Norwood, N.J.: Ablex, 1980).

2. See Kenneth Goodman, "Reading: A Psycholinguistic Guessing Game," *Journal of the Reading Specialist* 4 (1967): 126-35; and Frank Smith, *Understanding Reading* (New York: Holt, 1971).

3. Andrew Wilkinson et al., *Assessing Language Development* (Oxford: Oxford Univ. Press, 1980).

4. Roger C. Schank, "The Structure of Episodes in Memory," in D. G. Bobrow and A. Collins, eds., *Representation and Understanding: Studies in Cognitive Science* (New York: Academic Press, 1975).

5. Teun A. van Dijk, *Text and Context: Exploration in the Semantics and Pragmatics of Text* (London: Longmans, 1977).

6. Frederick Bartlett, *Remembering: A Study in Experimental and Social Psychology* (Cambridge: Cambridge Univ. Press, 1968).

7. Beaugrande, p. 21.

How Do Users Read Computer Manuals? Some Protocol Contributions to Writers' Knowledge

Patricia Sullivan
Purdue University

Linda Flower
Carnegie-Mellon University

Computer manuals challenge those of us who study nonfictional writing to consider carefully how people read and use texts as they learn to perform complex tasks. We have always had notions about how people read and learn difficult material, rarely stated notions that we took primarily from our own reading habits and our literary reading training. Our theory has been essentially a linear one. We have normally expected that readers begin at the beginning of a piece, make some hypotheses about what is going on, and read to confirm or disconfirm those notions—moving either word-by-word through the text or skimming by reading the first sentence of each paragraph. And in most cases these expectations about how readers will read make sense. Indeed, structurally there is a compelling linearity to almost all modern prose. But in the area of functional prose we are finding that other reading patterns may well direct readers.

Detailing these other reading patterns has been aided by the emergence of a document—the computer manual. Because computer manuals now reach audiences that vary widely in computer knowledge and sophistication, because the economics of the computer industry are beginning to dictate that manuals be usable, and because the immediate feedback users receive alerts them to how well a manual is working, the problems inherent in producing good manuals have quickly come to the attention of professional writers. Further, because the computer can monitor everything the user types into it, that monitoring device can be coupled with protocols of users at work to give us detailed records of a session. Using the feedback computers and protocols are giving us, we can begin to develop a different portrait of the readers of functional documents like computer manuals.

The central question posed to those writing computer manuals (Can the manual be used successfully?) constitutes a rich and compelling test for a functional text. Fully answering it requires a "user-based" approach to when and how readers actually read functional texts. But the text's success can be verified. When we consider this possibility of verifying success in light of such trends as the tremendous growth of computing in nonspecialist fields and the government's policies of ensuring public understanding of documents (i.e., the plain English movement), we see the dovetailing of new research methods with current public needs. It is little wonder that the functional reader/user has become the focus of study for several groups—technical writers, instructional designers in the military, and document design researchers. These groups aim to understand how documents are read and used in practice and also aim to use that understanding to construct strategies technical writers can employ while writing and testing functional documents. Because of the progress these researchers are making, we will devote the first section of this paper to highlighting what is known and what we need to know about functional readers/users. Then we will discuss a study of the reading patterns of six new users of a computerized catalog in the Carnegie-Mellon University Libraries. We will contend that testing based on user protocols[1]—process records of people talking aloud as they work—can aid technical writers, both in constructing a model of functional readers/users and in building a text that accommodates several audiences. In the final section, we will suggest how the study of functional writing and of its readers/users can profit the writing classroom.[2]

How Can We View the Reader/User?

Researchers interested in functional prose frequently observe situations in which the traditional, linear model of reading[3] does not usefully portray how the audience behaves. The readers of reference manuals, for example, usually do not read the entire text, front to back. In some cases, they read very little of the text at any sitting but refer to parts of it frequently. The question the researchers face is: How then do functional readers use and read the text?

Technical Writing Teaching

One understanding of functional readers comes from traditional approaches to teaching technical writing. This understanding of the reader has been built on three points: (1) a report serves a variety of audiences and purposes that the writer needs to identify and keep in mind,[4] (2) audiences read the sections of a report selectively and in an order driven by their own purposes,[5] and (3) both writers and audiences share a knowledge of what kinds of information are likely to be contained in a particular section. Thus, the picture of usage that has begun to dominate technical writing instruction suggests that a report reaches many audiences, and not all these audiences read the report thoroughly—many only read the sections that suit their purposes. While this view still implies a word-for-word reading of the sections selected by a particular reader, it recognizes the functional character of reading at work and allows a break from the usual linear approach to reading.

Instructional Design Research

Another view of readers can be derived from the military's research into how to produce training manuals their personnel can use. Sticht and others,[6] working from the premise that workers do not read the same way that students read, developed a distinction between read-to-do tasks and read-to-learn tasks. Interviews gathered in navy training schools by Sticht, Fox, Hauke, and Zapf on reading at the work site showed that most reading could be classed as read-to-do tasks (78%) rather than read-to-learn tasks (15%). In reading-to-do, readers would go to the text for specific information about a procedure and follow that information, using the text as an external memory store and never bothering to learn the details of the instruction—only where to find the proper information. Such a reading pattern focused attention on how to perform the act rather than how to learn, remember, or understand the information in depth.

The dominance of read-to-do tasks in the workplace led the military researchers to study literacy in more specialized ways and to develop a set of guidelines for the writing of training literature.[7] This method trains writers to spot topic-oriented approaches to training procedures (e.g., three paragraphs of technical description about what constitutes an unsafe storage room) and then gives them guidelines for revising the topical focus to a more usable performance focus (e.g., the description of the messy storeroom is revised to something like, "Don't leave oily rags lying around").

Such instructional design research calls attention to the reading patterns likely to be used in typical military jobs, and forces us to recognize that there are many kinds of functional documents that are not read front-to-back for an understanding of the material. Instead, many workers search for the material they want and read only the pertinent information. This is very important for writers, many of whom are trained as careful readers. If the users are going to read only parts of a document, and make selections of what to read with an action in mind, then the information important for the readers has to be located in the sections they will read.

To date, however, the military has not progressed past the general guideline stage in their understanding of how to structure materials that will be accessible to the users. Perhaps the nature of job tasks in the military is such that most training literature can be subdivided into manageable modules, and thus the placement of information is not a key issue beyond that point. But in the area of computer manuals the situation is a bit more complicated. There is ample testimonial evidence that computer manuals are used for specific reference by computer professionals (both technicians and computer scientists) and for learning and specific reference by new computer users, a mix of audiences and purposes that suggests we cannot adopt a simple read-to-do model for structuring manuals. For example, a person reviewing the EMACS (a text-editing program) manual to find out how to move a chunk of text is often expecting that there are several ways to move text and is looking for the best method for the situation at hand. This person will normally read to make a decision about which set of procedures to use before invoking a read-and-act strategy. Thus, we need to examine the reader/user patterns more carefully if we are going to make suggestions for writing computer manuals in a more detailed way than has the military.

Document Design Project Research

A third view of the reader has been emerging from work in document design initiated by the Document Design Project. Marking a new direction for document design in the private sector, the project (funded by the federal government in the late seventies) was a cooperative venture among American Institutes for Research (Washington, D.C.), Siegel and Gale Associates (New York), and the Communications Design Center (Carnegie-Mellon University).[8] In that project, AIR reviewed the state of document design research, adopted a psycholinguistic approach to the question of readability (particularly in the realm of government regulations and documents), and produced writing and teaching aids for document designers; Siegel and Gale focused on legal form redesign, both for general consumer documents like apartment leases and for banking forms; and Carnegie-Mellon studied the writing process, the reading of technical prose, and the design of hospital consent forms.[9]

This emerging view of the reader as a cognitive (or purposive) information processor starts with the reader/user. Where the military view is based in analyzing the task, this document design view is based in understanding the functional users as they read and use documents. To focus this understanding in the process, the Communications Design Center (CDC) has applied protocol studies to functional documents. Using a protocol (a taped record of a person talking aloud while completing a task—e.g., reading and understanding a text), the CDC researchers began to trace the processes of reading and writing.[10] In computer manuals they found that this tracing, when coupled with computer feedback on correctness of action, became a very powerful tool both for evaluating the success of a manual and for studying the computer-manual user.[11]

Protocol-aided revision helps writers diagnose where users have trouble in texts and what kinds of errors result from that trouble. It is similar to a long-used and poorly documented technique described by M. Atlas, called the user edit,[12] which has been used widely in such diverse situations as the military and the testing of Heath kits. Protocol-aided revision, however, differs from the user edit in collection and use. In a user edit the user reads the manual aloud while using the terminal or facing a piece of equipment, and the writer takes notes that direct the revision. This method is inexpensive, and directs the writer to problems evident as the user reads; as Atlas points out, however, such a front-to-back reading may not reveal problems of access. Protocol-aided revision sometimes uses a task similar to the user edit; for example, in revising the TOPS-20 introduction, which was a set of tutorials, it made sense to ask subjects simply to work through a tutorial. But in general the task is chosen to reflect the purpose of the manual. Protocols are also either video- or audiotaped for playback; this makes them more expensive than a user edit. But the taping also changes the revision process, because the writer replays the session for help in identifying and diagnosing the text's problems (e.g., what makes particular sections of the document confusing, where precisely users' comprehension problems are, and where the errors in sections are). This means that the revisor is not at the mercy of his or her immediate perceptions.

Although few studies of the functional reader of computer manuals have been completed, a number of studies have tried to use this protocol method to learn more about the functional reader. For example, Flower, Hayes, and Swarts[13] approached a federal regulation for small-business owners with the premise that the reconstructions or "revisions" readers made to the text during reading in their effort to understand it might suggest the sorts of revisions they needed from the writer. The study revealed a vigorous attempt on the part of readers to revise highly definitional prose into more comprehensible "scenarios" specifying human agents acting in a meaningful context. A struggle to build a meaningful context is also reflected in K. A. Schriver's study of the differences between humanists and scientists in their approaches to reading graphs that accompany text.[14] Humanists are more likely to move back and forth between the two, spending time building a propositional model for the graph and checking it against the text; scientists are more likely to leave the text when they see the reference to the graph and quickly say what the graph is, focusing on the high-level relationships and not dealing with propositional structures. In both these studies readers unfamiliar with the meaning (or form) of the material given spent time creating a scenario or propositional framework for the document.

Protocols of people talking aloud as they use a document can contribute to a model of the functional reader because these records are quite specific about reading patterns. The protocols follow readers through interactions with a text and with a system, charting what problems they represent to themselves, how they locate a section to read, how much they read, how they interpret the text, where they pause, where they question the text or add to it, when they decide to leave the text, and in general how they respond to the text. Thus, we can use the patterns we locate to build models of functional reading for particular types of tasks. Though new, protocol analysis is a promising path to a model for the functional reader of computer manuals and other documents.

How Users Orient Themselves to a Manual: One Case

Consider this situation as a test case: in order to provide the appropriate educational materials, we needed to predict how users would orient themselves to the Carnegie-Mellon University Libraries' on-line card catalog (LS/2000) and what problems they would normally have in dealing with the system (both in moving around and in using it to do their research). It was a situation in which a useful theory about how people read such a manual could aid in decisions about developing educational materials and programs. Thus, this case study can help us make our emerging notions of functional reading more concrete.[15] Given a question to answer—such as "Does the library have Eliot's book that inspired the musical *Cats*?"—an orientation manual to the system, and no previous experience with a computerized catalog, how do these students proceed? What do they read in the orientation manual?

When do they read the manual? And what does their behavior suggest for writers/editors of this document and similar documents?

To study the reading patterns in this reading-to-orient, we had six Carnegie-Mellon undergraduates try to use the LS/2000 catalog to answer typical questions students take to a library card catalog. We were careful to make the situation as similar to actual students' experience as we could. Based on catalog-use research, each person was given four questions that asked for the information most frequently sought in the catalog: a title, an author, and two general subjects. The questions were asked verbally so that the users would have to contend with their own spelling abilities. And they were instructed that they could use the orientation manual or the on-line help (a screen that contained definitions of terms, like lc subject search or call number search), but they could not ask anyone for help.

All six subjects had trouble using the system, but by the end of the session they also liked all the information they could locate using LS/2000. They did not like the manual, though. To a person, they stopped using it halfway through the session. Two of the subjects commented, while having trouble with an aspect of the third question: "I could try to find it in the manual, but I'm having trouble finding anything there." Abandoning the manual, in favor of hunting through the system and using whatever strategies seem successful, is a typical reaction to a poorly structured manual, so we examined what the users tried to find in the manual and where they looked for this information. In order to diagnose the text's inadequacies we (1) traced the user actions to determine how they tried to use the manual and (2) examined the user errors in conjunction with the text, to discover where the text gave the error-recovery information (if at all). From these analyses we were able to make more detailed suggestions about how the manual should be revised.

How Do These Users Act?

Because all users referred to the manual while trying to answer the first question, we focused on the first question and tried to develop an understanding of how the users actually used the text to help them search the catalog. Below is a protocol of a user's attempts to answer the first question (reading is italicized):

> Let's see. Do we have Eliot's book on cats that inspired the Broadway musical? OK. So I need to find . . . I wonder if "cats" is the title? Anyway . . . Well I'll try that as the title. *Choose the type of search you wish to perform. 1 author . . . 2 title . . . 3 corporate . . .*

4 by other . . . I want 2. So I'll type it and hit Return. Good . . . cats
Return . . . *No match this entry. Return to continue* . . . Wonder if
they don't have it or if that isn't the title or I'm sure I spelled
it right. Let me check this book. *Getting Started and Sample
Search* . . . *4.* OK. Yeah. It tells about Carl Sagan. Maybe I should
do an author search. I can follow this example on the next page.
Good. *Suppose you wanted* . . . *Carl Sagan. You would type 1, the
number of a search by author.*
  So I choose 1. Oh. Elliott, then Return, Return. *No match this
entry. Return to continue.* I wonder if I spelled it right? Maybe it's
one "l" or one "t." I'll try one "l" and abbreviate . . . Elio . . .
umm . . . Hey, that's it . . . But how do I get to the book? Let me
see if this book says how . . . [scans table of contents . . . decides
no . . . tries out ways until gives up and writes down what he has].

This typical user does several things we expect: (1) he tries to use the
table of contents to locate the places where the information he seeks is
likely to be, (2) he uses pictures of actual screens to confirm that he
has found the place in the text that matches his question about the
system, (3) he applies his computer knowledge to the system (e.g., use
of the return key to enter commands and the use of truncation or
abbreviation to avoid spelling errors or simplify data entry), and (4) he
scan-reads for answers. But this user, typical of the six we tested, also
surprises us when he: (1) tries to reason out the method rather than
reading any of the orienting material, (2) does not use the text until he
has failed, and then goes to the text with some notions of what might
be useful to read, and (3) reads very little of the actual text (this is true
for the computer screen as well as the text—he misses the "or enter a
keyword" on the first screen and does not know about the most
powerful type of search). Figure 1 summarizes the way the six subjects
oriented themselves as they worked to answer the first question.

How Do These Users Read?

The patterns all six subjects displayed for using the manual support
this model of how people actually approach and read such a manual.
Their method is especially sensible when we realize that these people
are interested primarily in finding a book rather than in understand-
ing/learning the subtleties of the catalog. Several features of the reading-to-orient need to be examined in light of our notions of reading:

1. No one carefully reads (i.e., reads most of the words) more than
   two sentences at a time.

2. Most of the users begin to use the catalog before they read the
   manual.

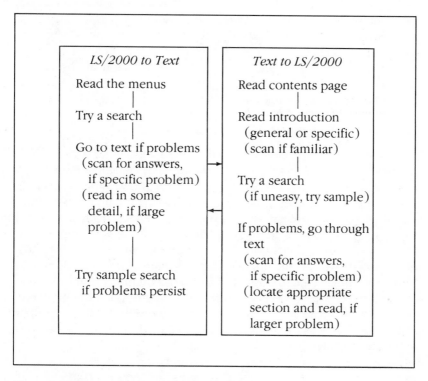

Figure 1. Reading and orientation to LS/2000

3. This manual is used primarily to answer questions that arise when users fail.

4. Most readers do not read the introduction first; nor do they generally read all of it, even though the introduction is only three short paragraphs.

5. Most readers do not read any section in its entirety.

Two logical explanations for these reading patterns may suggest why this model is limited to this case: (1) the text was poor, and (2) in menu systems readers expect that all orientation will be found in the computer. Both explanations have some merit here. The text used in the protocol test had problems, and often the subjects read the menus first and tried to construct an answer from their content alone (see protocol example). But neither explanation eclipses the frankly worrying possibility that this model characterizes typical orientation behavior for people learning computer systems. Why? First, there is no evidence that the subjects knew the text was less than adequate before they even glanced at it. Second, subjects had questions almost immediately that the menus did not answer. Even if the subjects expected the system to be self-sufficient, they were disabused of that notion almost instantaneously. Still, these alternative hypotheses urge caution in applying this model beyond orientation to LS/2000.

What Did the Findings Mean for Writers?

In this case, the orientation manual needed substantial revision. The original writers had assumed that readers/users would orient themselves by reading the document cover to cover and working the sample search before doing any personal searching. That assumption was not viable, given our observations of how the students actually proceeded to use the catalog. Instead, the manual, aimed at the general populace (undergraduate students who look for books when they have to), needed to be written and arranged for the minimalist reader. Prose had to be cut to the bone, information had to be highlighted in ways that would attract the attention of someone flipping through the brochure, strategies had to be adapted to encourage people at least to glance at every page, and more screens had to be included for those people who looked for pictures as guides to information.

In order to convey the essential concepts for LS/2000 as economically as possible, the writers studied the use patterns for computerized catalogs (to identify which searches are most commonly used), identified the problems users typically had with this system, and tried to structure as much information as they could into tables or simple procedures. The protocols helped them (1) focus on how the audience actually used the document produced, (2) identify the problems users had with the system so that those problems could be featured in the manual, and (3) arrange information in such a way that users would find it quickly and easily.

How Can This Study Contribute to the Training of Writers?

This study can serve both as an illustration of writers' using user protocols to revise a document, and as a method a writer can use to diagnose problems a functional reader may have with a text. A classroom illustration might be structured: distribute a portion of the original text (Appendix A) and have the students evaluate it; then distribute the protocol example above and have the students examine the user's response alongside the text in order to check their perceptions of what should be revised and also to generate a list of goals for a revision of the text; then have the students examine the revised text (Appendix B) for evidence that the user's problems have been addressed.

Such an exercise allows students practice in anticipating user feedback, working with that feedback to give direction to revision, and evaluating the results of one revision. But the more substantial contribution to teaching functional writing provided by this and other protocol studies lies in the method for writing computer manuals (and other functional documents) that it demonstrates. By developing a writing assignment that gives a person (or group) a short document for revision using protocols,[16] a teacher can help the writers come to terms with the functional reader more concretely, assess the usefulness of a functional document in considerable detail, and revise the document with a reader/user in mind.

What Does This Study Tell Us about Functional Reading?

This study also adds information to our picture of the functional reader. Though not an experimental study designed to be conclusive in its findings, this case study shows users behaving consistently. They read only sections of the document, they skip the orienting material in introductions, and they read primarily to answer specific questions rather than to learn or do. How typical their behavior is to the orientation process is an open question. Is that behavior typical to users orienting themselves to systems that are menu-driven? Is it behavior typical to users who must learn how to cope with a system in order to perform some task or solve some problem (which may make them impatient with the task of learning the system)? Further study along these lines seems warranted.

This study of users reading as they orient themselves to LS/2000 contributes to our understanding of the functional reader/user by giving evidence about how people choose to read a passage in a computer document. Taken with the growing body of document-design research, it illustrates the growing importance of reader behavior to writers of functional documents. What people look for in a computer manual, how they decide what to read, and how much they actually read are questions important to writing researchers, technical writers, and teachers of writing. They are of particular importance in situations in which we are committed to testing whether (and how well) our writing works.

Appendixes

Appendix A: Original Cover and Introduction for LS/2000 Manual

ILS
CARNEGIE-MELLON UNIVERSITY LIBRARIES
INTEGRATED LIBRARY SYSTEM

WHAT IS ILS?

The Integrated Library System, known as ILS, provides access to a catalog of holdings of all branches of the University Libraries. The system is available to you from terminals placed in the libraries and currently contains about 8,000 test records.

ILS is designed to be used by new users who are not familiar with on-line catalogs. As a user you won't have to worry about destroying any part of the system or "breaking something." The system is designed only to DISPLAY any information you request of it.

ILS will PROMPT you as to the next step in your search and will tell you when you've done something wrong. It will also suggest ways to help you fix your mistakes. As you progress in searching ILS you will be able to shortcut these step-by-step directions and use the short commands on pages 10 and 11. If you need help you can type HELP followed by a CARRIAGE RETURN; ILS will respond with instructions.

Notes

1. The format is 8½ by 11 paper folded in half, with wide columns.

2. The title of the system, ILS, is given, with the name of the library between the acronym and its decoding (Integrated Library System).

3. The table of contents consists of phrases and page references arranged into traditional format and placed on the cover.

4. The introduction to the catalog—"What is ILS?"—takes up a page and includes information of a general nature about the catalog: name, what generally it contains, the size (8,000 items was the size of the test data base), information to reduce fear (like "Don't fear breakage"), where step-by-step instructions are, and how to access on-line help.

Appendix B: Revised Cover and Introduction for LS/2000 Manual

LS/2000

A computerized catalog of materials in C-MU Libraries

books
journals
government documents
technical reports
musical scores
records

Copyright 1984   Prepared by
Carnegie-Mellon University Libraries   Peggy Seiden, Pat Sullivan

---

PROMPTS / MOVING AROUND
STARTING A SEARCH / OTHER SEARCHES
SEARCH CHOICE / AUTHOR SEARCH
TITLE SEARCH / SUBJECT SEARCH
SHORTCUTS / LOCATION CODES

Notes

1. The format is 8½ by 14 paper stagger-folded to form natural tabs, with wide columns that allow for tables. The logo marks it as an official library publication.

2. The title of the system is stated but never decoded, because all references to the catalog are being standardized as LS/2000. (Notice that the name of the system changes; this happens because Avatar was bought by OCLC, Inc., and OCLC changed the name of the catalog.)

3. The table of contents is replaced by the tabs (Prompts/Moving Around, and so on, are the tabs on the brochure). The tabs clue us to a reorganization of material. Notice that since people use the manual to help them with specific errors, information about system prompts (paragraph 3 of the original introduction) is expanded to a table that helps people decipher what the system is saying.

4. The introduction is condensed to the list of system contents on the revised cover. This revision takes into account both users' need to know what was contained in LS/2000 (the original does not contain that information concretely) and users' desire to read less. The paragraph on fear is deleted, and the writers try to make the system look easier through the easy-to-use tables that predominate in the revision. Further, because the system help is unstable, references to it are deleted.

Notes

1. There are several user process records that we can study when working with computers: (1) transaction logs, or keystrokes recorded by the computer, that give a list of what a user typed (and sometimes the times); (2) videotapes that record the screen and what the person said; and (3) audiotapes that record what the person said. The transaction logs record only what was actually entered into the computer, but the other two record strategies that users verbalize and any reading of a manual that they do. The most complete data combine the transaction log with an audio- or videotaped protocol. The question of what you get when you ask people to think aloud as they work is a serious one that is being debated in psychology. To follow the pros and cons of that debate see: K. A. Ericsson and H. A. Simon, *Protocol Analysis: Verbal Reports as Data* (Cambridge, Mass.: MIT Press, 1984); R. E. Nisbett and T. D. Wilson, "Telling More than We Can Know: Verbal Reports on Mental Processes," *Psychological Review* 84 (1977): 231–59. Even when we make a weak claim about what protocols can show—i.e., that they can give us data about when users refer to a section of a manual, what they read, and what they do after reading— protocols give us valuable data about the user.

2. The research discussed in this paper was funded by a grant from the Andrew W. Mellon Foundation.

3. We are calling the model of reading that underlies literary criticism, linguistic analysis, and psycholinguistic research the linear model. This reference does not imply a particular stance or theory about reading; instead it refers to the underlying assumption in these fields that reading is a making of meaning that happens when a reader processes a text front-to-back, one word at a time.

4. See J. C. Mathes and D. W. Stevenson, *Designing Technical Reports* (Indianapolis, Ind.: Bobbs-Merrill, 1976); and L. A. Olsen and T. N. Huckin,

Principles of Communication for Science and Technology (New York: McGraw-Hill, 1983).

5. R. W. Dodge and J. W. Souther, "What to Report," *Westinghouse Engineer,* July–September 1962.

6. T. Sticht, "Understanding Readers and Their Uses of Texts," to appear in *Designing Usable Texts,* ed. T. Duffy and R. Waller (in preparation), summarizes the military research on read-to-learn versus read-to-do reading tasks. Other relevant reading studies are: R. Kern, *Usefulness of Readability Formulas in Achieving Army Readability Objectives,* report no. 437 (Alexandria, Va.: U.S. Army Research Institute for the Behavioral and Social Sciences, 1980); T. Sticht, L. Fox, R. Hauke, and D. Zapf, *The Role of Reading in the Navy,* NPRDC TR 77-40 (San Diego, Calif.: Navy Personnel Research and Development Center, 1977); T. Sticht and D. Zapf, eds., *Reading and Readability Research in the Armed Services,* HumRRO FR-WD-CA-76-4 (Alexandria, Va.: Human Resources Research Organization, 1976); T. M. Duffy and P. Kabance, "Testing a Readable Writing Approach to Text Revision," *Journal of Educational Psychology* 74 (1982): 733–48.

7. R. P. Kern, T. G. Sticht, D. Welty, and R. N. Hauke, *Guidebook for the Development of Army Training Literature* (Alexandria, Va.: Human Resources Research Organization, 1976). See also W. Diehl and L. Mikulecky, "Making Written Information Fit Workers' Purposes," *IEEE Transactions on Professional Communication,* vol. Pc-24, no. 1 (March 1981): 5–9, who have adapted the military work to the more general arena of technical writing, adding a read-to-assess category. Diehl and Mikulecky give specific suggestions for writing technical read-to-learn and read-to-do materials. Read-to-learn material should include aids for understanding: questions, advance organizers, diagrams, and headings. Read-to-do material should aid the search for material and include indexes, guide words, graphic highlights, color-coded sections, and tabs.-

8. The Document Design Project newsletter published by American Institutes for Research relates the history of that grant. See *Fine Print,* nos. 1 and 2 (1979), and then *Simply Stated,* nos. 4, 9, and 15 (1980 and 1981).

9. For examples of the work sponsored by the project, see A. Siegel and D. G. Glascoff, Jr., "Case History: Simplifying an Apartment Lease," in *Drafting Documents in Plain Language, 1981* (New York: Practicing Law Institute, 1981); V. R. Charrow, V. M. Holland, D. G. Peck, and L. V. Shelton, *Revising a Medicaid Recertification Form: A Case Study in the Document Design Process* (Washington, D.C.: American Institutes for Research, 1980); D. Goswami, J. C. Redish, D. B. Felker, and A. Siegel, *Writing in the Professions: A Course Guide and Instructional Materials for an Advanced Composition Course* (Washington, D.C.: American Institutes for Research, 1981); D. B. Felker, F. Pickering, V. R. Charrow, V. M. Holland, and J. C. Redish, *Guidelines for Document Designers* (Washington, D.C.: American Institutes for Research, 1981); L. Flower, *Problem-Solving Strategies for Writers* (New York: Harcourt Brace Jovanovich, 1981); and C. J. Janik, J. H. Swaney, S. J. Bond, and J. R. Hayes, "Informed Consent: Illusion or Reality?" *Information Design Journal* 2 (1981): 197–207.

10. L. S. Flower and J. R. Hayes, *A Process Model of Composition,* Document Design Project Report no. 1 (Pittsburgh, Pa.: Carnegie-Mellon University, 1979); also in *Cognitive Processes in Writing,* ed. L. W. Gregg and E. R. Steinberg (Hillsdale, N.J.: Lawrence Erlbaum, 1980), 3–50.

11. S. J. Bond, J. R. Hayes, C. J. Janik, and J. H. Swaney, *Introduction to CMU TOPS-20,* vols. 1 and 2 (Pittsburgh, Pa.: Carnegie-Mellon University, 1982). Volume 2, pages 1–2, explains how PAR (protocol-aided revision) works. A detailed discussion of user protocols and computer manuals can be found in M. Dieli and J. H. Swaney, "User Protocols: A Method for Testing and Revising Documentation," Carnegie-Mellon University, typescript.

12. M. Atlas, "The User Edit: Making Manuals Easier to Use," *IEEE Transactions on Professional Communication,* vol. Pc-24, no. 1 (March 1981): 28–29, succinctly describes the user edit.

13. L. Flower, J. R. Hayes, and H. Swarts, "Revising Functional Documents: The Scenario-Principle," in *New Essays in Technical and Scientific Communication: Research, Theory, and Practice,* ed. P. V. Anderson, R. J. Brockmann, and C. R. Miller (Farmingdale, N.Y.: Baywood, 1983), 41–58. For other papers demonstrating how protocol analysis can be used to study, teach, and produce functional documents, see J. H. Swaney, C. R. Janik, S. J. Bond, and J. H. Hayes, *Editing for Comprehension: Improving the Process through Reading Protocols,* Document Design Project Technical Report no. 14, (Pittsburgh, Pa.: Carnegie-Mellon University, 1981); K. A. Schriver, J. R. Hayes, and L. S. Flower, *Editing for Comprehension: Increasing Writers' Sensitivity to Readers' Needs,* Technical Report (Pittsburgh, Pa.: Carnegie-Mellon University, 1985); D. Charney, "Redesigning Forms: An Experimental Method for Testing and Comparing Forms" to appear in *Information Design Journal* 4; M. Dieli, "Two Complementary Approaches for Revising User Documentation: Protocol-Aided Revision and Focused Revision Tasks," paper presented at the annual College Composition and Communication Conference, New York, March 1984.

14. K. A. Schriver, "Exploring Graphic Literacy for Humanists," paper presented at the annual College Composition and Communication Conference, New York, March 1984.

15. We would like to thank Peggy Seiden for her help in this study. She is currently studying how users learn to search; see P. Seiden and P. Sullivan, "Learning to Use an On-line Catalog: Possible Models of the New User," a paper presented at the American Educational Research Associates Conference, New Orleans, April 1984.

16. A typical assignment for professional and technical writing classes that has been used at Carnegie-Mellon has three phases: (1) a user protocol is gathered on the original document for diagnosis purposes, (2) the group revises on the bases of their evaluation of the document and on the demonstrated user needs, being careful not to overgeneralize about all users, and (3) another user protocol is collected to test the revision. To date, variations on this typical assignment have been widely used in technical and professional writing classes at Carnegie-Mellon. If you want more detailed class materials for this example, write to: Patricia Sullivan, English Department, Purdue University, West Lafayette, IN 47907. A different approach to structuring technical writing assignments around reading protocols is detailed in D. D. Roberts and P. A. Sullivan, "Beyond the Static Audience Construct: Reading Protocols in the Technical Writing Class," *Journal of Technical Writing and Communication* 14 (1984): 143–53.

Using Nonfiction Literature in the Composition Classroom

Maxine Hairston
University of Texas at Austin

Suppose you are a new teacher of composition, fresh from a graduate program in rhetoric that has introduced you to the new paradigm for teaching writing. Again and again in that program you have been told, "Teach the process, not the product," and you have been exhorted by one authority after another to work with your students *during* the process rather than to judge their work solely on the basis of their written products. You agree with master teacher Donald Murray's comment, "The process of making meaning with written language cannot be understood by looking backward from the printed page. Process cannot be inferred from product any more than a pig can be inferred from sausage."[1] Thus, you have no intention of using professional essays in your class; instead you will use the students' own writing as the reading material for the course.

Wonderful. But what are you going to do when you find that your departmental syllabus includes an essay anthology, and that you are expected to teach it? Does that mean you are going to have to give up your process-centered class and go back to the conventional classroom that you remember from your own days as a freshman, a classroom in which the teacher talked more about the contents of the reader than he or she did about writing? Should you take the chance of ignoring the syllabus and not have the students buy the essay anthology at all? Or should you tell them to buy it and then feel guilty because you don't use it?

Take hope. The answer to these questions can be "None of the above," because it really is possible to use an essay anthology in a composition class and still focus on the writing process. In fact, I think process-minded teachers can enhance their writing classes by including nonfiction essays in the course; properly used, they can begin to give students some insights into how the writing process works and can help them to strengthen their own writing abilities. But the phrase "properly used" is an important qualifier here. Too often, I am afraid, writing teachers use nonfiction literature in their classrooms for the wrong reasons and in the wrong way.

First, because most teachers are trained only in literature, and thus are uncomfortable when they find themselves talking about the craft of writing instead of a body of familiar material, they frequently complain that writing courses have "no content," and they use the essays to provide that content. But when discussion in the class focuses on finished products rather than on how those products came into being, the writing component of the course suffers. What *should* be the focus of any writing course—*the study of the writing process at all levels,* both amateur and professional—gets lost.

Second, because they worry about the perennial problem of devising good theme topics, teachers sometimes resort to using professional essays as models for the students to imitate in their own writing. For good reasons, the results are usually not happy. Faced with the prospect of trying to understand an essay by Virginia Woolf or E. B. White and then of imitating it, most students are going to be more intimidated than instructed. Often, as consolation for what they see as their own incompetence, they take refuge in the myth that real writers can write because they are inspired, not because they were ever taught to write.

I believe that both these ways of using nonfiction in the writing class are not only inefficient, they are often damaging. But there are several constructive ways for teachers to use nonfiction in a writing course, ways that will preserve the emphasis on the writing process and still allow both students and teachers to enjoy the intellectual and aesthetic rewards of reading well-written professional essays. For it is a pleasure to introduce students to the stimulating ideas and beautifully crafted prose of writers like John McPhee, Joan Didion, and Loren Eiseley, and students, particularly freshmen, do benefit from reading them. They can also benefit from occasionally reading less dazzling professional writing, that of their writing teachers.

Some of the ways in which I have incorporated nonfiction writing into my classroom are these:

> Using essays to teach students to read *rhetorically,* that is, from the writer's point of view.
>
> Using simulation exercises to help students understand how an essay gets written.
>
> Bringing my own professional writing into class.
>
> Using portions of professional essays to illustrate strategies for revision.

Using professional writing to emphasize the value of facts and specific details.

Reading Rhetorically

I think the first way to use nonfiction in a composition course is to teach your students to read *rhetorically,* that is, to show them how to focus simultaneously on the content of an essay and on the process by which it was written. All of our students should understand that *every piece* of nonfiction is written in response to what Lloyd Bitzer calls a "rhetorical situation."[2] Bitzer says that every rhetorical situation has three components:

1. The *exigence* or occasion or demand that sets up the need for a response. Rhetoric can exist only when there is some problem that needs to be solved or change to be effected.

2. The *audience* to which the discourse is directed. Rhetoric *requires* an audience, one that can act or be influenced.

3. The *constraints* that influence the rhetor; these include the writer's intentions and knowledge and the means available for persuading readers. It also includes the limitations under which the writer works.

You can help students to analyze the rhetorical situation of an essay by giving them these guidelines for their reading.

1. What occasion or question do you think impelled the author to write this essay? What need does it meet, or what problem is it addressed to?

2. Who is the audience that the writer is trying to change or influence? What attitudes, knowledge, and assumptions would such an audience have that the writer would have to keep in mind? What questions would the audience have in mind that they would expect the writer to respond to?

3. What change or action does the writer hope to cause? That is, what is the writer's intention?

4. What means does the writer use to influence the readers? Identify examples of those means, and analyze how well they are used.

5. Does the essay work? That is, does it respond adequately to the situation or problem that caused it to be written; does it answer the questions that its readers would have in mind, and would those readers be likely to act or to change their opinions after reading it? Why do you think it works or doesn't work?

This set of guidelines establishes a rhetorical approach to all reading that goes on in your class—student papers as well as professional essays—and makes every discussion about reading a discussion about writing. The approach makes students look at the writing process and begin to understand what a writer goes through in order to bring an essay into existence.

For example, suppose the class were to analyze Virginia Woolf's feminist argument from *A Room of One's Own* that is often anthologized as "If Shakespeare Had Had a Sister." This piece of writing came into existence in response to the need to explain why there have been so few women artists before the twentieth century. As such it is clearly a rhetorical piece, designed to persuade. The audience would be both men and women who believe the claim that women's having produced so few works of art shows that they are inherently less creative and artistic than men. But these would not be people who hold the belief *a priori;* if given good reasons, they could be persuaded to change their minds. Otherwise there is no point in Woolf's writing, since she excludes from her audience anyone from a culture that holds women are inherently inferior or any unreconstructed male chauvinists.

The chief question that Woolf's interested readers would have in mind as they read would be, "If women are not naturally less creative than men, why is it that until recently there have been so few women musicians or artists or poets?" This is the question that Woolf keeps in her mind as she begins to write, and an important part of her writing process is looking for ways to answer it. She does it chiefly by showing her readers that circumstances, not lack of talent, account for women's not having produced many great works of art. She appeals to her readers' intellect with evidence, deduction, and the argument from circumstance, but she also draws her readers in as agents of their own conversion by appealing to their imagination and experience. Without their active involvement in the rhetorical drama Woolf creates, the piece does not work. But for most readers in Woolf's audience, it probably does work because not only has she anticipated their questions and answered them, but she has also taken account of their experiences and their feelings. She has responded to the *rhetorical situation.*

Simulation Exercises

A second way in which you can use professional essays to teach the writing process is to engage in simulation exercises in which you and the class try to put yourselves in a writer's place as he or she goes through the process of creating a piece of nonfiction writing. Working together, construct an imaginary scenario of a writer's actions, mental and physical, from the time that he or she started to write an essay until the time it was finished. Of course you would want to stress that the scenario is imaginary, since no one knows exactly what goes on in someone else's mind as he or she writes; nevertheless it can be useful.

Take, for example, George Orwell's famous essay "Marrakech." After asking the students to read the essay carefully and reflect on it, you could start the scenario by theorizing about what occasion or situation might have made Orwell decide to write the essay. Probably it would help to tell the class about Orwell's lifelong concern with the misery of the poor and with colonialism and racial exploitation; you might want to quote from his essay, "Why I Write." Then the class might think of some incident that could have provoked Orwell's anger so that he wanted to write a protest about the wretched conditions of the poor and the average person's callous indifference toward them. The readers he wants to reach are Englishmen and other white Europeans—the tourists to whom the laboring natives are invisible and who profit by their misery. Now Orwell has a point he wants to make and an audience for whom he wants to make it.

The next two questions to ask in constructing this scenario are (1) How is he going to make his point? and (2) What resources does he have to draw on? The answer to the first question is that initially he has to catch his readers' attention and then he has to gain their sympathy. He knows that one way to catch their attention is to make some startling statement, and that's what he does in that famous first sentence, "As the corpse went by, the flies left the restaurant table in a cloud and rushed after it, but they came back a few minutes later." Now, he asks himself, what resources can I use to follow up and make my point about the poor? His answer, of course, has to be that he'll use examples. Where will he get them? From his own experience—that's the most effective evidence he could have, so he uses incidents from his own travels in Africa. Then he might ask himself, "What comparison can I make that will dramatize my point?" One that would come naturally from the material is that poor people are like draft animals and are treated in the same way. So he might think, "Aha! I can play on the English people's love of animals and show them that they get outraged about cruelty to animals but don't pay any attention to worse cruelty to people. And I'll use myself as an example because I've done it too."

So this is the way Orwell might begin to write his essay, gradually accumulating his material and shaping it to say what he wanted. You might go on to analyze some of the paragraphs in the essay, discussing why he selected certain details, why he used dialogue in some places, and what effect he is trying to get with his images, and identifying places where he moved down the ladder of abstraction in order to support a generality. Of course, students may provide several reasonable rhetorical scenarios for a particular essay, but such variety is also useful because it helps them to understand how many effective ways they can find to develop their ideas. The important point about having them recreate such imaginary writing situations is that when they experiment with this kind of analysis they are learning to talk about the writing process. Inevitably, they will become more conscious of their own writing processes and of the options they have when they write.

Using Your Own Writing in the Classroom

As an important variation on these process scenarios, I frequently bring in my own professional writing and talk about it. By doing so, I can create a rhetorical scenario that has real authority and sometimes considerable drama. I usually begin by describing my rhetorical situation, telling them *why* I am writing—that is, what demand or need I am responding to—who the audience for my writing will be and what I know or conjecture about that audience, and what constraints I am working under—word limits, deadlines, and so on. Then I talk about the problems I am having and what I think may be causing them.

For example, last semester I wrote a grant proposal to apply for the Mina Shaughnessy fellowship, and I shared my writing process with the students as I went along. First, I explained to them what the fellowship is and why I wanted it (they were intrigued to learn that their teacher wanted time off to write a book about teaching the writing process). Then I explained that I had two audiences. The first readers would quickly screen the thousands of proposals on the basis of the all-important abstract. If the proposal survived that round, a second group of careful readers would read it and ask tough and specific questions. By carefully reading the announcement for the competition, we theorized about what qualities the screening committee would be looking for—usefulness, relevance, broad application, originality—and we went over the abstract to see if it met those criteria and to be sure it did not exceed the word limit.

Then we read the announcement again to determine what specific qualities the second audience would be looking for and what questions they would probably have as they read the proposal. We came up with these:

What kind of book does she intend to write?

Why is it needed?

Who will benefit by it?

What else has been done in this area?

What qualifications does she have to write such a book?

Can she do it in the time specified by the grant?

Does she convince us that the results of the proposal are worth spending money on?

Finally, we talked about the constraints I was working under. One important one was that the proposal could not be more than ten double-spaced pages; another was that it absolutely had to be in the mail by November 1—no extensions.

During the three weeks that I worked on the grant proposal I brought in my planning notes and then my rough drafts and showed the students how the work was progressing. I talked about my chronic writing problem, a tendency to overexplain, and got them to help me identify places where I was telling the audience things they really didn't need or want to know. I showed them three beginning paragraphs and got them to help me choose the best one, keeping in mind that I had to get the audience's attention and confidence immediately. We talked about voice—they convinced me that my tone was too casual—and we debated about how much information I needed to include about my credentials, given my space limitations. By the end of the three weeks they were deeply involved in my writing process and worried about whether I was going to meet my deadline. They also learned that their writing teacher has problems too, and they found that consoling and heartening.

Using Professional Writing to Demonstrate Revision Strategies

A third way you can integrate professional writing into teaching the writing process is to use the strategies suggested by Paul Escholz in his essay "The Prose Models Approach: Using Products in the Process," included in the 1980 NCTE book *Eight Approaches to Teaching Composition*. He recommends introducing students to prose models "on an individual basis during conferences" after they have completed one or two drafts. They are then likely to have specific questions or problems that the instructor can respond to by referring them to prose models that demonstrate how a professional writer has dealt with that kind of writing situation.

Such an instance might occur when the professor tells students that they are taking too long to get into their subjects and are going to lose their audience because they don't make a commitment soon enough to

give the audience signals about what to expect. To find a strategy for
meeting their problems the teacher might suggest that they look at the
paragraph Hemingway uses to introduce his essay "When You Camp
Out, Do It Right."

> Thousands of people will go into the bush this summer to cut
> the high costs of living. A man who gets his two weeks' salary
> while he is on vacation should be able to put those two weeks in
> fishing and camping and be able to save one week's salary clear.
> He ought to be able to sleep comfortably every night, to eat well
> every day and to return to the city rested and in good condition.[3]

The teacher could also direct students to this opening paragraph to
illustrate how an author simultaneously announces a subject and ingra-
tiates himself with readers:

> Everyone must have at least one personal experience with a
> computer error by this time. Bank balances are suddenly reported
> to have jumped from $379 into the millions, appeals for charitable
> contributions are mailed over and over to people with crazy-
> sounding names at your address, department stores send the wrong
> bills, utility companies write that they're turning everything off,
> that sort of thing. If you managed to get in touch with someone
> and complain, you then get instantaneously typed, guilty letters
> from the same computer, saying "Our computer was in error, and
> an adjustment is being made in your account."[4]

A student who is having trouble working out a conclusion for his or
her paper—and they're much harder, of course—might be referred to
this paragraph, with which Alan Moorehead concludes an essay about
encountering a gorilla.

> That was the end of the show, and it had lasted I suppose a
> couple of hundred seconds. Yet still, after wandering through Africa
> in the last few years, I rate this as the most exciting encounter that
> has come my way; and I remember how, no longer any need for
> silence, the guides with their pangas slashed a path for us to return
> through the bush, and how they grinned and were pleased because
> we were pleased, and how I went down the mountain like a young
> gazelle in two hours straight, never a touch of fatigue, never a
> thought for my blistered feet after such a happy day.[5]

I find it particularly useful to refer students to professional writers'
work to illustrate how writers use metaphor to persuade—Martin Luther
King, Jr.'s "I Have a Dream" speech, for example—or how they use
concrete personal examples to make their points—Jessica Mitford or
E. B. White, for example. John McPhee's essays demonstrate how a
writer can make his writing come alive through details, and Ellen
Goodman's columns show how a writer can construct an argument on
the basis of her own experience.

Escholz recommends that a writing teacher keep a small collection of nonfiction in his or her office to supplement an essay reader and over a period of years develop a file of selections that illustrate solutions to students' recurrent writing problems. He concludes his essay by saying,

> The main problem with the traditional prose models approach has been that teachers tend to present the models too early in the process. . . . It has been assumed that problems are best solved before they ever arise. But writing does not work that way. Students must be permitted to discover their own writing problems. . . . Writers can best learn from what other writers have done when they find themselves in similar situations.[6]

In other words, you cannot expect students to benefit appreciably from simply *reading* professional essays and having writers' strategies pointed out to them. But after they have practiced constructing some imaginary writing process scenarios and then find themselves facing the same kinds of problems other writers typically encounter, they are ready to learn from professional examples. And they must realize that one cannot simply lift a solution from another writer; each writer has to adapt a particular strategy to his or her specific rhetorical situation. We can learn from other practitioners of our trade, but we cannot solve our writing problems in precisely the ways they use.

Using Essays to Show the Weight of Facts

Finally, I find that using nonfiction literature in the composition classroom helps to improve my students' writing because by studying it they can learn that if they want to be taken seriously as writers they must learn to add the weight of facts to their writing. They cannot get by with writing a series of generalizations or simply repeating their unsupported opinions, no matter how strong and virtuous those opinions may be. Students resist accepting that truth for a number of reasons. For one thing, they are not used to writing for any audience but their teachers, and they may still believe that teachers value correct form more than content. They are also not used to trying to make their writing interesting to a reader, since they have had no rhetorical situation in mind as they write—why bother to dig out facts when no one but the teacher will read the paper anyway?

But the truth about what real readers expect from a writer begins to dawn when they read the work of writers like Annie Dillard and Carl Sagan from a rhetorical point of view and ask themselves why we take the work of such writers seriously. What have they done that makes us pay attention and commands our respect? The answer is that they use examples and facts, and they teach us something. They pay their readers the compliment of assuming that they are intelligent and will not simply accept unsupported statements; therefore they go to the trouble to find specific facts and experiences to illustrate their points. If that takes research, they do it. If it takes examples, they find them. Eventually students will realize that if they want to be taken seriously as writers, they too must give their writing the weight and depth that come only from concrete details and specifics. But they have to read good nonfiction in order to understand that, and most of them come to college without having done so. That is why we have to help them by introducing them to the works of good essayists.

But in spite of the legitimate ways in which nonfiction can be profitably incorporated into a composition class, I would argue strongly against making it the center of a writing course or using it to give the course "content." A writing course has its own content, and that is the students' and teacher's writing and the writing process itself. Only if we use professional essays in ways that throw light on that process and help students to better understand "how writers work," as Mina Shaughnessy puts it,[7] can we justify their place in the writing classroom. But if we do use essays properly, we can enhance the teaching of writing and make it not only intellectually richer but more fun.

Notes

1. Donald Murray, "Writing as Process: How Writing Finds Its Own Meaning," in *Eight Approaches to Teaching Composition,* ed. Timothy R. Donovan and Ben W. McClelland (Urbana, Ill.: National Council of Teachers of English, 1980), 3.

2. Lloyd Bitzer, "The Rhetorical Situation," *Philosophy and Rhetoric* 1 (Winter 1968): 1–15.

3. Ernest Hemingway, "When You Camp Out, Do It Right," *Toronto Star,* 26 June 1920; reprinted in *The Riverside Reader,* ed. Joseph Trimmer and Maxine Hairston, vol. 2 (Boston: Houghton Mifflin, 1983).

4. Lewis Thomas, "To Err Is Human," in *The Medusa and the Snail* (New York: Penguin, 1981), 37.

5. Alan Moorehead, "A Most Forgiving Ape," *No Room in the Ark* (New York: Harper, 1959); reprinted in *The Riverside Reader,* vol. 2.

6. Paul Escholz, "The Prose Models Approach: Using Products in the Process," in *Eight Approaches to Teaching Composition.*

7. Mina Shaughnessy, *Errors and Expectations: A Guide for Teachers of Basic Writing* (New York: Oxford Univ. Press, 1977), 76.

An Integrative Approach to Research: Theory and Practice

Jill N. Burkland
Michigan Technological University

Bruce T. Petersen
Michigan Technological University

As teachers of writing at a predominantly technological university, we often hear students ask why the freshman composition sequence is not a straightforward course in technical writing. Many students appear to believe that a set of universal writing rules exists which will make them, in all situations, good writers. They imagine that their writing courses should be little more than training for their careers. This "practicality" is mirrored by a society that makes increasing demands on our profession to solve the "literacy crisis" through courses in composition. This demand for literacy has not been accompanied, however, by any similar call for literary, historical, or philosophical study. In short, we seem confronted by a call for literacy which ignores the very context of what has historically been considered the curriculum of literacy.

This change in what passes for literacy has created, in turn, fundamental changes in the nature of our profession. Already we talk to professors willing to consider first their perceived "duty" to service courses. Composition comes to serve, in these teachers' classes, only the utilitarian ends of teaching students about organization, library research, and format.

We are concerned, then, by a growing belief that writing can be taught as mere technique, devoid of the symbolic content of novels, essays, history, or philosophy. We find ourselves frustrated and most of our students bored by the repetition of essays, personal experience papers, and research papers on such social issues as abortion, the ERA, pornography, the drinking age, or the draft. For us, moreover, the problem is more significant than student boredom. We want our students to learn not only how to do research, but also how to understand the process of research and of responding to reading in ways that made them active composers of meaning. In the midst of a writing-across-the-curriculum program designed to encourage writing in all disciplines, therefore, we began to look for ways to incorporate literature, nonfiction essays, scientific writing, history, and philosophy into the earliest writing classes.

It may be useful here to briefly review our concept of research. Research begins when a person wants to know something about a subject, issue, or experience that is not immediately understandable. Research is a twofold process. On one hand, it is a search inside of oneself, what Donald Murray calls "recollecting."[1] On the other hand, research is a search outside of oneself, a discovery and integration of what is known with what is not yet known. Both of these processes constitute research. Such research is not done only in the service of a "research paper," but is rather a way of thinking about both reading and existential experience. Richard L. Larson, in discussing his doubts about the concept of the research paper, argues that the "best service we can render to [students] is to insist that [they] recognize their continuing responsibility for looking attentively at their experiences; for seeking out, wherever it can be found, the information they need for the development of their ideas; and for putting such data at the service of every piece they write."[2] This chapter describes how we integrate reading and writing in a class that includes some type of research paper as its main component. In the first part of the chapter, we outline a theoretical rationale based on recent work in cognitive psychology, composition, and literary theory. In the second part, we detail the pedagogical practice deriving from this theory with particular focus on teaching the research paper.

The Concept of Process

Any teacher of composition or of literature over the past decade recognizes that we have experienced a radical shift in our approaches to both subjects. The concept of process is ascendant. In composition, process pedagogy and theory have become what at least one author terms the "paradigm" of the discipline.[3] The rise of audience-based or reader-response criticism in literature study parallels the interest in process in composition. Reader-response criticism and process pedagogy in composition share fundamental precepts about perception and about the structures and functions of our brains. These shared concepts have recently been noted in journals devoted to composition and in journals devoted to literary criticism.[4]

Psycholinguists and reading and composition theorists now agree that the processes of reading and writing are active. David Bleich, Louise Rosenblatt, Linda Flower, and James Britton, for example, all say that composing occurs, that is, meaning emerges, from an affective use of language, when readers and writers are motivated to make sense of experiences, memories, associations, and texts through language. Like Lev Vygotsky, these authors believe that our minds process both sense and symbolic experience through personal associations, from previous experiences, and out of already developed and developing cognitive schemata. The process of composition and the process of reading are based, under this theory, in a matrix that *composes* meaning as we read, write, and interpret. While each theorist has his or her own terminology for the action of this mental center, they all agree about its existence and function. Flower calls the action "writer-centered prose," Britton "expressive writing," Bleich "re-symbolization," Rosenblatt the "evocation of the poem."

James Britton's work in composition derives from the personality theories of George Kelly and the linguistic school of Edward Sapir. Britton defines expressive writing, therefore, as an element of the individual personality. Expressive writing is language "close to the self . . . [which] has the functions of revealing the speaker, verbalizing his consciousness, and displaying his close relation with a listener or reader."[5] Expressive writing is thus a record or explanation of the feelings, moods, opinions, or preoccupations that a writer experiences as he or she works with a topic.

Linda Flower bases her theory of composition on cognitive models developed at Carnegie-Mellon University. She defines "writer-based prose" as "a verbal expression written by a writer to himself and for himself . . . [it] reflects the associative, narrative path of the writer's own confrontation with her subject."[6] Writer-based prose is thus a cognitive center for coherence; that is, writer-based prose is a function of the brain through which thought becomes articulate.

These separate but similar theories of writing share obvious epistemological assumptions with the work of reader-response literary criticism. David Bleich, for example, argues that "any new perceptual experience stimulates an emotional response immediately, and our thought about this experience is a reaction to an emotional response plus the experience, rather than to the experience alone."[7] We understand and interpret what we read by relating the reading experience to prior knowledge, and through this affective matrix we compose meaning.

Louise Rosenblatt, like Bleich, sees the reading experience as a "transaction" between the common experiences "already present in the personality and mind of the reader" and those similar experiences condensed by the text.[8] The composition of meaning, or what Rosenblatt calls the "evocation of the poem," depends on the brain's ability to develop coherence from the disparate elements of text, reader, and social moment: ". . . a poem, then, must be thought of as an event in time. It is an occurrence, a coming together, a compenetration, of a reader and a text. The reader brings to the text his past experience; the encounter gives rise to a new experience, a poem."[9]

Bleich's and Rosenblatt's views of the reading process have direct relations to Britton's and Flower's theories of composition. All four believe that our initial response in either writing or reading is motivational and affective. In addition, all four see the making of meaning as a recursive process in which the mind actively *composes* the texts and data it encounters. This common acknowledgment of recursiveness suggests that there is a mental activity which governs concomitantly our reading and writing processes and, in turn, provides a rationale for integrating reading and writing for the individual student. In addition, these authors and other contemporary educational theorists have argued that reading and writing have a social context.

Not so long ago, reading and writing were conceived as solitary, or at most dual (author-reader), activities. Modern composition theory and reader-response criticism both argue that reading and writing are social acts; that is, readers and writers develop knowledge by exchanging information. The occasion of this exchange has been called an interpretive community by literary critics and a peer group by composition teachers. Louise Rosenblatt, for example, says, "Perhaps we should consider the text as an even more general medium of communication *among readers*. . . . We may help one another to attend to words, phrases, images, scenes that we have overlooked or slighted."[10] James Britton describes, in similar language, the importance of talk to a writing peer group: "The relationship of talk to writing is central to the writing process. . . . Talk relies on an immediate link with listeners; . . . the rapid exchange of conversation allows many things to go on at once—exploration, clarification, shared interpretation, insight into difference of opinion. . . ."[11]

This emphasis on the social nature of learning and knowledge is of particular interest in light of the common criticism that "process" composition and "subjective" literary criticism cater to narcissism and egocentric thought in students. In fact, quite the opposite is true. Rhetorician James Moffett, for example, argues that composing only takes place when a writer makes sense out of a chaos of uninterpreted facts, reading, and experience and then shares this new knowledge with others.

> The subject matter of student writing . . . needs to be materials not previously interpreted or abstracted by others . . . but central is the process of *expatiation* that takes the interplay of inner voices back out into the social world, where the give-and-take of minds and voices can lift each member beyond where he or she started.[12]

Moffett's view is shared by a variety of modern rhetoricians who emphasize the complex interrelations of writer, subject, reality, language, reader, and time.

One of the major difficulties that students face when they read texts written in the distant or even recent past is a problem of context. Their own sense of a social connection to the author can be radically affected by their knowledge or lack of knowledge about a specific time period. The context of time presents particular problems for readers and writers who, like many of our students, do not possess a broad repertoire of past reading experience. Jonathan Culler, in *The Pursuit of Signs,* argues that a text's meaning depends on a reader whose view of time is both immediate, or synchronic, and historical, or diachronic.[13] We may put this another way: a reader attempts to understand a text both within the context in which the author wrote it and within the context in which the reader reads it. Often, readers' responses to a text spring from their attempts to recreate it as both a historic and an immediately personal document. The unraveling of a reader's questions may require further reading of the text, outside research, or exchange of information with classmates. It always depends on the connections between a historical reader and a historical writer; that is, readers attempt to create a social context whenever they read. Because of this, even a "small" historical question may significantly affect how readers come to understand any text.

We will use one of our student's research projects as an example of how reading and writing can act in concert to help students create social contexts for their reading. The student in this example had an interest in, perhaps even an obsession with, hunting. As he read Ernest Hemingway's "The Short Happy Life of Francis Macomber," his responses centered on the guns Hemingway describes. The student decided to find out as much as he could about the 6.5 Mannlicher, a gun with which he was unfamiliar, and the gun which, readers will remember, kills Francis at the story's end. The student discovered that the 6.5 Mannlicher has a tremendous and overpowering kick. No one familiar with it or its use could hope intentionally to hit an object at the distance from which Margot Macomber fires. Other students in the class told us that Hemingway always attempts to depict literally and accurately the information about the tools of hunters, fishermen, bullfighters, and others. From these two pieces of knowledge the student constructed a theory of the story's end—that the narrator and not Wilson is correct about Margot's intentions. He derived this theory of the story from a seemingly minor question—in fact, a question considered important by no critic of whom we are aware. Experiences such as this convince us to approach reading and writing as mutually reinforcing *composing* processes.

From Response to Research

Over the course of the freshman year, we want our students to become alert readers, conscious of their own research processes and of the useful research processes of their peers. We want students to be able to formulate a variety of questions from their initial responses to a text. And we want them to have a variety of strategies for using the resources of their own minds, their peers, the library, and other people to answer their questions. The basic strategies discussed in this chapter could be applied to any number of other assignments, from informal readers' journals, to bibliographies, to critical investigations of texts, to almost any paper that might be assigned in a course that asks students to read and write.

During the first term of the year we assign readings designed to encourage students' memories and associations of places, experiences, people, and events that they might be willing to share or consider worth sharing with their peers. In moving to the second term, we ask students to begin to move outward in their research efforts—since all their writing in the first term can be done by using various methods of recalling their pasts. We do, however, continue to ask for personal associations and responses to the texts as the first step in the process.

We use the same reading-response strategies to begin all research assignments. We start by reading several texts and writing what we call "narrative responses"; that is, we ask students to write down anything that pops into their heads as they hear the story being read. They are told not to wait until the end of the story and then to look for a unified response, but rather to jot down comments and questions in progress. This method of developing a protocol of a student's reading has been found useful in reading research. Our intent, however, is to encourage students to keep a record of their associations, questions, and thoughts as they read. This recording of thought, or putting thought into words, is important. James Britton has called such spontaneous writing "shaping at the point of utterance."[14] He says that "when we come to write, what is delivered to the pen is in part already shaped, stamped with the image of our ways of perceiving."[15] Clearly putting this immediate response to reading in writing is one component of the connections between the two processes. This writing done, students share their responses, reading them aloud to the class, and then we try to categorize the different kinds of comments we find. We list these responses and then place them into categories, most commonly (1) interpretations, (2) questions aiming toward interpretation, (3) factual questions, (4) personal associations, and (5) personal reactions or evaluations.[16]

We can use our students' responses to Ernest Hemingway's short story "The Old Man at the Bridge" to illustrate these categories. By interpretation, we mean general comments on what the text means; for example, one student wrote: "War seems to be hardest on innocent victims." Questions aiming toward interpretation reflect a student's search for meaning, as in, "Why does Hemingway have the soldier as the narrator of the story?" In addition, texts raise several factual questions, for example, "What country is this?" "What war is this?" or "Who were the Fascists?" Students respond with a variety of personal associations, from memories of grandparents to recollections of other war stories they have read. Personal reactions and evaluations include everything from "This is a really sad story" to "I don't understand what Hemingway is trying to say here." We use these responses to direct our discussion of the stories read. The class arrives at possible interpretations, discusses what light their associations and reactions might shed on an understanding of the texts, and shares information in an attempt to answer many of the factual questions raised. Thus, our classes immediately become involved in using the resources of their peers as a first step in research.

We will use three Hemingway short stories ("The Old Man at the Bridge," "Ten Indians," and "The Short Happy Life of Francis Macomber") to illustrate the rest of the process with which we begin all research-oriented assignments. Having introduced students to our method, we make an assignment of what we call a research report:

> Formulate an appropriate question for research, learn the answer to that question through research in the library or elsewhere, and then describe both the research process you went through and what you discovered in answer to your question. Finally, discuss briefly what insights your research has given you on the story.

This assignment has three purposes: first, to help students begin to analyze their own researching processes; second, to get students used to the process of reading-questioning-searching-answering; and third, to familiarize students with the resources of the library and of other sources in our community. Once students have read the stories and written their narrative responses, we talk in class about what puzzles them, identify the questions and areas of confusion in their responses, and make lists of questions we want answered. With this extensive list, we then discuss which questions are "researchable."

Researchable questions, our students usually decide, are ones that could conceivably be answered. For example, "Who were the Fascists in Spain?" "What Indians lived near Petosky around 1900?" and "What laws cover big-game hunting in Africa?" are all questions which promise to be researchable. We also rephrase or expand purely speculative or interpretive questions to open them for investigation as well. For instance, the question "Where is Nick's mother in the story 'Indian Camp?'" might be more useful as a research question if changed to "Does Nick's mother appear in any of the Nick Adams stories, and if so what is she like?" Another question, "Why are the Indians drunk in 'Ten Indians?'" could be revised to "What problems are associated with alcohol and the American Indian?"

Each student is asked to settle on three or four questions that he or she would like to investigate. The first method of investigation we encourage students to use is peer inquiry. Students meet in groups to discuss each other's questions, to elucidate the text wherever possible, and to formulate new questions that might be more easily researchable. We try in every way we can to lead our students to discover their own, real questions, questions that engage them and to which they want to know the answers, questions which, once answered, would help them to better understand the text.

Students select a question, research it, report back to the class on the progress of their research, exchange information, and suggest other sources. The final report consists of an introduction to the problem or question posed by the paper, a procedure section (i.e., a narrative of the writer's research activities), a discussion of the findings, and a final note on the relevance of the answer to the story. The many discoveries that students have made and shared with the class in response to Hemingway's work include the meaning and etymology of the word "quid," the immediate causes of the Spanish Civil War, the laws governing big-game hunting in Kenya today, and the causes of the high rates of alcoholism among American Indians. However, more important than the factual discoveries students make are the narratives of their investigations. In sharing their papers with each other they share a wealth of information not only on specific questions in the texts but also on how to go about finding the answers to questions raised by a text.

The Research Paper

Our second paper is assigned to fulfill our university's requirement for a research paper. Again we will use our unit on Hemingway to describe how the method works in an extended paper. The paper is initiated with the reading of several stories (our examples come from "Soldier's Home," "In Another Country," "Indian Camp," "Big Two-Hearted River," "A Way You'll Never Be," "Capital of the World," "A Day's Wait," and "Up in Michigan." A varied selection is important to allow students a wide range of research opportunities. Students write the same kinds of responses as they read this time, again looking for interpretations, associations, factual questions, etc. In looking over initial responses to "In Another Country," for example, students will find a number of questions and comments about the war and Hemingway's reaction to it, for example: "What war is this?" "I didn't know there were Communists in Italy"; and "I think that Hemingway really was in Italy during World War I." From such initial responses students can develop specific questions. For example, the first two questions above might be turned into the more specific question, "What was the status of the Communist Party in Italy during World War I?" And the third question could be revised to read, "Why did Hemingway go to Italy as an ambulance driver in World War I?" Other responses might center on the medical issues raised by the story: "Was that kind of therapy with machines really used, and did it work?" or "I think the machines were just to give soldiers hope, which might help them survive." From these observations students can move to questions like: "What role does mental attitude play in the healing process?" or "What kinds of physical therapy were used on World War I veterans?"

Some students might connect the events in "In Another Country" to the subject of veterans' benefits, leading to questions such as: "How have medical benefits to veterans changed since World War I?" or "What kinds of assistance have disabled vets of the Vietnam War received?" These questions from a single story represent, in only a very limited way, the possibilities for student exploration and discovery.

After these initial steps are taken, we begin to talk about focusing on some organization that can lead to a paper. We put off this discussion until after students begin to do research, because our experience tells us they will otherwise lock themselves into finding the kind of question that one teacher will like or that will be easy to research or, worse, pose false questions that lead not to topics they want to explore, but rather to a topic they feel they can, as our students put it, "blow off," i.e., write on without doing any research. (Of course, any topic can be expanded, but what we want to avoid is a too-easy sense of assurance and satisfaction with their "old" knowledge of a topic.)

We once again begin with narrative responses to a text and work to develop a comprehensive list of questions from the class, and then work with the class to expand or refine questions to make them suitable for research. The Hemingway story "Up in Michigan" has served, in many classes, as a model. For instance, a yes-or-no question like "Did Hemingway struggle to get along with women?" can be narrowed and broken down into several questions more easily investigated, such as, "What kind of relationship did Hemingway have with his mother?" or "Why couldn't Hemingway establish a good marriage?" or "How do the unhappy love relationships in Hemingway's stories compare to those in his life?"

With the help of editing groups, then, each student decides on a question on which to work. We ask them next to write one-page proposals, stating their questions, what stories they come from and why they are interested in them, what they know about them, and how they plan to begin researching them. We hold conferences with each student to discuss these proposals, approve or offer suggestions on questions, and suggest possible sources for research.

A sample of the questions our students have developed in response to a variety of Hemingway stories may be of use here.

1. Did World War I veterans experience the same kinds of traumas when they returned home that Vietnam veterans did?

2. What were the different attitudes in the United States about prohibition in the 1920s?

3. What caused the downfall of Seney, Michigan, and who was responsible?

4. What role does bullfighting play in Spain's culture today?

5. How did the Spanish Civil War affect the relationship between church and state in that country?

6. What are some of the differences between children of one-parent and those of two-parent families?

7. What evidence do we have to support or deny the existence of ESP?

8. Is Nick Adams really Hemingway?

9. Why was Hemingway obsessed with death and how is that related to his committing suicide?

10. What causes some people to become habitual liars?

11. What are the dangers of stress and how can they be overcome?

12. Is faith-healing a real phenomenon or a hoax?

13. What was the bonus army, and why wasn't it successful?

14. What are the new regulations for the disposal of chemical waste, and are they enough?

The variety of research questions, while theoretically predictable, is one of the greatest values of this open-ended method of questioning. We have had no two questions exactly alike, and not one of our students has had serious trouble finding a question for research. We encourage students to revise, expand, or narrow their topics as they do their research, and to branch off in whatever direction their interests lead them as they work, but to make sure they have at all times a controlling question to guide them.

The "Zero" Draft

After students have spent about ten days on library research and interviewing, and after they have prepared annotated bibliographies and taken notes, we ask students to write a "zero" draft of their research paper in class. A "zero" draft is an extended free-writing.[17] For this free-writing, students are not allowed to use their notes; instead they write down everything they want to say or can say about their research and what they have found about their question. The purpose of this draft is fairly simple. We want students to begin the actual writing of their papers with a piece of what James Britton has called "expressive writing." Expressive writing has been described by a wide variety of theorists in both cognitive psychology and composition. Britton, who bases the concept on the work of Edward Sapir, Susanne Langer, and Lev Vygotsky, defines expressive writing as language "close to the self . . . [which] has the functions of revealing the speaker, verbalizing his consciousness, and displaying his close relationship with a listener or reader."[18] Expressive writing is a record and evaluation of the feelings, moods, opinions, or preoccupations writers experience as they compose. We want our students to express what, in fact, they *know* as opposed to what they have simply recorded in their notes. By writing the "zero" draft, they locate those areas of their topics that need further research and study. In addition, this draft forces students to begin to focus and organize their papers into logical form.

After writing their "zero" drafts and reading them to each other and to themselves, students need to rethink their topics in order to add needed detail or support from outside sources, to reorganize, and to think about how they might approach a particular audience. Each "zero" draft is then revised, using the notes they have written about it as a guide, and the students submit this second draft to us at a small-group conference.

Developing a Thesis

The teacher and the group make suggestions for revisions, and suggestions about how the student might focus the paper even further by adding a thesis. This does not mean, of course, that the general topic changes, but it does require students to become conscious of composing, even imposing, a meaning on what they have been discovering. We cannot too strongly point out that the students have to say something about the topic, i.e., take a stand or make an argument. These papers are not simply reports on a subject. After this session, students revise again and read their next drafts to their peers in small groups. This peer discussion has two main purposes: to offer a chance for editing and to review the process of research students have used in preparing the paper. There are two important points to be made here. First, we constantly emphasize that the research students do is not done only in the service of a "research paper." On the contrary, it is our intention to encourage habits of active reading and thoughtful writing; the paper that emerges from this work can take any number of forms both in content and format. Second, the research the students do during this period can be applied to the rest of the writing they would do in the term; the writing of this paper does not end the usefulness of their research.

A Critical Paper

Finally, we usually assign one paper requiring students to make some critical or evaluative comment on the texts they read. Up to this point in the year, our students have been attempting to shed light on their understanding of literature by looking inside themselves for associations to their own feelings and past and by investigating outside of themselves for information they don't know. Now, with the final paper, we ask our students to integrate these processes while they search carefully in the texts for concepts, themes, or ideas about which they want to write. A representative assignment might be the following:

> Figure out, from the stories you've read, Hemingway's (or Darwin's, Freud's, Plath's, Mansfield's, Plato's, Thomas's) views on some

> subject (death, bravery, parenthood, sex, friendship, marriage, etc.)
> that interests you. Then show the class why you think what you say
> is true by using specific evidence from one or more of the texts.

We ask students to write responses in which they discuss ideas, make associations, and ask interpretive questions for each of the texts they read. Students make lists of single words or phrases that complete the sentence, "This is a story about ＿＿＿＿＿＿," where "＿＿＿＿＿＿" is the student's summary of the story's meaning. Students then look back at the texts and their own responses and try to answer the question, "What is Hemingway (etc.) saying about ＿＿＿＿＿＿?"

Students study the text carefully for answers, just as they have studied other research materials and their own memories in earlier papers. We spend several class periods discussing our summaries, comparing the ideas, plots, and situations in these stories with other stories we have read earlier, and talk about how the knowledge we have gained from our various research endeavors might reflect on the general interpretations we are now forming. We look for patterns and contradictions, talk about our own reactions and associations, and consider carefully what our combined research into Hemingway and related topics might tell us and in what ways it might help direct our present investigations. Some of the conclusions students have drawn about Hemingway's short stories include:

> "Old Man at the Bridge" and "A Clean, Well-Lighted Place" show Hemingway's belief that a man must have some responsibility to give him purpose, or he will waste away or die.
>
> In "The Snows of Kilimanjaro," "Soldier's Home," and "A Clean, Well-Lighted Place," Hemingway expresses his belief that the more clearly you see and understand life, the more dissatisfied you become with it.
>
> In "Up in Michigan" and "Ten Indians," Hemingway shows the misunderstanding and uncertainty often associated with young-love relationships.
>
> In "Big Two-Hearted River," Hemingway uses symbols to describe Nick's thoughts and feelings as he makes the adjustment from war to civilian life.

We are always pleased with the variety of ideas students raise. Of course, to those versed in literary study, many of these concepts are not new, some may seem rather simplistic, and others appear to contradict established critical opinion. To us, it is more important that these are students' ideas and concepts and that the students are prepared to take the responsibility to demonstrate proof for their ideas. Students are asked to support their observations and interpretations with specific references from their texts, from brief new research, or from previous research, and to develop short but carefully constructed arguments to prove those ideas.

Conclusion

Our experience with this method is that most students, having worked for a year with us, come to move with relative ease and confidence through reading they originally think is too thorny, complex, or "stupid" to spend any time with. They discover that literature not only has "something" in it, but that they can have a major role in composing that "something." They discover that they have within themselves the resources to pursue both inner and outer research which can help them understand difficult texts because they have helped each other develop strategies for exploring their own experiences, for asking questions, and for seeking answers outside of their experiences. Reading literature, in particular, has been for them demystified, made accessible, because they now know that its meaning is not a "secret" held only by literature professors but something composed by the active questioning and writing of readers.

Notes

1. Donald Murray, *Write to Learn* (New York: Holt, Rinehart, & Winston, 1984), 18.

2. Richard L. Larson, "The 'Research Paper' in the Writing Course: A Non-Form of Writing," *College English* 44 (Dec. 1982): 811–16.

3. Maxine Hairston, "The Winds of Change: Thomas Kuhn and the Revolution in the Teaching of Writing," *College Composition and Communication* 33, no. 1(Feb. 1982): 76–88.

4. See Bruce T. Petersen, "Writing about Responses: A Unified Model of Reading, Writing, and Interpretation," *College English* 44 (Sept. 1982); Joseph Comprone, "Literature and the Writing Process: A Pedagogical Reading of William Faulkner's 'Barn Burning,'" *College Literature* 11 (Winter 1982): 1–21; Anthony R. Petrosky, "From Story to Essay: Reading and Writing," *College Composition and Communication* 33 (Feb. 1982): 19–36. See also David Bleich, Eugene Kintgen, et al., "The Psychological Study of Language and Literature: A Selected and Annotated Bibliography," *Style* 12 (Spring 1978): 113–210; Inge Crosman, "Annotated Bibliography of Audience-Oriented Criticism," in *The Reader in the Text: Essays on Audience and Interpretation,* ed. Susan Suleiman and Inge Crosman (Princeton: Princeton Univ. Press, 1980); and Bruce T.

Petersen, "A Selected Bibliography," in *The Language Connection,* ed. Arthur Young and Toby Fulwiler (Urbana, Ill.: National Council of Teachers of English, 1982).

5. James Britton, Tony Burgess, Nancy Martin, Alex McLeod, Harold Rosen, *The Development of Writing Abilities (11–18).* Schools Council Research Studies (London: Macmillan Education, 1975), 90.

6. Linda Flower, "Writer-Based Prose: A Cognitive Basis for Problems in Writing," *College English* 41 (Sept. 1979): 20.

7. David Bleich, *Readings and Feelings: An Introduction to Subjective Criticism* (Urbana, Ill.: National Council of Teachers of English, 1975), 5.

8. Louise Rosenblatt, *Literature as Exploration* (New York: Noble & Noble, 1965), 42.

9. Louise Rosenblatt, "The Poem as Event," *College English* 26 (Nov. 1964): 126.

10. Louise Rosenblatt, *The Reader, the Text, and the Poem* (Carbondale: Southern Illinois Univ. Press, 1978), 146.

11. Britton et al., 29.

12. James Moffett, "Writing, Inner Speech, and Meditation," *College English* 44 (Mar. 1982): 234.

13. Jonathan Culler, "Semiotics as a Theory of Reading," in *The Pursuit of Signs* (Ithaca, N.Y.: Cornell Univ. Press, 1981), 47–49.

14. James Britton, "Shaping at the Point of Utterance," in *Reinventing the Rhetorical Tradition,* ed. Aviva Freedman and Ian Pringle (Conway, Ark.: L & S Books, 1980), 63.

15. Ibid.

16. Readers familiar with research into readers' responses to literature will recognize the categories into which our students' responses fell. See, in particular, Lee Odell and Charles R. Cooper, "Describing Responses to Works of Fiction," *Research in the Teaching of English* 10 (1976): 203–25.

17. For an explanation of free-writing see Peter Elbow, *Writing without Teachers* (London: Oxford Univ. Press, 1973).

18. Britton et al., 90.

Combined Reading-Writing Instruction Using Technical and Scientific Texts

Anne Eisenberg
Polytechnic Institute of New York

The term "math anxiety" became popular a decade ago to describe the fear and urge to avoid that people—particularly young women—feel in regard to mathematics. The subsequent analysis of this anxiety has led to many innovative programs designed to overcome the difficulties both young and older learners have understanding the introductory principles of mathematics.

I would like to propose a different term—science anxiety—to a different audience: not students, but teachers of reading and writing who instruct engineering and technical students, but who are uncomfortable using engineering subject content, preferring instead the more familiar materials of the social sciences or literature. There are excellent reasons for this discomfort: many teachers feel intellectually dishonest using materials they understand either incompletely, or at least less fully than do some of their students.

But such materials have significant teaching potential. If their reading or writing skills are weak, students who have immersed themselves in mechanical systems, circuits, or programming can use that knowledge, in the form Bruner calls their "coding systems," to help them understand and interpret technical materials when they are used as the basis for reading/writing improvement. It is this understanding that reading and writing teachers versed in psycholinguistic theory want to draw on; ironically, it is their own lack of such understanding that causes them to hesitate. In this article I will discuss some of the compelling pedagogical reasons to use science content as the basis for combined reading/writing instruction for engineering and engineering technology students, and some of the ways teachers weak in science or engineering might go about doing this confidently and without fearing that they are doing an intellectually dishonest job.

The Skills Model and the Psycholinguistic Challenge to the Skills Model

How should science content be used in the reading/writing class-room? It's essential to understand that science should *not* be the new bottle into which one pours the old wine of "skills lessons." That is, the teacher about to embark on integrating science content into a reading/writing classroom should cast a cold eye on the pervasive skills model, for its use may very well undercut all one wishes to accomplish with the use of science content.

The skills system, which has its antecedents in the work of William S. Gray, posits specific skills or abilities associated with various levels of reading and suggests that the primary job of the reading teacher is to teach the skills associated with these levels.[1] Throughout the United States, schools and community colleges embraced this model, resulting in an underemphasis on the role of prior knowledge and experience stated broadly by such cognitive psychologists, composition theorists, and reading researchers as Jerome Bruner, James Britton, K. Goodman, Frank Smith, and R. W. Shuy.[2]

Despite conflicting findings on the effectiveness of instruction organized by skills, between 1940 and 1970 there was no challenge to the skills model, which "held sway at all levels of school reading in the United States."[3] During the past decade, however, the skills model has been subject to increasingly sharp criticism from theorists who say that it is "a wrong model [which has led to] the wrong kinds of instruction."[4] R. E. Shafer, who characterizes secondary reading instruction as a plethora of kits, study guides, skill builders, and reading machines, puts the issue sharply:

> In spite of three decades of development, including revision of certification requirements, extensive preparation of teachers in college and inservice programs, and a plethora of instructional materials on the market, these programs do not seem to be ful-filling their mission. Could it be that the skills model, the founda-tion for the programs themselves, has feet of clay?[5]

Fortunately, during the past fifteen years ideas from the fields of psycholinguistics, linguistics, and cognitive psychology have led to a fundamental questioning of the skills model and its application in reading programs. This has led, in turn, to a conflict between those who see reading as a process of skills that can be consciously learned, and those who see reading as an aspect of general learning behavior that shares basic rules of hypothesis testing and confirmation and, as such, is firmly rooted in one's past experience. These ideas, in turn, have led to a reevaluation of the sorts of materials that might be employed in the teaching of reading.

It is important to examine the ideas of Smith, Goodman, Brown, Shuy, Britton, and Bruner, because their thinking provides an alternative to the skills model and a way, therefore, for the reading/writing teacher to use technical and scientific materials to extend rather than limit student abilities.

Psycholinguistic Models

Frank Smith equates reading with comprehension and says that comprehension and learning are basically inseparable: they both involve relating new experience to what is already known. Smith argues, "It is what we know that makes our experiences meaningful"; however, he does not postulate a new or special ability for comprehending language: "The process by which we make sense of the world in general—relating the unfamiliar to the already known—is all we need to make sense of language as well."[6] Smith defines the fluent reader as one who predicts meaning and samples the surface structure of a text to eliminate uncertainty. Readers predict what a writer is about to say because they have the ability to make such predictions generally, and because they have the necessary prior linguistic knowledge of how speakers and writers are likely to express their intentions in surface structure. The reader selects among alternatives by sampling, looking for limited "matches" or correspondences with their expectations, rather than by decoding surface structure exhaustively.

Kenneth Goodman's model of the fluent reading process shares much with Smith's. Like Smith's, Goodman's model is psycholinguistic. And it shares with Smith's model emphasis on (1) the significance of comprehension; (2) the fact that the reading process cannot be broken up into subskills to be taught, nor can it be subdivided into categories like code-breaking without making qualitative changes in the process; and (3) the contention that reading instruction should be carried out with text materials using natural, meaningful language within the conceptual grasp of learners.

Linguistic Models

The importance of the reader's prior knowledge and experience, including oral language experience, is also supported by literature from the field of linguistics suggesting that pragmatic and semantic components play a crucial part in the fluent reading process.

In his foreword to *Linguistic Theory: What Can It Say About Reading?* (1977), E. Brown points out that "the potential set of inferences from linguistics to the applied problems of reading must be explicitly delineated and argued; they are not necessarily straightforward or immediately apparent." There is a danger of "facile generalizations from the theoretical descriptive science of linguistics to the culture-specific task of reading."[7] Yet there are important reasons for looking at linguistics and its relation to the reading process.

Brown points out that there has been a shift of emphasis in linguistic studies away from syntactic issues confined to the sentence and toward an elaboration of extrasentential considerations such as discourse constraints, context, intentionality, and reference:

> A number of the more prominent cognitive models of reading (such as the works of Kenneth Goodman and Frank Smith) have emphasized the role of semantic expectations in reading comprehension to such an extent that one can predict a relatively easy accommodation of these models to the new linguistic formulations. . . . This type of vital interaction of semantic-contextual theory with problems in reading may be especially useful in helping us think about teaching strategies for the development of reading comprehension in the middle grades.[8]

R. W. Shuy, in discussing the relationship of reading to linguistics, points out that many aspects of linguistics besides phonology and grammar can be brought to bear on the act of reading: "Teaching programs [continue] to focus on onset skill development at stages in which more appropriate strategies would involve larger and larger chunking of the language accesses." He recommends programs to help develop middle-level reading skills that make use of the reader's pragmatic knowledge. By pragmatics, Shuy means "the broader role of context as it is related to the benefits and attitudes of the participants in a communication event."[9] P. Griffin defines pragmatics as "facts existing independent of language structure per se, but facts that are needed to encode and interpret language on any occasion for its use."[10]

James Britton is also concerned with the relationship of prior experience to language learning. He equates the word "learning" with learning from experience. As the scientist formulates hypotheses, puts them to the test, and reframes them, so, according to Britton, does a person engage in language behavior, "with the aid of language in the light of further experience in order that our predictions may be better."[11] He concludes that the new can be incorporated only at points where it relates to what is already in a person's world-representation, and that language is the key organizing principle in constructing each person's world-representation.

What types of materials and teaching strategies are suggested by Goodman and Smith's psycholinguistic models, by Shuy and Griffin's contextual theories, by Britton's general language theory? Clearly their ideas sharply oppose those underlying the skills model, and suggest instead another direction for classroom instructors. These theories suggest the use of materials that are not fragmented, that make available all the reading cues—graphonic, syntactic, semantic—simultaneously, and that draw on the prior knowledge, experience, and interest of the reader. Students' familiarity with and interest in the content would allow them more readily to make use of their general linguistic competence.

In the Classroom

Let us say, then, that you have decided to use science content in your classroom and, further, that you choose not to present it as a series of fragmented "skills"—such as "reading for inference" or "reading for supporting details"—but instead to use science materials as the basis for developing reading and writing skills in the holistic way presented by Smith.

If your background is in the liberal arts, you may say, "Yes, I agree the skills model is reductive. But I still can't deal with a second-year physics text." The answer to this is that second-year physics texts are not the only source of materials. Consider, instead, a range of materials that may be approached by historical period, by rhetorical model, or by theme. That is, there are many materials you might legitimately organize and then analyze in terms of the way they are written, the time at which they were written, and their central arguments. Following are some examples of ways you might go about integrating science content in your reading/writing classroom.

By Historical Period

Are you interested in teaching your students how to read and write instructions? Consider a historical approach, in which you begin with instructions written in an ancient Egyptian surgery and end with instructions for how to operate a word-processing program. Or the students might begin with Anaxagoras or one of the works attributed to Hippocrates; among the more famous of the latter, for those instructors who are interested, are "A Case with Cheyne-Stokes Breathing" and "A Case of Remittent Fever." The class might read the instructions and then discuss their content and the author's way of presenting the material. In the same way, students might look at Roman instructions for road building to see how the instructions are written and how the author manages to make the material clear to the user, and then at some modern instructions—both ones that are written well and ones that are written poorly. Students could write instructions for tasks with which they are familiar, such as changing a tire, operating a word-processing program, or changing a printer ribbon, incorporating what they have discovered. None of these assignments is "too technical" for the liberal arts–trained instructor, yet they will have valid technical content for the student. At the same time, they are a way to develop reading and writing using materials that have built-in interest to the technical student.

There are other historical periods to consider, if one's tastes do not extend to Greek or Egyptian surgeries. From the Middle Ages there is fascinating source material, including "Granted That the Stars are Living Beings, On What Food Do They Live?" (from *Quaestiones Naturales* by Adelard of Bath) and "Of the Reasons Why Birds Migrate" by Frederick II, in *The Art of Falconry*. The scientific revolution provides an unparalleled source of clearly written, accessible materials. Copernicus' "A Theory That the Earth Moves around the Sun" is a stimulating and elegantly written discussion (from *Concerning the Revolutions of Heavenly Bodies*), as is Galileo's "Proof That the Earth Moves" from *The Sidereal Messenger*. Bacon's "The Methods of Acquiring Knowledge" is appropriate, as are Newton's "On Scientific Method," "On Experimental Method," and "On Hypotheses." Those using journals in class may be interested in excerpts from his "Accomplishments of the Plague Year." Vesalius' preface to his book on the mechanism of the human body as well as his "Examination of the Uses of the Veins and Arteries" is also interesting, and Leeuwenhoek's blunt, fascinating letters are outstanding, especially his landmark "Observations Concerning Little Animals" and "Though My Teeth Are Kept Usually Very Clean."

By Rhetorical Model

Let us say you are interested in developing your students' abilities to read/write science using the genre of the laboratory notebook. Here is an area accessible both to the liberal arts–trained teacher and to the technical student. Further, it offers many lively opportunities for classroom instruction.

One might start with the story of Le Monnier, the eighteenth-century astronomer, who observed Uranus twelve times, but decided that it was a fixed star, not a planet. The great discovery fell instead to Herschel, who identified Uranus correctly in 1781. Historians have since decided Le Monnier's mistake was due at least in part to his habit of writing measurements on scraps of paper—including a paper bag originally containing hair powder.

There are other readable, dramatic examples of record keeping in science, examples that the students could read and then relate to the laboratory notebooks and records that they are learning to maintain in their technical classes. For example, one might have them read the documents in the case of Daniel Drawbaugh *v.* Alexander Graham Bell. Bell filed a patent application for the telephone in 1875; Drawbaugh sued, claiming the invention for his own and producing witnesses who testified he had discussed a crude telephone with them. But this personal testimony did not convince the Supreme Court, which rejected Drawbaugh's claims largely on the basis of his inability to produce a single properly dated piece of paper describing the invention.

A third, contemporary instance of the importance of laboratory notebooks is provided by the case of Gordon Gould, who as a young physicist filed an application for a basic laser patent in 1959. Gould failed to get the patent, which was awarded instead, in 1960, to Charles Townes and Arthur Schawlow. Gould went to court, claiming he was the true inventor, and basing his challenge in part on his research notebook, which showed, among other items, a sketch, a statement of the main idea, and a derivation of the acronym LASER—Light Amplification by Stimulated Emission of Radiation. In October 1977, after a series of litigated oppositions, Gould was granted a patent for optically pumped laser amplifiers, the world market for which has been estimated at between 100 million and 200 million dollars. When one looks at the history of science, one grows increasingly respectful of the importance of journals—and not only for their potential legal significance but particularly for the ways they help the writer understand the ramifications of an insight.

More difficult than notebooks, if one is shopping for a rhetorical format, are scientific articles, for many are addressed by definition to specialists within a field, rather than to generalists, and consequently are difficult for both students and teachers to penetrate. There are, however, many scholarly articles that are accessible. Among them are the writings of Linnaeus and of Edward Jenner, in particular "An Inquiry in the Causes and Effects of the Variolae Vaccinae, Known by the Name of the Cow-Pox." In microbiology, readable papers exist by Robert Kock ("The Etiology of Tuberculosis"), Louis Pasteur ("A Method by Which the Development of Rabies after a Bite May Be Prevented"), Joseph Lister ("On the Antiseptic Principle in the Practice of Surgery"), Ronald Ross ("On Some Peculiar Pigmented Cells Found in Two Mosquitos Fed on Malarial Bloom"), and Gregor Mendel ("Experiments in

Plant Hybridization"). Other accessible classics include excerpts from Charles Darwin's *On the Origin of Species,* from Hugo DeVries's *The Mutation Theory,* and from Claude Bernard's *Introduction to the Study of Experimental Medicine.*

Here is one final example combining historical documents with a focus on rhetorical model. Let us say in this case that you would like your students to be able to read and write clear abstracts. This is a valuable ability for a technical student, one he or she can practice in laboratory reports and term reports while still in school. You could teach this ability using a combination of historical documents and contemporary ones. For instance, you might start with a landmark paper such as Joseph Lister's "The Antiseptic Principle in the Practice of Surgery," in which he discusses the metamorphosis of the Glasgow Infirmary during the nine months he employed carbolic acid to treat fractures and wounds. The paper is divided into the traditional sections of introduction, procedure, results, conclusion, and implications. The instructor might start by having the class read the paper at home, follow that with a classroom discussion, and then assign the writing of an abstract. Afterwards, the class could practice abstracting contemporary papers, as well as one another's term papers. Students who have already tried their hand at writing abstracts in their lab reports will appreciate the challenge to state their findings clearly and directly.

By Theme

There are many promising ways of organizing readings by theme. Among those that suggest themselves are the following: (1) A unit on "The Context of Discovery." Scientists write vivid, often highly readable accounts of the moment at which their discoveries are revealed to them. Einstein sat on a trolley car conducting *gedanken* experiments; Friedrich Kekulé stared into the fire and saw a vision of linked snakes. Other writers who discuss this moment include Darwin, Poincaré, Kepler, William James, Marie Curie, and James Watson. (2) A unit on "Science as Debate." When Koch stood before the Physiological Society of Berlin and read his paper on the etiology of tuberculosis, the august body rose as a group to applaud him. But that doesn't always happen: the announcement of a new discovery is as likely to be greeted with brickbats as with applause. The history of science is the history of conflict, of new ideas and the heated arguments they spark. These arguments rage from the letters columns of the professional journals to public debates, in the thrust and counterthrust of papers and rebuttals. Several excellent topics include the issue of spontaneous generation (Pasteur et al.) and the topic of astro-archeology (Hawkins et al.). (3) A unit on the patent. Samuel Hopkins received the first patent in 1790. Since then, business has been brisk. Among the more lively documents are Mark Twain on suspenders, Lillian Russell on dresser trunks, and Mary Phelps Jacob on brassieres.

Conclusion

There is a world of documents in science and engineering available to the nonscientist enterprising enough to teach reading/writing. Such teaching has a satisfying reward: students arrive at the awareness that reading and writing are often overlooked but vital activities in science. One of the best services we can do for technical and scientific students is to train them in these abilities.

Notes

1. W. S. Gray, "The Major Aspects of Reading," in *The Sequential Development of Reading Abilities,* ed. H. M. Robinson, Supplementary Educational Monographs no. 90 (Chicago: Univ. of Chicago Press, 1960).

2. J. S. Bruner, "Going Beyond the Information Given," in *Contemporary Approaches to Cognition: A Symposium Held at the University of Colorado* (Cambridge, Mass.: Harvard Univ. Press, 1957); J. Britton, *Language and Learning* (Harmondsworth, England: Penguin, 1970); K. Goodman, "Psycholinguistic Universals in the Reading Process," *Journal of Typographic Research* 4 (1970): 103–10; F. Smith, *Comprehension and Learning* (New York: Holt, 1975); and R. W. Shuy, ed., *Linguistic Theory: What Can It Say About Reading?* (Newark, Del.: International Reading Association, 1977).

3. R. E. Shafer, "Will Psycholinguistics Change Reading in Secondary Schools?" *Journal of Reading* 21 (1978): 305.

4. C. R. Cooper and A. R. Petrosky, "A Psycholinguistic View of the Fluent Reading Process," *Journal of Reading* 20 (1976): 184–206.

5. Shafer, 310.

6. Smith, 10 and 92.

7. E. Brown, *Linguistic Theory: What Can It Say About Reading?* ed. R. Shuy (Newark, Del.: International Reading Association, 1977), iv.

8. Ibid., vii.

9. Shuy, iv, vii.

10. P. Griffin, "Reading and Pragmatics: Symbiosis," in Shuy, *Linguistic Theory,* 124–25.

11. Britton, 31.

IV Using Literature and Teaching Literacy

Integrating the Acts of Reading and Writing about Literature: A Sequence of Assignments Based on James Joyce's "Counterparts"

Joseph J. Comprone
University of Louisville

The Critical Background

Even casual readers of Joyce know something about his epiphanies. For Joyce, writing was akin to religious experience. Certainly it demanded a commitment from the writer perhaps equaled in the history of literacy only by early Christian and Gnostic writers, who used the exegetical method not only to describe sacred documents but to inform the process of their writing. Much has been made of the sudden though—once recognized—cumulative discovery of meaning in Joyce's major characters, whether in the more mimetic stories of *The Dead* or the more directly symbolic novels. Initiated readers, of course, shared in the epiphanies of characters: Stephen's renunciation of religion and embracing of art becomes the reader's generalizations on art, religion, and their frictions in the twentieth century; Leopold's gradual objectification of his understanding of Molly, and of what Molly is to him, gives significant symbolic meaning to Molly's interior monologue in the final section of *Ulysses*. This realization, in turn, allows readers to make similar generalizations on passion and love in the twentieth century, and through all time.

These standard critical responses give readers objective guides to their own individual responses to Joyce's texts. They provide a cultural framework within which the act of reading can effectively take place. There is, however, something missing in all this critical give-and-take on any major author, including Joyce. This missing element is best suggested by this question: Where is the reader and how does he or she function within this objectified critical context? More specifically, how are the reader's creative responses assimilated into this more abstract context without losing their essential identity? The implications of this question become far more complex when we consider, as current reader-response theory suggests, what happens *during* the reading of a particular literary work. Are Joyce's epiphanies, as they occur in a text and are explained in objective terms by critics, identical for readers and critics? In other words, is the process through which we, as readers, discover the meaning of a Joycean epiphany the same as the product of textual analysis that is embodied in the work of a critic? The acts of reading and criticism, recent literary theory suggests, are different in kind. Criticism, or interpretation, simply put, is a process of reconstruction, drawing from textual cues, the shared conventions and backgrounds of readers, and structural ways of knowing. Reading, drawing from these same general areas (the text, conventions and shared skills, and common ways of knowing), is primarily a process of deconstruction. The processes share a number of features, but the role and perspective of the critic is essentially different from the role and perspective of the reader. A tendency to ignore this basic fact has led a good deal of recent literary theory and practice astray, a tendency perhaps most apparent in recent critical arguments concerning the function of objective and subjective response during and after reading. David Bleich convincingly argues the prior nature of the affective, the fact—corroborated by Louise Rosenblatt in her transactional theory—that readers *begin* to identify with a text primarily through emotional and individual psychological response, by tying what they feel to what they know about reading literature in general and to their ability to contextualize and decode the symbols in the text.[1] The process of subjective response merges with the process of experiencing a literary text. Each is autonomous and interdependent. Bleich goes on to argue that reading is essentially a way of knowing, that what is known and how it is to be known is always defined by the knower, never by the known, and that teachers and critics ought to shift attention from what Rosenblatt calls the textual "blueprint" to the kinds of responses a reader is encouraged to synthesize while reading.[2] Searching out the subjective sources of felt response and collectively sharing those sources with others should, Bleich argues, clarify and define the acts of reading and negotiating meaning.

It was important for Bleich to establish the place of subjective response in the act of reading.[3] But it is important now, with recent reader-response theory in mind, to point out that any complete dichotomy between subjective and objective is a false one because it separates and atomizes what, during reading, is an interdependent, holistic process. In fact, this dichotomy appears only during textual reconstruction, as the reader takes on the role of critic, relating what E. D. Hirsch calls the "meaning" of a literary work to its "significance," which Hirsch defines as the broader social/cultural importance we give the self-contained meaning of a literary reading experience.[4] Readers do become critics, but they function first as readers experiencing a text or their criticism rests on sand.

Rather than constructing meaning out of individually perceived and separately realized subjective and objective responses, experienced readers combine the two. They construct from the material of feeling and knowledge the organism of meaning, which grows into existence organically, much in the way that eighteenth- and nineteenth-century romantic-expressive critics, epitomized by Coleridge, described when they used the plant rather than Newton's mechanistic universe as the dominant metaphor when defining a literary work.[5]

Perhaps a construct from Jean Piaget will help clarify this interdependent process. In the process of growing and learning, Piaget suggests, people "assimilate" information from their world, through their senses. The process of assimilation itself is made, of course, even more complex by the fact that remembered information from previously assimilated experiences—from reading, observation, various relations with the world—interacts with current information. Piaget also suggests that people "accommodate" information that is received through the senses to their inner frames of experience and learning. Their picture of the world, constructed from past assimilations of sensory experience, becomes itself an agent, a filter, a framework for new information. This intricate synthesis of assimilation and accommodation allows the organism to remain somewhat stable and balanced without closing it off to the constant flow of new information.[6]

The Pedagogical Foreground

The type of literary theory I have been discussing, currently termed reader-response criticism, has much to offer teachers who wish effectively to combine reading and writing about literature in either composition or literature classrooms. The sequence of writing exercises that follows encourages students to use writing to objectify and integrate their objective and subjective responses to a complex text— James Joyce's short story "Counterparts." This description begins at its end, with a final writing exercise in which students are asked to discuss the story's significance within a defined rhetorical context, and proceeds from this final assignment to a description and analysis of a series of assignments that gradually lead the student to the point at which the final assignment becomes a natural culmination of a complex writing process. The complete assignment sequence encourages students to integrate subjective and objective response in a natural learning process in which the kind of epiphany many critics describe when they interpret Joyce exists in the participating reader—not in the text or in some highly abstract professional reading of the poem. Certainly there are elements of traditional reaction to the story contained in almost every student's response to the final assignment, but these traditional reactions are part of, not *the* dominating influence on, the overall student response.[7]

Application of the learning theory that I describe here must be grounded in a particular situation if we are to get any practical results from it. Let us hypothesize a college reader of "Counterparts" to begin establishing this situation. In developing this hypothetical student reader, I will be following the lead of Wolfgang Iser, who assumes an "implied" reader for every literary work. This implied reader is created by a synthesis of textual networks of traditional cues to meaning (imagery, point of view, style, for example), the reader's tacit knowledge of these literary conventions, and the shared knowledge—in writer and reader—of the language itself.[8]

Our implied reader is capable, and has read some serious and a good deal of popular literature. She has no trouble decoding; she reads rapidly enough to process complex systems of information and slowly enough to be affected by style, imagery—all those cues inherent in literary texts that alert readers to shifts in perspective on meaning. Ideally, she is not reluctant to bring her feelings and memories as well as her opinions and values to a literary text, but she will, because this is an English class, strive to produce what, in traditional contexts, we might call an "objective" final interpretation of "Counterparts." She is, in other words, a fluent but not terribly experienced reader; she has read for pleasure *or* she has read for knowledge. She has not often, however, experienced the kind of reading that synthesizes these two aims. She is not Iser's ideal reader, ready to participate fully in the story while she integrates the experience of reading with the rest of her knowledge, to use the understanding of the whole experience of reading "Counterparts" as a symbol for a new or revised social or cultural value. Nor, on the other hand, is she a reluctant reader, a reader of informational prose alone, or a disabled reader, restricted to newspaper prose.

What will our student be *able* to do with "Counterparts"? Certainly she will effectively process the story's surface structure—its basically chronological narrative, the third-person-limited point of view, and the protagonist's center of consciousness, although she may be neither able nor willing to name those literary devices as she reads. Her reading of literature, her hearing of stories as a child, her experience with well-told gossip, as James Britton suggests, would have prepared her to link up with these nonvisual literary cues, to use them in marking her reading trail.[9] Her experience in reading literature in English classes will have reinforced these natural literary experiences. By the end of her first reading, she will have shared a formed experience; she will know, however subconsciously, that the meaning of this story focuses on Farrington. She will most likely expect to learn something about human character in general from Joyce's treatment of Farrington, but this aim will remain subordinate to her experience of the character himself, at least during her first reading of the story.

What else will she be able to do? Certainly, she will be able to link particular subjective responses with her experience of the story. Despite her objective identification with Farrington because he is the story's center of consciousness, our student would most likely feel some combination of negative emotions (anger, frustration, irritation) in response to Farrington's prevarication and implied laziness, even early in the story. She may not, as Bleich suggests, give much play to these affective responses because she is reading this story in an English class, where she assumes objectivity reigns; but they are there nonetheless, and they may, early in her reading, actually dominate her responses to the story. And—later in her reading, when she may think that objective, nonvisual understanding is predominant— these subjective responses are still there, cumulatively affecting her reaction to Farrington. Kenneth Burke would argue, on this issue of subconscious subjective response, that our reader was providing a perfect example of literary identification, with part of herself—in this case the objective—sharing Farrington's experience on the surface level, while another part of herself—in this case the subjective—experiences a negative tension and a sense of being different from Farrington.[10] At the close of her reading, when Farrington beats his son simply because he is frustrated with his own life, this gradually developing stream of negative subjective responses may, and I would argue *should,* become the climactic point in our student's reading experience, a point where her developing subjective and objective responses—her emotional reaction against what he does—result in her taking on a new and more abstract perspective on the meaning of the story.

It is at this point that, as teachers, we might ask ourselves what this student, fluent as she is, might still need to learn about reading. What she needs, I would argue, is the ability to make this pivotal shift in perspective, to accomplish what Iser and other reader-response critics point to as essential to the reading of all serious literature—the synthesizing of new meaning out of the simpler subjective and objective

patterns of meaning that have been evolving from the reading experience so far. Our implied reader, in other words, learns how to balance
two ongoing processes at once: the one evolving from her developing
stream of subjective responses, cumulatively organizing themselves
into patterns; the other developing from her growing awareness of
textual patterns that have been inherited from the literary tradition and
employed by Joyce in conscious reaction to this tradition.

What our hypothetical student-reader needs most is a teacher who
can use textual patterns and literary conventions to discover textual
focal points. These are points in the text where a critic-teacher, conscious of how literary reading works, can assume an important friction
between the developing patterns of the story, the reader's subjective
responses, and the tacit knowledge of literary convention both in the
reader and, presumably, the author. These focal points can be ideal
opportunities for using writing to clarify the reading process, to bring
into objective perspective the interworkings of the mind.

Establishing the existence of focal points within the phenomeno-
logical process of reading, however, does not necessarily imply that
only the teacher knows where meaning exists in a complex text. It
simply means that a teacher, experienced and well-informed in reading
literature, can know where meaning is likely to occur in the process of
reading. Teachers may not know all focal points, nor do they always
know the best. But they can make the educated guesses that will most
often produce an occasion where writing will help a student reconcile
or work out a complex problem in defining meaning. In planning a
sequence of writing exercises that will effectively prepare a student for
discovering meaning in the process of reading, the teacher is often
working deductively, beginning by devising a final assignment and
then building exercises that help the student work toward that assignment by focusing on textual focal points. Writing can be an immense
help as students respond to these important textual places.[11]

A Sequence of Illustrative Assignments

This process might begin with the teacher directing the student reader
to the final paragraphs of "Counterparts." The teacher might ask the
student to go back over the reading experience up to this point in
the text in order to synthesize subjective and objective responses.
The following assignment, then, might serve as a final exercise on
"Counterparts":

> Imagine yourself a social worker who has been assigned to the
> Farrington family. You have just heard the child, Tom, describe the

> final scene in the story, in which Mr. Farrington beats his son for
> letting the fire go out. The family's fate has recently altered for the
> worse: Farrington has lost his job; state aid and charity have not
> been enough to pay debts or buy necessities; and Mr. Farrington
> drinks incessantly, sometimes abuses his wife and children, and
> refuses to search for or take any job that is "below his station."
> Write a case report to your superintendent in which you use an
> analysis of Mr. Farrington's character to explain the causes of the
> family's reduced state, considering both facts about Mr. Farrington
> from the story and your own feelings about him. You are writing
> the report because you hope to convince your superintendent that
> something must be done to have Mr. Farrington treated for his
> psychological and physical problems. Only then, you feel, will the
> family's problems be solved.

This assignment would be an effective one to place at the end of our student's reading experience because it functions at a transitional point between the meaning and significance levels of the reader's apprehension of the story. It demands a generalization from the student that draws together several complex perspectives on Farrington's character. That generalization, because it remains within the context of the reading experience that has been generated by the text and the student's responses to it, organizes the meaning of the story for this student. Yet the assignment also brings the student to the threshold of a statement of significance because it contains a rhetorical context—the social worker reporting to a superintendent on the Farrington family—that will encourage the student to apply the generalization of meaning (an overview of Farrington's character) to a general social and moral issue—the effects of behavior such as Farrington's on other people, particularly his family. In responding to those effects in this particular story, our student will have at least begun to understand Farrington's behavior and its effects as a somewhat typical pattern of social conduct. She will have brought the meaning of this particular story into a broader, more abstract social context.

Looking back, then, on her reading experience, our student will need to integrate, simultaneously and organically, subjective and objective responses; she will need to reconstruct what has been assimilated and accommodated during reading, as one perspective on Farrington is gradually synthesized with another. To accomplish this reconstruction, she will need to be able to integrate objective and subjective responses to Joyce's manipulation of point of view.

As a reader, she will probably first experience Farrington's point of view with relatively little interference by reactions from outside the character's experience. Indeed, most of us, as readers, feel along with Farrington, at first. We are with him as he runs off to the tavern for a drink during working hours; we are with him as he procrastinates on the job and fails to finish his copying by the end of the working day; and certainly we are with him when he feels satisfaction with his verbal retort to Mr. Alleyne, in front of the office staff and Miss Delacour, at the end of the day.

During this early stage of response, however, our student's emotions, although subordinate to her identification with Farrington's point of view, might create an underlying stream of negative subjective reactions to Farrington's behavior and thought. This tension between objective response to point of view and subjective reaction to Farrington's character might then culminate in a reversal in perspective on Farrington during the reading of the second half of the story. This reversal would be gradual; it occurs because our reader has been decentering, distancing herself from the story's point of view. This distancing occurs because she has come to experience contrasts between Farrington and a series of other characters, in a series of well-defined scenes. She comes, in other words, to see Farrington as others see him—both others in the story and others outside the story.

First, she might notice Farrington's somewhat pathetic need to get reinforcement from his drinking buddies by retelling his put-down of Mr. Alleyne. Then, she experiences Mr. Farrington's equally pathetic responses to the young woman from the Tivoli, and his inability to make any contact with her, which in turn might come to suggest sexual inadequacy and frustration in Mr. Farrington. Finally, our reader experiences Farrington's humiliation in the arm-wrestling match with Weathers, and sees—along with O'Halloran—that Farrington's rage is a product of his own inadequacy and frustration, not of the injustices of the world and its treatment of him, as he might wish others to believe.

While reading the second half of "Counterparts," our reader's subjective response might well become dominant. Her frustration and anger with Farrington would increase, and the fact that she must continue to experience the story primarily through Farrington's eyes simply reinforces her negative reactions to him. This sequence of contrasts in the second half of the story, which reverses the discovery process that was established by structural contrasts in the first part of the story, results in a tension within our reader that is resolved and synthesized in the final scene. This resolution might begin when our reader notices the facts of Farrington's domestic life. Early in the second half of the story, in an understated and subordinated clause, she learns that Farrington is married. Still later in the story she discovers that Farrington has five children. These seemingly small pieces of information prepare our reader for the final scene by alerting her to the fact that other people are relying on Farrington, that his behavior does not affect only himself, that his egocentrism might well have caused a great deal of suffering for his family. This, in turn, might cause a retracing on our reader's part, in which she goes back over Farrington's earlier actions and reconstructs a new and more completely negative interpretation of his character. At this point she will be ready to do the final assignment described above, because she will have reached a point at which her reaction to Farrington merges with more abstract social values.

The Early Stages of Response

The questions I wish to consider at this point return us to our consideration of teaching reading and writing. What kinds of earlier writing exercises would best prepare our implied student reader for the challenge of this final assignment? More specifically, where might our implied reader focus her attention as she assimilates objective and subjective reactions to Farrington's character? These pedagogical questions lead me to a consideration of the function of expressive writing in the process of writing about a literary work. My goal here is to help the student become conscious of the reasons behind her rejection of Farrington.

James Kinneavy and James Britton have contributed most to our understanding of the purpose and function of expressive writing. Britton explains how expressive discourse fits into a central position in all language learning.[12] Children, at very early ages, transform egocentric and social speech, speech for oneself and speech for others, into what Lev Vygotsky—the Russian psychologist—first called "inner speech." Inner speech, Britton contends, then develops gradually into expressive discourse, which then functions as the base upon which transactional discourse (writing to get something done in the world of practical affairs) and poetic discourse (literature and any language that is used for its own sake) develop. From my perspective in this paper, expressive discourse *is* the language of learning. It is thought becoming meaning.[13]

Kinneavy adds philosophical resonance to Britton's developmental definition of expressive discourse by defining expressive discourse as writing or language in which the self is primary audience, and he draws on existential philosophers and phenomenologists (Sartre, Merleau-Ponty, Husserl, Gusdorf) to explain the primarily teleological nature of all expressive discourse.[14] Self-development according to tentatively understood goals is the aim of expressive discourse. Being works into becoming and takes on the structures and forms that are appropriate to the object of thought as it is being discovered. Peter Elbow has described this process, when it is applied to composing, as the writer's "emerging center of gravity."[15] This center of gravity takes shape as the writer writes; Mina Shaughnessy has called it the record of an idea developing.[16]

Expressive writing, then, can become our student's means of making discoveries as she reads, and—carefully assigned—expressive exercises can give teachers control over the student's writing process without establishing a teacher-dominated classroom. How might a teacher use expressive writing to begin and to develop our student's reconstruction of the experience of reading "Counterparts"? She might be asked to take on perspectives during her earlier responses to the story that will help her combine subjective and objective responses. She might be asked, for example, to list places in the story where she noticed what she felt were surprising pieces of factual information. This question might elicit references to the facts that Farrington was married and had five children. This objective reference might then become a way to get our reader to specify her subjective reactions to Farrington at this point in the reading experience. What effects did these textual facts have on her evolving sense of Farrington's character? Following a recursive pattern, our student's subjective reactions to Farrington might then become the basis of an objective, physical description of two or three people our student had known who evoked emotional responses similar to the ones evoked by Farrington. These objective descriptions might then become the basis of the student's recording, in an interior monologue, her emotional reaction to Farrington's beating of his son in the story's final scene.

Here is a sample list of exercises that would specify these general strategies:

1. Describe, in detail, your emotional response to the narrator's initial description of Mr. Farrington. Does he remind you of someone you once met, knew, or read about in literature? Do you like him, dislike him, feel repulsion or attraction? Write this description rapidly, without stopping.

2. Go back over the first three or four pages of the story and find objective reasons for your feeling toward Mr. Farrington. If the reasons or details that you find do not support your initial feelings, then you should revise your emotional response to Mr. Farrington.

3. Tell, in a brief paper, what you think the story's narrator thinks of Mr. Farrington. Be objectively analytical. Make a list of the evidence in the story that you believe illustrates the narrator's attitude toward Farrington. Does the narrator seem distant from Farrington; does he ever seem to treat him humorously? Is the

> narrator intimately involved in Farrington's situation? Does the
> narrator seem to feel the same way toward Mr. Alleyne as
> Farrington does?
>
> 4. Write a brief response to Farrington's character from the point
>   of view of the narrator. Use the first person. Imagine the
>   narrator of the story talking to you directly about Mr. Farrington,
>   explaining what he thinks of him.

These four expressive exercises, during which the student tries out
various subjective and objective perspectives on Farrington, help students revise and shape their responses to the story. They can then
conclude this first stage of reshaping the story's developing meaning by
doing a transactional exercise in which they address a small group of
peers. In contrast to the expressive writing they have done up to this
point, transactional writing puts the results of this self-discovery process in front of other readers of the story for reaction. Here is a sample
of a transactional exercise that might be used at this point in the
student's reading process.

> Go back over your expressive responses to Farrington. Write a
> paragraph in which you describe what you believe the assumed
> author is saying about Mr. Farrington. Then write several paragraphs
> in which you explain the reasons behind the assumed author's
> purpose in presenting Farrington as he does. Work in workshop
> groups, combining different interpretations of the assumed author's
> purpose into more complex ones.

Students might go on at this point to produce dialogues that represent their interactions with each other concerning this exercise. Whatever students do at this point should help them translate their personal,
expressive responses to the first four exercises into more publicly
negotiated statements of meaning. Listening to and talking with others—
always pointing to the transactional writing in hand—helps students
project their construction of meaning statements into a public context without ignoring or destroying their initial expressive responses.
Through all this, of course, the teacher also benefits by having a written
record of the personal and collective responses of students' reading
experiences up to this point in the story. This record, read and
analyzed, can become an important means of developing effective final
assignments and evaluation guidelines.

The next or middle section of "Counterparts" brings readers closer
to Mr. Farrington. We, as readers, might identify with him as he thinks
about his planned evening's carousing and is then confronted by Mr.
Alleyne because he has not finished his copywork. On a more objective
level, experienced readers recognize Joyce's manipulations of narrative
structure here. Despite our distaste for a good deal of Farrington's

thought and action up to this point, however, we must feel with Farrington and come to know his frustrated rage and his hatred of Mr. Alleyne if we are to see both the positive and negative aspects of his character. We, in other words, must see his side of the story as well. We probably identify with Farrington because Mr. Alleyne is a pompous stuffed armchair, a "manikin" displaying the trappings of bureaucracy.

Experienced readers also, however, keep in their minds as they read the more objective and distant narrative perspective on Mr. Farrington that was established in the first section of the story. As they reread this second section students might have a better chance of developing this more complex response after they have written this exercise:

> Write for reading to the rest of the class a brief paper in which you argue that Mr. Farrington was justified in not finishing his work and in looking forward to a night on the town. Present what you believe would be Farrington's ideas.

After reading aloud and discussing these writings with the rest of the class, students should review their writing in response to the first part of the story as preparation for writing a third-person character-sketch of Mr. Farrington. This sketch should expand upon a significant action represented in the story. Students may embellish the action with new details, but they should strive to capture what they believe to be the essential nature of Mr. Farrington's character as they describe the action.

Summary of the Learning Theory Informing This Sequence of Assignments

This sequence of written responses fulfills the learning function embodied in all expressive discourse. Students shape their felt and thought responses to the experience represented in the text; in the process, they experience meaning while they move toward more clearly written and abstract expressions of that meaning to the larger community of readers. The student, armed with this record of responses, should now be ready to move up a level of abstraction to consider the social significance of this story. Here again, an informed reader will need to work gradually through several levels of abstraction, beginning with the need to play the role of a social worker, and proceeding to the need to feel with and analyze Mr. Farrington's sense of failure with his friends, his intense frustration, and his ultimate mistreatment of his son. Only then would the student-reader be prepared to show both empathy and critical objectivity in doing an interpretation of Farrington's character.[17]

The exercises could be done in oral or written form; probably a combination of both would be most productive. Their purpose would be to help our implied student-reader use both subjective and objective responses to build upon one another in a process that would help her objectify her reading experience. The audience and purpose of these exercises need not be described because the rhetorical context in this kind of expressive discourse is implied in the learning situation itself. These exercises are means of clarifying discoveries that are necessary if our student is to make a final, symbolic statement on the meaning of this reading experience. The student's teacher, however, must be careful to respond to these earlier, expressive exercises as a trusted expert (Britton's phrase was "trusted adult" because he was discussing younger learners[18]), whose goal is to help the student clarify her own responses. The teacher-reader, in other words, looks over the shoulder of the student-reader, helping her put her subjective and objective responses into assimilated form. The final assignment, in contrast, will demand that the teacher take on the role prescribed in the assignment's rhetorical context and make a more definitive evaluation of whether or not the student has accomplished the assignment's rhetorical purpose.

I am inclined to go on at this point to discuss the kind of response a teacher might reasonably expect from this final assignment. That, however, is the subject of another essay. Simply establishing the movement from lower to higher levels of abstraction, within the context of an ongoing give-and-take between subjective and objective perspectives on the experience of reading, provides at least a foundation for more productive sequences of assignments. If these assignments are at all successful, they should help bring reading literature and composing interpretive responses together as mutually sustaining activities.

Where does this leave us in our interpretation of "Counterparts"? Farrington does not discover much about himself in this story. Unlike Stephen Dedalus, he does not become more conscious of the pattern of his life, nor does he recognize or accept his own part in his or his family's suffering. He does become a bit more conscious of the gradual pattern of decay that has come to take hold of his life, but he does not come to take the more objective stance toward his life that a true Joycean epiphany would demand. The implied reader, particularly after the final scene, does not feel that Farrington will use a discovery made in this story to redefine his life and behave differently.

For our student-reader, however, the experience of reading, expressed and objectified in stages of response, might well result in a vicarious epiphany, in what John Gardner might call a moral response to fiction.[19] Bringing together emotional and rational reactions in ways that generate shifting perspectives on Farrington can result in an organic and complex understanding of Farrington's character. He is a man who is unable, either by nature or acquired character, to see the relationship between what he does—what he chooses to do, Aristotle might have said—and what he is. In the process of sharing in this and other reading experiences like it, our student becomes not simply a fluent but an able reader, using reading and writing to compose and interpret the world around her. She has gone through what Gardner says all writers of fiction go through:

> The necessity of choosing between conflicting emotions or emo-
> tionally charged ideas, the necessity of choosing what to put first,
> and the necessity of meeting the arbitrary demands of form . . . fully
> awaken the artist's critical consciousness . . . and govern what it is
> he puts down. In revising, the creative artist repeats this process,
> coming with each revision to fuller and more totally conscious
> awareness of his feelings.[20]

Notes

1. David Bleich, *Subjective Criticism* (Baltimore, Md.: Johns Hopkins Univ. Press, 1978), 39. "Resymbolization," Bleich argues, is always motivated by subjective need (39). Objective response occurs *after* the reader experiences affective reactions. Louise Rosenblatt, in *The Reader, the Text, the Poem* (Carbondale, Ill.: Southern Illinois Univ. Press, 1978), argues that the poem is "evoked" as the reader moves between text-as-blueprint and his or her own experience and feeling (49). The result of this transaction is a paradigm of meaning for each textual experience that is both anchored in literary and linguistic convention and adapted to the subjective experience of each reader (48–50).

2. Bleich, 99. Bleich here establishes the epistemological contention that aesthetic reading is, by nature, subjectively motivated, and thus—as a way of knowing—can direct itself toward objectivity only through a collective negotiation of meaning within a community of readers (100).

3. Bleich discusses the pedagogical implications of his subjective theory in *Readings and Feelings: An Introduction to Subjective Criticism* (Urbana, Ill.: National Council of Teachers of English, 1975).

4. Hirsch distinguishes *meaning*—"an affair of consciousness" (23)—from *significance*—always a "meaning to" something else (63) in *Validity in Interpretation* (New Haven: Yale Univ. Press, 1967). Meaning, Hirsch contends, can be objectively validated, although the experience of reading may vary from reader to reader (16). In a later note I have explained how Michael Riffaterre, in *Semiotics of Poetry,* uses the term *significance* to refer to the meaning of the whole poem that readers hold in their heads and revise as they work their way through the literal-representational, or linear, level of the poem. Hirsch defines significance by relying on the writer's and reader's combined uses of an

inherited hermeneutic tradition; Riffaterre—with other semioticians—defines significance within the framework or network of words (signs) as they operate within a particular text, although that text may, of course, partake of the semantic weight of other texts. See *Semiotics of Poetry,* 29–31.

5. M. L. Abrams, "The Psychology of Literary Invention: Unconscious Genius and Organic Growth," *The Mirror and the Lamp* (New York: Oxford Univ. Press, 1953), 184–225. This chapter in Abrams's book explains aesthetic theory in terms of the organic metaphor; interesting ideas evolve when the organic metaphor is applied to the process through which readers make meaning.

6. See Jean Piaget, *The Construction of Reality in the Child* (New York: Basic Books, 1954), 350–57.

7. I should acknowledge here the contributions that participants in a pre-convention workshop on "The Function of Expressive Discourse in the Process of Learning to Write," at the 1982 Conference on College Composition and Communication (San Francisco), have made to the development of the kind of assignment sequence described in this article. Special citation should be given to Katharine Reavley, Hepzibah Roskelly, Warren Seekamp, and Georgia Disman, Ph.D. students at the University of Louisville who served as my assistants in conducting this workshop. Their general work on assignment sequencing has influenced this article a great deal.

8. Iser describes the reading process as a transaction between author and reader in which the "strange thought" of the author becomes a theme from whose perspective the reader judges and reconstructs his or her own thoughts as he or she reads, in *The Implied Reader* (Baltimore, Md.: Johns Hopkins Univ. Press, 1974), 293.

9. Britton associates literature with what he describes in children as speech from a spectator's rather than a participant's perspective in *Language and Learning* (New York: Penguin, 1970), 107–10.

10. Kenneth Burke, *A Rhetoric of Motives* (Berkeley and Los Angeles: Univ. of California Press, 1969), 21.

11. In *Semiotics of Poetry* (Bloomington, Ind.: Indiana Univ. Press, 1978), Michael Riffaterre describes the relationship between "marks," or places in the text where the representational and poetic-figurative levels of meaning converge, and "gaps" in a poetic text (9–11), which exist on the literal-mimetic level. These gaps are filled and the poem's significance is completed by the developing figurative level of a poem (12). This figurative level, at first only dimly sensed by the reader, establishes itself in tension with the mimetic or representational level of a literary work. As readers are confronted by "ungrammatical" gaps that they cannot close in the poem's literal-mimetic level, they make this figurative level more dominant. When a sufficient number of textual gaps have been filled by the reader's evolving paradigm of figurative meaning, the reader begins to read directly to this deeper, paradigmatic meaning. Gaps and inconsistencies on one level become the "marks" of meaning on another: "It is . . . a way of speaking that keeps revolving around a key word or matrix reduced to a marker" (12). These key words, or markers, are simply buttons that readers push to bring the whole, symbolic meaning of a work to bear on surface inconsistencies of text. Transferred to "Counterparts," we might suggest that the reader's developing sense of Farrington as a symbol of failure comes to resolve the reader's perception of superficial, textual inconsistencies. The

overbearing truth of Farrington's destructive character, for example, explains away the seeming inconsistency between Farrington's earlier need for comradeship and his later rejection of comradeship in the final scenes of the story.

12. James Britton, Tony Burgess, Nancy Martin, Alex McLeod, and Harold Rosen, *The Development of Writing Abilities (11-18),* Schools Council Research Studies (London: Macmillan Education, 1975; distributed in the United States in paperback by the National Council of Teachers of English, Urbana, Ill.), 81-87. Britton writes at greater length about the function of expressive discourse in *Language and Learning,* but this is his briefest and most general description of expressive writing.

13. Lev S. Vygotsky, *Thought and Language,* trans. Virginia Hanfmann and Gertrude Vaker (Cambridge: MIT Press, 1962), 130-53. Vygotsky devotes this final section of *Thought and Language* to, first, a descriptive definition of inner speech—predicative, condensed, elliptical, oriented to direct apprehension of meaning—and, second, a qualitative definition: inner speech "is a function in itself. . . . Inner speech is to a large extent thinking in pure meanings" (149). It is, to paraphrase Vygotsky, a "subtext" to the spoken word, where motivation and psychological process are articulated in a kind of semiverbal thought-language.

14. James L. Kinneavy, *A Theory of Discourse* (New York: Norton, 1980), 393-449.

15. Peter Elbow, *Writing without Teachers* (New York: Oxford Univ. Press, 1973), 35-37.

16. Mina P. Shaughnessy, *Errors and Expectations: A Guide for Teachers of Basic Writing* (New York: Oxford Univ. Press, 1977), 228.

17. This sequence of writing exercises and classroom dialogue follows the general pattern of learning described in James Moffett's *Teaching the Universe of Discourse* (Boston: Houghton Mifflin, 1968) and *Active Voice* (Montclair, N. J.: Boynton/Cook, 1981).

18. Britton analyzes the various roles that are open to teachers as they respond to students' expressive writing in *The Development of Writing Abilities (11-18),* 118-28.

19. John Gardner, *On Moral Fiction* (New York: Basic Books, 1978), 201.

20. Gardner, 200-201.

The Self and the Other in the Process of Composing: Implications for Integrating the Acts of Reading and Writing

Katharine Ronald
University of Nebraska at Lincoln

English departments today recruit composition specialists to "handle" their students' writing problems while the rest of the faculty gets on with the more important business of teaching reading, or literature. In those upper-level literature courses, students are evaluated primarily on their writing, but that writing must reflect the quality of their "reading" of a literary work and of the "literature" in its area. The professors of these courses tend to look for evidence that students have mastered their reading, not their writing, leaving the business of teaching writing to other classes, other teachers. At the same time, many departments and composition specialists have banned literature from their writing classes, believing that it "gets in the way" of teaching writing. The trend has been toward departments in which literature people and composition people studiously avoid encroaching on each other's territories.

James Murphy is among those arguing that we are already in the same territory and that departments must acknowledge that fact. He claims it will take "curricular courage" to heal the split between reading and writing, a split he sees as distinctly American and decidedly recent.[1] Toward that end, several theorists have been writing recently about ways to reintegrate reading and writing in both composition and literature courses. Most of them find that curricular courage through some form of expressive discourse.[2]

Two recent articles on the connections between reading and writing illustrate this move to expressive writing in both literature and composition classes. However, neither essay moves beyond reporting the results of expressive writing exercises to an exploration of why asking students to write for themselves helps them shape later drafts and more critical readings. This essay will try to provide an account of the function of expressive discourse and an argument for why it can serve as a link between reading and writing in any college classroom.

Elizabeth Flynn, writing in *College Composition and Communication* in October 1983, talks to teachers of literature who are beginning to use exploratory writing in their classes. She argues that such tentative response statements are not ends in themselves, but can lead to more formal, transactional writing, the traditional sort demanded in both composition and literature courses. Flynn points out a crucial difference between the early stages of response, where students "tend to participate in the events depicted in the literature and have difficulty stepping back from them to make judgments and find a coherent pattern of meaning," and the later, more distanced writing where students have succeeded in creating a whole meaning for the literature that makes sense to others.[3] Flynn presents three drafts of an essay written in response to John Updike's "A & P," drafts that move from noting descriptive details from the story to organizing those details to make the point that Sammy is "antiestablishment." The student's view changed, she says, through social exchange in the classroom and a "return to the text," that is, the text of "A & P," not the text of the student's initial exploratory response or subsequent drafts.

Mariolina Salvatori, writing in *College English* in November 1983, emphasizes the integration of reading and writing that a rereading of *both* kinds of texts produces. She uses Wolfgang Iser's concepts of consistency building and wandering viewpoint to show students how dissonance in the process of reading literature can translate into increased awareness of the dissonance in their own first drafts: "By enabling students to tolerate and confront ambiguities and uncertainties in the reading process, we can help them eventually to learn to deal with the uncertainties and ambiguities that they themselves generate in the process of writing their own texts."[4] Salvatori, too, uses student writing as examples, but her assignments are not in a linear progression from response to analysis of literary texts. Instead, Salvatori points out the "intertextual" and "intratextual" nature of her student's writing, as "Mary" moves among papers that refer to other papers, picks up on ideas in responses to short stories, and, generally, uses reflection on earlier writing to form later drafts. The literary text and the text of a student's writing come together, Salvatori says, as the student "actively interacts with the text she composes as that text composes her."

Both of these teachers, then, see some form of expressive discourse as the link between reading and writing. They have moved beyond those teachers who, despite the work of James Britton and James Kinneavy, tend to think of expressive writing as purely emotive or personal and who relegate it to journal-keeping or initial response statements without any clear connection to the "real" writing that follows. However, neither Flynn nor Salvatori offers much explanation of *why* their students' writing improved as a result of expressive exercises.

The answer may lie in two parts of the definition of expressive discourse. Kinneavy provides the first: expressive writing has the self as the primary audience; it is "psychologically prior" to all other forms.[5] Britton adds to this definition the restriction that expressive discourse operates with the speaker/writer in the role of "spectator." As opposed to participants, spectators use language to step back from experience, to reflect and to evaluate.

Drawing from cognitive psychologists' studies of language acquisition and operation, Britton posits that we use language to objectify and categorize our experience. We symbolize experience in language in order to deal with it, and then we can symbolize and categorize the representation itself. When we cast ourselves as observers of our own experience in language, which writing and literature both by their very nature do, we are operating in what Britton calls the role of the spectator. A spectator's language is motivated by the desire to evaluate and understand experience. It is talk that goes back over experience, usually with a sympathetic listener. For example, people will discuss a car accident much differently over dinner than while they were explaining it to the police; or friends will share the same story of a party over and over again, sometimes simply to enjoy it, sometimes to understand its dynamics more clearly, and sometimes to form bases from which to structure their behavior at the next. In other words, a spectator's language serves to distance the speaker from the subject and allow for reflection and understanding. Spectator language, therefore, becomes an appropriate way to foster learning, particularly about the form and function of language itself. Britton says: "A spectator uses this freedom for the purpose of paying attention, in a way that a participant is unable to, not only to the pattern, the form, taken by feelings of participants in an experience, but also to forms of other kinds."[6]

In fact, Britton defines "literature" as the most sophisticated written form of a spectator's language, in the sense that the author invites the reader to observe and evaluate a shared world. One of the reasons literature and composition have not worked well together is that teachers have ignored the aims of the discourse they ask their students to read and write. Typical assignments in writing classes using literature ask students to write essays in the participant's role: informative analyses of themes and characters or persuasive arguments about intended meaning for public, distant, or even unspecified audiences. In other words, teachers have told students to read in the spectator's role and write in the participant's, ignoring the basis of both in expressive discourse.

I want to suggest that because a key dimension of expressive writing is the spectator's stance, such writing lends itself to responding to literature. Just as readers of literature become spectators while they follow and evaluate the unraveling action of a novel, student writers become spectators of their own thought processes while they use expressive discourse. The writing they produce embodies their developing responses to the literature they are reading, and the very act of writing for themselves allows them to monitor and objectify that response. Both expressive and literary discourses demand a self-conscious "looking back" at the text so far, at both the story and the student's responses, in order to discover meaning, and a looking forward to devise expectations for what is to come. Such reflection allows students the freedom to explore and explain their purpose to themselves before going public.

Expressive writing, then, is writing for oneself and reflecting on that writing. Flynn and Salvatori, too, use the terms "participation" and "reflection," although not exactly in Britton's sense. Flynn says that her students moved from participating in the story to achieving critical distance on it, while Salvatori describes how her student moved from passive reproduction of the text to active involvement and reflection. What is crucial, however, are the spaces between the drafts of these students, in which they have taken on the role of spectator. They have become their own audiences, their own readers, and thus are able to synthesize their own voice and meaning ("I") with those of the class, the teacher, and the demands of the assignment (the "other"). Through expressive discourse, these students have become better writers and readers. I would like to offer some theoretical suggestions for *why* expressive writing leads to this improvement.

Expressive Discourse as a Means of Integrating Reading and Writing

First, writing teachers have gained new insights into how they can productively intervene in the composing processes of reading and writing by borrowing from learning theorists and cognitive psychologists. Part of the goal of writing courses has traditionally been to train students to become effective readers, or editors, in the fullest sense of the term: an editor is a writer who reads his or her own work objectively, or a writer who can move easily between the role of "I" and the role of "other." In other words, an effective writer has the ability to "decenter" from his or her own thoughts on paper, or, to use Linda Flower's terms, to change writer-based to reader-based prose.

Research in both reading and writing shows that this ability to reflect on a process in process marks more fluent readers and writers. Readers must attend not only to what is in front of them at any given moment, but they must also hold onto what has come before in order to fit new information into old. Writers, too, must have a sense of where they have been in order to keep going. Experiments have shown that the writing process virtually stops when the writer cannot look back to track his or her progress.[7] Since expressive discourse demands this sort of looking back and pausing, it can help students achieve the more distanced, decentered stance that research shows is the hallmark of better readers and writers.

Besides focusing on the ability to reflect or look back, research in cognition shows that learners need to look forward in order to make predictions about what is coming next. Otherwise, learners become trapped in the present without any strategy for handling that experience. Psycholinguistic reading theory, particularly, has proven how important the ability to predict is to efficient reading.[8] Recent literary theorists, too, have focused on how expectations lead readers to arrive at meaning. Expressive writing exercises that ask students to write at different stages in their reading of a short story, for example, help develop this crucial skill of prediction by making students conscious of its operation.

Both of these cognitive skills, reflection and prediction, have personal bases, and teachers should explore those bases with their students as one way of intervening in the composing processes of reading and writing. Language in the role of spectator needs to become a more conscious part of the classroom. As Britton has explained, a spectator uses language in order to evaluate and predict according to personal memory, experience, and belief.[9] Given that a spectator is particularly aware of how those individual assumptions shape his or her evaluation, one of the basic premises in an argument for expressive discourse as a teaching strategy is its ability to increase this awareness. Writing sequences such as the ones Flynn and Salvatori describe are designed, first, to show students how their predictions and evaluations shape the texts they read and write—and with that consciousness comes control.

Students often lack a useful sense of their own control over the reading and writing processes. Typically trained to read for information rather than pleasure, and not trained to write in many contexts other than for a teacher, college freshmen tend to be extremely passive participants in both activities. They often expect knowledge or information to be given to them rather than taking an active role in obtaining or shaping that knowledge. Such students wait for the teacher to tell them what a reading "means," for example, or how to make their next paper more "correct." In general, students tend to think of reading and writing in terms of conventions rather than effectiveness. They seldom see these discovery processes as opportunities for learning in which their personal stance is central. Expressive writing exercises can help teachers counter this tendency because they encourage students to take control of their own reading processes, and give teachers strategies for intervening in both reading and writing to show students how prediction and evaluation—language in the role of spectator—are at work as they compose.

When assignment sequences such as Flynn's and Salvatori's ask students to comment in writing on their own responses during reading, to take on the spectator's stance, the reading and writing processes become integrated in new ways. Such sequences also can show teachers more clearly where to intervene in both processes because they slow each down and play up their interdependence. Students working through these assignments use their writing to discover and shape their creation of a text as they read, and teachers can direct students to the areas where their expectations do not match what occurs in the text. This sort of interdependence differs from the relationship of reading and writing in the traditional literature and composition class, where writings are often "based" on readings, or reading is used as a common ground for writing assignments, which sometimes have as their hidden agendas a test of interpretation or comprehension. This approach separates the reading and writing processes in artificial ways.

Often such assignments ask students to read an essay and write in imitation of its structure, or to read a short story and write about it as if it were something other than a dynamic event. Students who are asked to imitate the descriptions of E. B. White, for example, or to defend the narrator's decision in "Shooting an Elephant" are not given the opportunity to engage with these texts in a productive way. Such assignments fail to show students how their responses play a part in shaping the meaning of the texts they read and write. The texts they read, then, become obstacles rather than opportunities for students to reason about how they shape what they read and incorporate it into their own personal schemes, and the texts they write become formulaic rather than exploratory, making students passive participants in the acts both of reading and writing. Because it works from the cognitive skills common to both processes, however, expressive discourse can help teachers integrate reading and writing in ways that will improve students' control of both.

Because expressive writing is also based on what cognitive psychologists have found out about how learning happens, it can help teachers integrate language skills in general into their writing courses. Learning theory has demonstrated that language is the foundation of all learning, the mechanism by which people create their representations of the world. Behind a theory of using expressive discourse lies the belief that people learn to construct and revise this representation by using all the resources of language, by reading, writing, speaking, and listening. Bruner, Oliver, and Greenfield have shown how the mismatch, or inequilibrium, between cognitive and verbal skills leads to increased competence in both.[10] Expressive writing exercises bring this inequilibrium to the conscious level for students and show teachers where to help their students learn by matching their writing and reading. Reseeing through the lens of their own writing clarifies the student's vision of meaning in what they have read. Teachers like Flynn and Salvatori have interrelated language activities in their classrooms, as students write about what they have read, talk about what they have written, and listen to others' responses.

Such an integrated approach to language and learning is not new, nor is it solely the product of modern research into cognitive processes. On the contrary, the integration of reading and writing is supported by an argument in the history of rhetoric which modern teachers have often neglected or misunderstood. The rhetorical tradition which began in fifth-century Greece and persisted into the twentieth century was based on rhetoric as a form of learning and communication. The Greeks, who realized the potential that reading and writing added to oral skills, were the first to fully develop a theory of rhetoric as a mode of learning and discovery. The Romans systematized that theory into a coordinated approach using reading, writing, listening, and speaking. Quintilian's *Institutio Oratoria,* which outlined a pedagogical theory based on integration of all these language skills, has influenced educational practice in Western history for almost two thousand years. At the heart of his theory is the belief that learning proceeds through practice with all the forms of language.

Yet modern English and composition teachers tend to separate rather than integrate these forms, particularly reading and writing. Even assigning those two labels to teachers in English departments, defining them as either literary scholars or composition specialists, reflects a serious split between reading and writing. And, since 1914, the oral elements of composition have been regarded as the responsibility of speech, not English, departments. Murphy says the split has "allowed writing to become isolated from the writer, from the rest of the curriculum, and from the orality and reading which were its natural allies."[11] He suggests that modern teachers and departments look to their heritage in rhetorical history and practice in order to remake their teaching into a system which will approach language skills in an organic, rather than fragmented, way.

Expressive writing assignments can begin to accomplish that re-integration of reading, writing, speaking, and listening. Expressive discourse collapses the rhetorical triangle and thus focuses the writer's attention on the writer, as he or she moves among the roles of reader, speaker, listener, responder. Expressive sequences slow the composing process down, first of all, and thus make both students and teachers more conscious of its parts and how they are connected. Expressive writing, because it is private discourse, at first makes the writer into the subject on the page and then into the reader of that discourse. Beyond providing an argument for reintegrating reading and writing, teaching expressive discourse suggests another line of inquiry: how does the writer's self change as it moves outward from its role as initial subject and audience? What happens as students consciously examine the changes that the "I" goes through from the varying perspectives of "other" as the text is composed while reading or writing?

Expressive Discourse as a Combination of the "Self" and the "Other"

Plato and Aristotle were the first teachers to recognize and confront the idea that one thinker could embody the stances of "I" and "other" at the same time. That realization came with the decentering that the written language brought to Greece in the seventh century B.C. Plato's rhetorical theory argued for a private search for truth, but it also encouraged the dialectician to move back and forth among various positions of "self" and "other" in order to reach a synthesis of the two ways of looking at the world. Plato wanted his students to be aware of their simultaneous roles as the "one" and as part of the "many." Aristotle's rhetoric argued for a speaker's ability to know another's views, to be able to take on and to make predictions about others' backgrounds, beliefs, and feelings in order to present more effective arguments. He devoted half of Book II of the *Rhetoric* to a study of the states, the causes, and the effects of human emotions in order to teach speakers how to recognize them in themselves and in audiences. He wanted his students to be able to "decenter" from these emotions and therefore control them. Plato thus called for a "study of souls"; Aristotle answered that call when he advocated internalizing the charac-teristics of the types of human beings in order to study oneself.

Today we would call this ability the development of a "sense of audience." Yet that sense has either been neglected or taught mainly from the outside, with artificial audiences tacked on to writing tasks rather than discovered or created from within the thinker, as Plato and Aristotle suggested. The result is the fragmentation of writer and audience that parallels the separation of reading and writing, listening and speaking. Part of a strategy for recombining those language skills involves helping students arrive at a sense of themselves in the roles of both "I" and "other" as they practice them. Jerome Bruner and Jean Piaget point out that in language learning, a sense of "simultaneity," the realization that things have names, is the first step toward decentering and developing the ability to learn.[12] In the same way, Plato and Aristotle were arguing for the composer's simultaneous sense of being an "I" and an "other." Modern writing teachers strive for that sense by encouraging students to find a "voice," in order to become more aware of an "I" operating in the writing, or to "think about audience," in order to adjust that voice to an "other." But these directions keep the sense of "I" and "other" separate. Teachers need more effective ways of helping their students achieve the awareness of simultaneity in both reading and writing.

Expressive exercises make this activity more conscious by encouraging students to ask themselves: How is the self that I am now different from the one who began reading this story? The same process works in their own writing as students take up the spectator's role, or the role of "other" in relation to their own texts. They ask themselves the same questions when they become readers of their own work: How can the "I" that I see in this draft be changed to fit the "other" I have become as I read it?

Such exercises help students achieve the sense of simultaneity that marks learning and the ability to make connections and generalizations. They also lead students toward developing what George Mead has called a sense of "internalized other."[13] His concept of successively individual "internalized others" can be explained by defining those "others" as variations of the "self" in the spectator role. Those individualized senses of "other," or roles that the "I" takes on, become synthesized, according to Mead, into a more generalized sense of "other," or a sense of audience. That synthesis can also be described as the "fictionalized audience" Walter Ong describes.[14] Developing that sense of audience becomes the first step toward a move from personal to transactional discourse. Expressive writing helps students make that move by fostering their consciousness of a voice developing through drafts of a paper, a consciousness of the expectations inherent in the form of the discourse, and a consciousness of an "other's" specific reactions to that discourse because, at first, the students take on that role of "other" themselves.

Besides working to help students discover and control the internal sense of "self" and "other," teachers using expressive discourse must also consider how external forces determine and define that sense. Expressive writing begins as a private act; because language is shaped by each individual's experience with speaking, listening, reading, and writing, however, it is shaped by the social world as well. Sociolinguists study the relationship of social structure to symbolic systems and conclude that the meanings we give to words and texts are a result not only of personal association but also of social interaction with defined groups. Literary scholars, too, argue over the assumptions that must be shared before any worthwhile critical debate can take place. E. D. Hirsch discusses how scholars and readers must agree on what a text "means," by agreeing on the author's intention, before they can begin to undertake any serious interpretation of the work's significance.[15] Reaching that agreement becomes an elaborate process in itself that involves exploring the social and personal contexts surrounding the work. And I. A. Richards devotes *The Philosophy of Rhetoric* to a study of how assumptions about meaning derive from layers of contexts, and how "the stability of meaning comes from the constancy of the contexts that give it its meaning."[16] Those contexts, Richards suggests, evolve from shared conventions in a defined community of readers.

Those conventions may be personal or social; most likely they are a combination of both. Teachers eliciting expressive discourse by using literary texts as the basis of an assignment need to think about what assumptions or conventions must be acknowledged and shared within a class in order for responses to be negotiated into a collective understanding of meaning. Obviously, expressive exercises emphasize the personal connections between a text and a reader, whether that text is one's own or not. However, those connections are, in part, derived from socialization and from public, cultural norms. Moreover, the classroom is a social environment, where working through assignments depends on verbal interaction among the group. Part of the process of producing meaning, as both sociolinguistic and literary theory show, is social. Teachers using expressive discourse to teach composition, then, must consider what kinds of shared interpretation need to take place in their classes and how that sharing might occur.

Flynn and Salvatori both point to the contribution of other students' responses in developing a final draft of a paper. Small-group reading and talking exercises follow easily from expressive writing, providing a bridge from a student's personal response to a public statement. In those groups, writers read one another's work, listen to others' responses, and, in the process, try to explain their meaning to those who are confused by their writing. The process may be rather messy, but that is all to the good when students are trying to arrive at a synthesis of "I" and "other." Many assignments in traditional literature and composition classes emphasize unity and coherence at the expense of complexity. Expressive writing, on the other hand, can help students deal with their complex, even dissonant, reactions in stages that can lead to a final paper that incorporates that dissonance.

Students experience dissonance when their assumptions about and associations with the symbols in a literary text or the texts of their own writing do not correspond with those of other readers. Several modern theorists have provided methods by which to accommodate such dissonance, and their suggestions can show teachers using expressive responses how and when to help their students reach some shared interpretation of the experience. In *Readings and Feelings,* for example, David Bleich encourages teachers to use class time to engage in what he calls "negotiating meaning"—arriving at a shared interpretation of what a text "means to me."[17] For Bleich, such negotiation, and the act of reading in class in general, becomes a social phenomenon. He suggests that students, after individually working out a tentative idea of meaning through responses, collectively arrive at a more definite and generalized meaning as a group. Thus, although students must approach a text at first by relating it to their own personal constructs, eventually they need to generalize that knowledge by discussing their understanding of meaning within a social group. In this way the roles of "I" and "other," the one and the many, are expanded to incorporate the stances of the group and can be translated into strategies for reading and writing that will make sense to that group.

Different disciplines approach the question of how groups arrive at a shared meaning in different ways, and their insights can help teachers direct students' oral and written responses in class toward this more generalized synthesis of "self" and "other." Researchers in sociolinguistics, for example, suggest, on one hand, that language structures are largely determined by social systems and, on the other hand, that language structures shape both the individual's and the culture's sense of reality. This view can reinforce the use of expressive writing sequences and help teachers intervene in them more effectively. Erving Goffman, for example, takes a "dramaturgical" view of how people interact in groups. In general, he sees each individual as a performer, presenting various "selves" to various groups; sometimes these roles are deliberate, but at times a person's performance may be controlled by the performance of others. Goffman defines "social roles" as the "parts" that each performer may play in response to different contexts.[18]

Teachers using expressive writing exercises can use Goffman's meta-phor of performance as they devise assignments and direct discussions. Expressive writing sequences require students to stand back from their original responses in order to evaluate the "self" or the "part" that they see there. Goffman's theory in *The Presentation of Self in Everyday Life* aims to increase individuals' understanding of the roles they play and, therefore, to increase their control over performances. In the same way, expressive discourse builds students' consciousness of various stances they adopt as they move among the roles of reader and writer. As students are asked to assume the role of "other" in relation to their own writing, they achieve the distance that allows them to evaluate their performance.

Another sociolinguist provides teachers using expressive discourse with a strategy for helping students translate their discovery of the relation between "self" and "other" into their own writing. Basil Bern-stein's distinctions between types of linguistic or speech codes can show how social roles and language are related. For Bernstein, when people share an immediate context (of place or personal experience, for example) they may often use a "restricted code" to communicate, a type of language whose meanings are particularistic, or idiosyncratic. People use "elaborated codes," whose meanings are more universal, when they are communicating in a more context-independent environ-ment.[19] In one sense, then, restricted codes focus on the "self," and elaborated codes on the "other." Bernstein believes that elaborated codes give the speaker more opportunity for reflection since they are not tied to a definite context. He suggests that access to the elaborated code is one of the marks of increased learning, or education.

To the extent that restricted codes rely on what Bernstein calls "condensed" symbols while elaborated codes use "articulated" sym-bols, his concepts are close to Flower's descriptions of writer-based and reader-based prose. Moreover, his descriptions can help teachers recognize those codes in student writing. Final writing assignments— such as Flynn's and Salvatori's—demand the use of an elaborated code, for example, since they call for explanation of a generalized meaning that others will understand. Students must synthesize their responses to the literature into a more universal statement about meaning, and then support that statement with those responses and with the text itself. Students working through earlier exercises may have used restricted codes to explain their initial response to themselves; however, by using writing to work through ideas in front of various other "selves," students' restricted codes become more elaborated along the way, more ready for a "public" reading. By showing students how context determines language, then, and by asking students to examine the contexts surrounding their roles as "I" and "other," expressive writing sequences can help students achieve the decentered stance on writing and reading that final assignments usually require.

Both Goffman and Bernstein see the definition of situation as the crucial variable that determines an individual's choice of role and language. If a person cannot play a certain role, he or she cannot produce the appropriate speech, and vice versa. And roles are determined not only by individuals but by groups. Teachers using expressive discourse, then, need to think about how the groups in their classrooms can help one another recognize and define those roles. Toward that end, teachers can borrow from recent work in literary criticism as well as in sociolinguistics on how groups arrive at a shared definition of context. Stanley Fish, for example, describes how literary readers form groups that agree upon ideas of what a text "means." His theory, outlined in *Is There a Text in This Class?* also helps to counter arguments that expressive responses are completely personal or idiosyncratic. Fish believes that the individual does "make" the text, but that the reader (or writer) is not a completely isolated or free agent. He or she is a member of a community whose assumptions determine the kinds of attention the text gets and, therefore, what it turns out to mean. Fish calls these groups "interpretive communities," and he suggests that they provide the basis from which writers write and readers read.[20]

Fish gives composition teachers a basis from which to explore how such communities can be recognized, shaped, and used to teach reading and writing. Expressive writing assignment sequences are intended to create such an interpretive community among the students and teachers in a particular class. Through examining their own and one another's responses, associations, and tentative statements about meaning, and through sharing those reactions as a group, students working through this sequence come to see themselves as part of a community at work on a particular task. They realize the reciprocal relationship between "I" and "other" and come closer to controlling what Bernstein characterizes as evidence of an elaborated code—the ability to hold the concepts of individual difference and group consensus in mind at once.[21] By playing roles within an expressive-transactional framework, students learn to combine their own and others' responses to what they read. Expressive discourse, as a result, can help students and teachers recognize and incorporate two ways of defining the "self" which Fish describes: the "self" who recognizes that it is constituted by conventional ways of thinking both socially and privately determined, and the "self" who stands back and surveys those conventions in order to evaluate and choose among them.[22] Becoming part of a community, in other words, helps students move toward a generalized sense of "other" without losing sight of the "I" that remains at its center. They are consciously operating in the role of a spectator. This ability to handle the dual role of writer/reader, creator/editor, marks more fluent writers—and accounts for the improvement that Flynn and Salvatori describe.

The exercises they invent certainly are a step in the direction that James Murphy suggests English departments follow—back to the classical notion of integrating all language arts. Because expressive writing makes students conscious of their revolving roles as "I" and "other," both as readers and as writers, it can help mend the fragmentation in our present curriculum. When students realize that their "reading" of their own work becomes crucial to their development as writers and when they come to see themselves as "composers" of the texts they read, they are *learning* in the classical sense of education, not merely mastering isolated skills. Teachers who consciously use expressive discourse, too, may learn to see themselves as members of a larger community. Finally, perhaps such an orientation toward the processes of reading and writing can lead the profession away from such arbitrary distinctions as "lit person" and "comp person." After all, we are all primarily interested in teaching our students how language shapes and communicates knowledge.

Notes

1. James Murphy, "Rhetorical History as a Guide to the Salvation of American Reading and Writing: A Plea for Curricular Courage," *The Rhetorical Tradition and Modern Writing,* ed. James Murphy (New York: MLA, 1982), 3–13.

2. See David Bleich, *Readings and Feelings* (Urbana, Ill.: National Council of Teachers of English, 1975); Joseph Comprone, "Recent Research in Reading and Its Implications for the College Composition Classroom," *Rhetoric Review* 2 (1983): 122–39; Bruce Petersen, "In Search of Meaning: Readers and Expressive Language," *Language Connections: Writing and Reading Across the Curriculum,* ed. Toby Fulwiler and Art Young (Urbana, Ill: National Council of Teachers of English, 1982), 107–23; and Alan Purves, "Language Processing: Reading and Writing," *College English* 2 (1983): 129–41.

3. Elizabeth Flynn, "Composing Responses to Literary Texts: A Process Approach," *College Composition and Communication* 34 (Oct. 1983): 343–48.

4. Mariolina Salvatori, "Reading and Writing a Text: Correlations Between Reading and Writing," *College English* 7 (Nov. 1983): 657–66.

5. James Kinneavy, *A Theory of Discourse* (Englewood Cliffs, N.J.: Prentice-Hall, 1971), 396.

6. James Britton, *Language and Learning* (Miami, Fla.: Univ. of Miami Press, 1970), 113.

7. James Britton and three of his colleagues at the London Institute Project on Written Language experimented with writing without scanning by using worn-out ball point pens and carbon paper. He reports that they were "acutely uncomfortable. . . . We could not hold the thread of an argument in our minds because scanning back was impossible." See James Britton, Tony Burgess, Nancy Martin, Alex McLeod, and Harold Rosen, *The Development of Writing Abilities (11-18),* Schools Council Research Studies (London: Macmillan Education, 1975), 35.

8. Psycholinguistic reading theory has formed the basis for seeing reading, and subsequently writing, as a process of reflection and prediction. Frank Smith's *Understanding Reading* (New York: Holt, Rinehart & Winston, 1982) gives the most accessible account for generalists and teachers of writing. Other, more technical, treatments of the reading process are Eleanor Gibson and Harry Levin's *The Psychology of Reading* (Boston: MIT, 1975), which offers an empirically based study of the role of physical movement, perception, cognitive strategies, and information processing to advance their thesis that reading is an "active, self-directed process." Charles R. Cooper and Anthony R. Petrosky, in "A Psycholinguistic View of the Fluent Reading Process," *Journal of Reading* 20 (Dec. 1976): 184-206, define and give a history of psycholinguistic reading theory in order to argue for teaching students strategies that fluent readers have displayed: hypothesizing, identifying distinctive features, guessing from context, using nonvisual information, and redundancy.

9. Britton, 109.

10. Jerome Bruner, Rose Oliver, and Patricia Greenfield, *Studies in Cognitive Growth* (New York: John Wiley, 1966). See especially chapter 1.

11. Murphy, 9.

12. See Bruner et al.; and Jean Piaget, *The Language and Thought of the Child* (New York: Harcourt, Brace, 1926); *The Construction of Reality in the Child,* trans. Margaret Cook (New York: Basic Books, 1954); and *Six Psychological Studies,* trans. and ed. David Elkind and Anita Tenzer (New York: Random, 1967).

13. George Mead, *Mind, Self, and Society* (Chicago: Univ. of Chicago Press, 1934).

14. Walter Ong, "The Writer's Audience Is Always a Fiction," in *Interfaces of the Word* (Ithaca, N.Y.: Cornell Univ. Press, 1977), 60.

15. E. D. Hirsch, *Validity in Interpretation* (New Haven: Yale Univ. Press, 1967), 126.

16. I. A. Richards, *The Philosophy of Rhetoric* (London: Oxford Univ. Press, 1936), 11.

17. David Bleich, *Readings and Feelings: An Introduction to Subjective Criticism* (Urbana, Ill.: National Council of Teachers of English, 1975), 80-95.

18. Erving Goffman, *The Presentation of Self in Everyday Life* (Garden City, N.Y.: Doubleday, 1959), 16.

19. Basil Bernstein, "Social Class, Language, and Socialization," in *Language and Social Context,* ed. Pier Paolo Giglioli (New York: Penguin, 1972), 164, 166.

20. Stanley Fish, *Is There a Text in This Class? The Authority of Interpretive Communities* (Cambridge: Harvard Univ. Press, 1980), 11.

21. Bernstein, 166.

22. Fish, 11.

Reading and Writing as Liberal Arts

Stephen N. Tchudi
Michigan State University

I would like to begin this essay by borrowing one of the great beginnings in literature:

> My father's family name being Pirrip, and my Christian name Philip, my infant tongue could make of both names nothing longer or more explicit than Pip. So, I called myself Pip, and came to be called Pip.

Virtually every English teacher will recognize that passage and most will have taught it; it is the opening of Charles Dickens's *Great Expectations.* I find it a reassuring opening. Although the reader has no idea of who Pip is or what is to befall or has befallen him, one's confidence in him is established by his secure assertion of his identity through his name: "So, I called myself Pip, and came to be called Pip." Of course, Dickens's use of the first-person narrative helps further our confidence in Pip, since, unless the author commits the literary sin of killing off the storyteller, we know that Pip will be around at the finish, alive, if not kicking.

There's more to the opening of *Great Expectations.* In the next paragraph, Pip describes his "first most vivid and broad impression of the identity of things," an impression gained "on a memorable raw afternoon towards evening" in a church graveyard. In a sentence that must be the envy of present-day sentence-combining advocates, Pip/ Dickens explains:

> At such a time I found out for certain, that this bleak place overgrown with nettles was the churchyard; and that Philip Pirrip, late of this parish, and also Georgiana, wife of the above, were dead and buried; and that Alexander, Bartholomew, Abraham, Tobias, and Roger, infant children of the aforesaid, were also dead and buried; and that the dark flat wilderness beyond the churchyard, intersected with dykes and mounds and gates, with scattered cattle feeding on it, was the marshes; and that the low leaden line beyond was the river; and that the distant savage lair from which

> the wind was rushing, was the sea; and that the small bundle of
> shivers growing afraid of it all and beginning to cry, was Pip.

That is a remarkable sentence for its compression, its impression of
gloom and terror (enough to make one doubt that the narrator *will*
make it to the end of the novel), and its shift from the landscape to
Pip's diminished sense of self. Pip was "afraid of it all"—"it," in this
instance, referring more to life itself than to the mysteries hidden in the
bleak landscape of southeastern England.

At this point in *Great Expectations,* not a word has been spoken.
When the first lines of dialogue appear, they make us fear for the very
life of the narrator:

> "Hold your noise!" cried a terrible voice, as a man started up from
> among the graves at the side of the church porch. "Keep still, you
> little devil, or I'll cut your throat."

That is life-and-death writing, the kind that grabs one by the shirt and
says, "Keep on reading; this is important!"

By the summer of 1982, I had not read *Great Expectations* for almost
twenty years, since I had last taught it to a group of ninth-grade students at Chicago's Kelvyn Park High School. However, I rediscovered it
that summer while in England leading a study group of American
teachers and simultaneously immersing myself in British literature. This
opening from Dickens caught my eye because the week before I had
heard David Holbrook, poet and educator from Cambridge University,
explain that "literature is existential." To summarize the arguments
presented in his book *English for Humanity,* Holbrook says that all
literature raises existential questions: "What is the meaning of life?"
"What am I doing here?"[1] In the opening of *Great Expectations,* Pip is
raising those same two questions, and Dickens devotes the rest of the
novel to answering them.

Listening to Pip struggle with those questions, I was reminded of
David Holbrook's conviction, stated in two earlier books, *English for
the Rejected* and *Children's Writing,* that children's writing does not
differ in aim or purpose from adult writing.[2] What children compose is
also existential, having to do with the meaning of life, the purpose of
existence.

David Holbrook's "existential" description of English meshes with a
classic justification for teaching the mother tongue offered by Benjamin
DeMott at the Dartmouth Seminar of 1966:

> English . . . is about my distinctness and the distinctness of other
> human beings. . . . [The English classroom] is the place—there
> is no other in most schools—the place wherein the chief matters

of concern are particulars of humanness—individual human feeling, human response and human time, as these can be known
through the written expression (at many literary levels) of men
living and dead, and as they can be discovered by student writers
seeking through words to name and compose and grasp their own
experience.[3]

DeMott, like Holbrook, sees an immediate connection between reading
and writing, between classic literature and student compositions.
Through the writings of Holbrook and DeMott one can visualize what
has long been an ideal of the English teaching profession: the "integrated" curriculum in which reading and writing flow naturally into
and from each other, where conventional compartmentalization of
reading skills and writing skills and literature is no longer necessary.

DeMott and Holbrook reach this position by two assumptions implicit in their views of language and learning. First, they both center
instruction in English on the student him- or herself. This is not simply
the idea of the "student-centered curriculum" as described by James
Moffett, where a curriculum evolves from the increasing verbal and
cognitive abilities of the students.[4] Rather, DeMott and Holbrook are
centering instruction on the very act of being human, with language as
the vehicle through which student writers and literary artists "name and
compose and grasp their own experience."

Second, both writers seem to me to be describing a view of English
as a "liberal art," by which I mean simply that they see English in the
schools as part of a broad and general enculturation, not taught solely
or primarily for practical ends. It is from that view of English that I take
my title for this essay, "Reading and Writing as Liberal Arts."

To some, my title may seem a truism: Of course reading and writing
are liberal arts. They are traditionally a part of the humanities; they are
usually ranked along with history, music, and art as the contraries or
antidotes to science and mathematics; they are part of liberal arts
requirements in schools and colleges.

At the same time, it seems to me that in the history of our profession, teachers of English have been anything but "liberal" in their
treatment of reading and writing. I suspect that many graduates of
American schools and colleges would be astonished at the view that
English is a liberal and humane art, something taught by people who
claim to be humanists. For those graduates, "reading" consisted of drills,
skills, comprehension tests and book reports. Literature study offered
more of the same: mastery and testing of names, dates, terminology,
and critical concepts. Writing (or more often, the duller-sounding
"composition") was first and foremost striving for correctness in what
teachers called "grammar" (meaning spelling, mechanics, usage, and

some aspects of style) and second trying to figure out something to say on uninteresting theme topics.

I am not one of those who delights in badmouthing the schools or teachers over an alleged decline in the quality of education. In fact, I believe reading and writing are being taught better today in this country than at any time in educational history. At the same time, I think English teachers and professors have missed the boat in not showing students that reading and writing are important and even pleasurable liberal arts. In striving to make writers of correct English, teachers have created people who don't like to write at all and who can hardly muster whatever skills of correctness they do happen to possess. In working to enculturate students and make them lifetime readers of great literature, teachers have killed off much of the joy of reading and graduated students who consciously choose never to read anything more challenging and rewarding than popular commercial literature. The profession has failed to help students come to discover language as a central and important feature in their lives.

Was there a time in the history of the profession that English was truly taught as a liberal art?

Not that I can discover.

In choosing my title, then, I am not arguing for a return to an imaginary golden era of literacy when reading and writing were integrated, when students read and deeply valued literature and when they wrote more eloquently and correctly than they do now. Rather, I am suggesting that the era of reading and writing as liberal arts lies somewhere in the future, and I want to suggest three principles teachers might follow to establish that era.

Reading and Writing Are Experiential

Writing in the *Phi Delta Kappan,* Beecher Harris once proposed "that we stop 'teaching reading' . . . and as a consequence [abandon] the complex that has grown up around it."[5] He observed that during the preschool years, children are relatively free to explore books on their own with help from an adult reader. The preschooler is not quizzed about content or comprehension and is allowed *not* to appreciate all of the books chosen by that adult. In school, Harris continued, all that changes: Reading begins to be "taught," and at that time reading "problems" emerge, problems only heightened and accentuated as youngsters proceed through the schooling process. Harris suggested doing away with the teaching of reading and replacing it with an approach based on the preschool model, with youngsters free to read books of their own choosing, with support from a friendly adult. It is his claim that in such a setting, children would learn to read on their own.

James Moffett is not quite so radical in his *Student-Centered Language Arts Curriculum.* He suggests that the essential reading "skill"—recognizing sound/symbol relations (phonics)—can be taught in as short a period as six months. After that, he contends, most of what are taught as reading skills are really perceptual and thinking skills, and they are learned through experience, imitation, and trial and error, not formal instruction.[6]

One can go 'round and 'round in the debates over learning to read "on one's own," but it is evident in the schools that reading instruction—including phonics, vocabulary, comprehension, and even spelling—stands in the way of experiencing books for many children. By the time "instruction" has ended, there is little time to sit down and enjoy a good book.

Reading is experiential in two ways. It is learned through experience, as Harris and Moffett suggest, and it centers on human experience, as Holbrook and DeMott have shown. The connection is not coincidental, for it is the perpetual human quest for *meaning,* for understanding experience, that makes people want to read and thus drives them toward teaching themselves to read. Nor does this experiential mechanism cease once people have mastered the fundamentals of decoding a text. As Louise Rosenblatt has reminded us in *Literature as Exploration,* literature is "a performing art": it "performs" for readers, entertaining and enlightening them; but readers also "perform" on literature, becoming more and more adept at analysis, interpretation, and meaning making.[7] Rosenblatt observes that this performance is not learned through studying a professor's lecture notes or through writing research papers on literary topics; good readers learn to read by experiencing texts and responding to them with nurturing by a concerned and more experienced reader.

A growing body of evidence also suggests that learning to write, like learning to read, is also "experiential"—a learn-by-doing skill that develops because it touches on important human experiences. In *Learning to Read through Experience,* a book that is as much about writing as about reading, Roach Van Allen and Dorris Lee outline their "language experience" approach, in which children learn to read and write by dictating and then reading their own stories.[8] Although children clearly must be "taught" the essential nature of the English transcription system (just as they must learn something of sound/symbol relationships in reading), once they get the idea of writing, they pretty much teach themselves "rhetoric."

James Britton has observed that "children *learn* by writing, . . . and if they learn by writing, they also learn to write by writing."[9] The work of Donald Graves and his colleagues at the University of New Hampshire supports Britton's claim.[10] Graves shows that when children are given opportunities to write from their own experience and to think of themselves as writers, their writing and language grow in powerful ways.

Space does not permit me to describe in detail the workings of this sort of "experiential" curriculum. (I have done so in considerably more detail in *Explorations in the Teaching of English* and *The English Teacher's Handbook* [with Susan Judy].)[11] Its philosophical roots, however, can be traced more or less directly to John Dewey. The professional English teaching journals, especially those of the National Council of Teachers of English, have discussed the nature of experiential learning for the better part of this century. The mystery, it seems to me, is why so many teachers at different levels of schooling are unwilling to let nature take its course and to let children learn to read by reading and to write by writing.

English Teachers Must Broaden the Dimensions of Reading and Writing

When I was editing the *English Journal* for NCTE, one of the book review editors, Carol Kuykendall, surprised me with a "Teaching Materials" column entitled "What's New?" It was a blank page. I published that column in May of 1980, persuaded by her argument that secondary school textbooks being published were little more than rehashes of older, conventional texts.

Since reading her non-column, I have been especially interested in spending time at the publishers' displays at conventions to determine, not whether Carol was right, but how right she was. I have observed that although textbook publishing goes through fads and cycles ("writing process" books are currently in; a few years ago "sentence combining" was the big selling point), the content remains remarkably static. In fact, if one looks into texts published throughout this century, one sees remarkably little change and growth. "Literature," as taught in American schools and colleges, has long been and is still principally British and American literature, presented chronologically, with little or no concern for the reader's experiential response. Composition, whether presented through the traditional rhetoric of the four forms of discourse or the contemporary "writing process approach," tends to focus narrowly on the writing of pseudo-academic expository essays.

Given the experiential nature of English, and given the fact that human experiences and emotions run an astonishingly broad spectrum, the textbooks seem to limit the potential of English studies. One cannot place exclusive blame with the textbook makers, for as salesperson after salesperson tells me at those exhibits, "We sell what teachers want to buy." Although one can fault publishers for being conservative and even for virtually plagiarizing one another's works, one cannot fault them for selling the books that most teachers want to buy. The limited dimensions of English are created by teachers, not publishers.

One of the greatest needs in teaching English in the coming years, I believe, is to expand the dimensions of the curriculum. Literature and reading materials can be extended in ways conveniently summarized by the "the three 'multi's' ":

Multicultural Reading. In the early 1970s, there was an awareness in our profession of the need to add multicultural literature to the curriculum. Black and ethnic literature courses were established and proved to be popular. Yet a decade later, many of those courses have disappeared, and, even worse, multicultural literature has not infused itself into *all* English courses. Our profession is still essentially teaching the literature of white America and white Great Britain.

Multidisciplinary Reading. The recent interest in "writing across the curriculum" has opened the way for its counterpart, "reading across the curriculum." This concept embraces more than the traditional "reading in the content areas," in which teachers help students learn to read their textbooks with greater comprehension. "Reading across the curriculum" (or, more simply, *multidisciplinary reading*) recognizes that "literature" in English can be redefined to include quality nonfiction, fiction, and even poetry and drama in other disciplines: science, mathematics, history, social science. Bringing that literature into the schools—whether in English or subject-area classes—increases reading interest for many students. Alleged "nonreaders" in the schools are often discovered to have strong reading skills when the reading program includes, say, *Scientific American,* a good supply of historical novels, and perhaps a copy of a computer magazine, as well as standard works by Dickens and Austen.

Multimedia "Reading." Throughout this century, English teachers have shown considerable interest in incorporating "new media" into their classes. In the twenties and thirties, the *English Journal* was filled with articles about radio and "photoplay" appreciation. The late sixties and early seventies found us interested in "media literacy," and in the eighties "computer literacy" is of interest across the entire curriculum. Yet historically the interest of English teachers in new media has been fleeting, and as enthusiasm wanes, one finds the traditional canon of British and American literature still firmly in place.

In some respects, the return to literature has been natural—even healthy. I hope that when the last Apple or IBM-PC has burned out in the school computer room, someone on the English faculty will note that good reading is still an important part of the curriculum. However, it is equally important that English teachers find ways to draw on the "literature" of the new media, especially television, in their classes. In the past, teachers have treated the new media rather as if they were literary objects, to be analyzed, dissected, and critiqued. (In the heyday of elective courses, it was common to find English departments teaching courses in "The *Grammar* of Film.") I believe English teachers would find more success with media if they were simply to use them as an integral, natural part of the classroom where—to paraphrase DeMott—language and humanness are the central concerns. When the media are treated this way, they cease being the rivals of print and simply become tools in the English teacher's attempt to broaden the base of literacy and to extend the dimensions of literature in the classroom.

The dimensions of writing need to be broadened as well. I think it is no exaggeration to say that the writing curriculum in American schools is dominated by teachers' felt needs to prepare students to write college freshman essays. From junior high school on, youngsters write mostly in the expository mode on set topics growing from schoolwork. In *Coming on Center* Moffett remarks that most school writing is, in fact, a test of reading.[12] School writing is thus narrow and—to students and teachers—dull.

In *Explorations in the Teaching of English* I asked the question, "Why *must* they always write essays?" I presented a list of "neglected" forms of composition, including sketches, profiles, autobiographies, satire, radio drama, poetry of all sorts, interviews, cartoons, pamphlets, fiction of all sorts, advertisements, parodies, jokes, newspapers, letters, telegrams, petitions, and television scripts (to name a few). From kindergarten through college, students ought to be encouraged to explore the full range of writing forms, the so-called creative or imaginative forms too. The existential concerns of students can be explored in many different discourse forms, and, in the long run, students who can write in diverse forms of discourse are better equipped for the demands of college and the "real world" than are those who have had a bland and steady diet of expository writing.

The Reading and Writing Curriculum Should Be Developmental

At this point, some readers may feel that in my zeal to extend the reading/writing curriculum and to base it in actual experience I have ignored and discarded some of the best parts of our traditions. "After all," the argument may run, "there are certain great books that all students should read. There are basic forms of discourse to be mastered. A curriculum based solely on student interests and 'existential' questions is no curriculum at all."

I understand that concern—it has been a common one in this century, first in the progressive movement, more recently in the elective curriculum movement. I want to address it by quoting J. W. Patrick Creber, who, in *Sense and Sensitivity,* argued that English teachers

> cannot accept any . . . dichotomy between the interests of the pupil
> and the interests of the subject. Such a distinction seems based on
> the false premise that the two are mutually exclusive or radically
> opposed. On the contrary, that method which is of greatest benefit
> to the child seems to be precisely the method which makes for the
> greatest vitality and sensitivity of language.[13]

As I read him, Creber is saying that our "disciplines" reflect human needs and interests (though that is sometimes forgotten in universities, where scholars pursue knowledge for its own sake). The classic books (including *Great Expectations*) are perfectly capable of holding their own with modern readers *if* presented at an appropriate time in those readers' intellectual and emotional development. Similarly, "logical organization" of discourse is a perfectly human trait which grows from the needs of one person to communicate effectively with another. Left to their own devices, people will organize their speech and writing, although they may not follow strictly the organizational patterns that have become canonized and ossified in school and college composition textbooks. As Creber argues, the needs of the students and the discipline must coincide. For too long English teachers and professors have ignored the developmental needs and interests of their students while promoting curricula distant from those students.

By contrast, it is possible to visualize a reading/writing curriculum in which students' growing emotional, psychological, and linguistic needs and interests mesh with the language arts activities. I have described the process of developing such a curriculum in *The ABC's of Literacy,*[14] and I recently had an opportunity to see it implemented in the secondary schools of Hampton, Virginia. By way of demonstration and summing up, I want to describe the procedure followed in Hampton and to describe its results in some detail.

In the fall of 1982, the Hampton English teachers (like teachers all over the country) were under fire for their alleged failure to teach "the basics." A number of high school principals were concerned that an elective curriculum was lowering standards and inducing bad habits of writing. The superintendent, under pressure from parents, had concluded that the English program was floundering because it failed to use a single textbook series. Although the English teachers in the district, along with their supervisor, Dr. Betty Swiggett, doubted that the curriculum was what was responsible for parental and administrative dissatisfaction, it was clear that the curriculum needed to be changed, and in more than superficial ways. I was invited to work with the teachers and selected parents and administrators in developing the new English program through a yearlong series of workshops.

We began the process by looking at Hampton students—their needs, abilities, and interests. I asked workshop participants early in the year to spend time writing descriptions of "typical" students at various grade levels. Naturally, some approximating and stereotyping was involved in such a process, but I pointed out that a good multidimensional, individualized curriculum would permit customizing of aims and objectives to meet individual needs as well. From informal discussions about the nature of kids came descriptions—broad generalizations. The seventh-grade team summarized a much longer report as follows:

> The seventh-grade student is entering junior high school in various stages of adolescence and is energetic but confused at new surroundings. He is going through an adjustment period where he is forming his own values, becoming aware of self, and beginning to accept new responsibilities. He is highly conscious of peer influence and sometimes questions or challenges self-worth and authority, yet at other times he recognizes his self-worth and realizes he has a role to play in society.

This is a very general statement, to be sure, but clear and accurate enough that the group could move on to my next question: "Given these students, what sorts of reading, writing, listening, and speaking activities are appropriate at that grade level?" This was simply another way of asking, "What are your broad aims, grade level by grade level?"

The seventh-grade team concluded that the greatest needs of their students were:

> *Reading:* The student will expand his/her range of interests through wide reading . . .
>
> *Writing:* The student will express ideas and feelings using a variety of forms: journals, summaries, notes, fables, scripts, poems, stories, and essays . . .

Listening: The student will develop listening skills through small-group discussions, listening to directions, speeches, stories, poems, and reports . . .

Speaking: The student will participate in oral readings, large- and small-group discussions, role-playing, and storytelling.

The focus for the seventh-grade curriculum became enlarging the students' universe of discourse. The curriculum planners did not see seventh grade as a place to teach the essay or the term paper, and there was no thrust toward bringing "the classics" into the junior high school.

   Those broad objectives were then presented in more detail as the planning teams developed specific units for each grade level. After considerable discussion, we had decided on a thematic organization for the curriculum, because we felt that an approach centering on themes (rather than, say, literary genres or chronology) provided the maximum possibilities for integrating reading and writing, while drawing on the strengths of the old elective curriculum and its individualized reading and writing programs.

   The seventh-grade team decided to break the year into four broad units:

Mythological Heroes (with a focus on myths as stories, not as fodder for analysis of allusions in literature)

Folk Heroes and Folkcraft (with particular emphasis on using Virginia's rich folkcraft tradition)

Popular Heroes and Conflicts (including biography and autobiography)

Family Courage and Challenges (with subthemes of identity, autobiography, and growing up in literature)

Through literature and writing, the curriculum would allow students to make contact with great stories from the past while making connections between "universal" issues and problems and their own concerns as adolescents. Among activities for the seventh-grade curriculum were

   —writing modern myths

   —keeping a scrapbook of personal writing

   —writing tall tales and adventures

   —storytelling

   —collecting folktales from the region

   —preparing a family tree

   —writing several fragments of autobiography

Any reader of this essay familiar with the seventh-grade curriculum in many schools will recognize some common activities and goals in the Hampton curriculum. It can also be argued that there are many other thematic units that would cover this same ground equally effectively. However, the point I want to emphasize very strongly is that the *developmental framework provides focus and rationale* for what, in many schools, is an unrelated hodgepodge of language activities, with no connection among the language arts. I think the Hampton curriculum shows quite clearly the truth of Creber's assertion that the needs of students and the needs of the discipline intertwine. (The unit titles for the balance of the Hampton curriculum are given in figure 1.)

English 7

> Mythological Heroes
>
> Folk Heroes and Folkcraft
>
> Popular Heroes and Conflicts
>
> Family Courage and Challenges

English 8

> Identity and Self-fulfillment
>
> Communication and Interpersonal Relationships
>
> Compassion
>
> Facing Reality

English 9

> Struggles and Conflicts
>
> Freedom and Responsibility
>
> Man's Hopes and Aspirations
>
> Influences of Media on Man

English 10

> What's In a Name? (Reviewing early childhood)
>
> Who Am I Now?
>
> What Am I Good For? (Making career decisions)

English 11

> America's Dream and Promise
>
> The Inner Struggle (Man and Himself)

The Struggle for Justice (Man and Society)
The Search for Values

English 12

Know Thyself
Conflict of Wills
Choice and Consequence
Foibles
Critics of Society
Quests

Figure 1. English Curriculum of the Hampton, Virginia, City Schools

In large measure, what I have called for throughout this essay is a *naturalistic* English curriculum for the schools of the 1980s and 1990s. It is a curriculum holding as its central premise that reading and writing and other uses of language are fundamental human processes and activities, and that they can be pursued with pleasure and vigor by most students. Over the years, however, the English curriculum has grown remote from its "natural" roots. Whereas English should be a learn-by-doing skill, it is often confined to workbooks and practice exercises. Whereas it should range broadly across all of literature and language, it is limited to a few select classics of print literature. Whereas it should be focused around students' developmental needs, it has become a monument to the interests of college English professors.

At the same time, the past twenty years have seen enormous growth in professional knowledge about the nature of language and learning. It seems clear that English teachers and professors have the "know-how" to develop substantial, integrated, naturalistic reading/writing programs. If the profession can implement that knowledge in coming years and decades, the teaching of English itself will have great expectations.

Notes

1. David Holbrook, *English for Humanity* (Atlantic City, N.J.: NFER, 1981).

2. David Holbrook, *English for the Rejected* (Cambridge: Cambridge Univ. Press, 1963) and *Children's Writing* (Cambridge: Cambridge Univ. Press, 1967).

3. Benjamin DeMott, quoted in *Response to Literature,* ed. James R. Squire (Urbana, Ill.: National Council of Teachers of English, 1968), 36.

4. James Moffett, *A Student-Centered Language Arts Curriculum K–13* (Boston: Houghton-Mifflin, 1976).

5. Beecher Harris, "Helping to Read: A Proposal," *Phi Delta Kappan,* May 1969.

6. Moffett, *Student-Centered Language Arts Curriculum.*

7. Rosenblatt, Louise, *Literature as Exploration,* 3d ed. (New York: Noble, 1977).

8. Roach Van Allen and Dorris Lee, *Learning to Read through Experience* (Englewood Cliffs, N.J.: Prentice-Hall, 1966).

9. Britton, James, "Talking and Writing," in *Explorations in Children's Writing,* ed. Eldonna L. Evertts (Urbana, Ill.: National Council of Teachers of English, 1970).

10. Donald Graves, *Writing and Thinking* (Dover, N.H.: Heinemann, 1983).

11. Stephen N. Judy [Tchudi], *Explorations in the Teaching of English* (New York: Harper & Row, 1981); and Stephen N. Judy [Tchudi] and Susan Judy [Tchudi], *The English Teacher's Handbook* (Boston: Little, Brown, 1979).

12. James Moffett, *Coming on Center* (Montclair, N.J.: Boyton/Cook, 1982).

13. J. W. Patrick Creber, *Sense and Sensitivity* (London: Univ. of London, 1965).

14. Stephen N. Judy [Tchudi], *The ABC's of Literacy* (New York: Oxford Univ. Press, 1980).

Select Bibliography

Patricia L. Stock and Karen K. Wixson

All the works cited in this bibliography explore issues common to the language acts of reading and writing, with the exception of several essay collections that provide the reader with introductory surveys of those disciplines that have substantially contributed to current knowledge about the relationships between reading and writing—i.e., the history and psychology of literacy, cognitive psychology, literary criticism, philosophy of language, reading theory, and composition theory. In this sense, the bibliography is not only an interdisciplinary one but also a guide to a second generation of research: the books and articles it cites posit theories or report research that presupposes a first generation of scholarship in the disciplines mentioned above. For this reason the following citations not only lead the reader to information about the relationships between reading and writing but also to other bibliographies that document the scholarship which invited the essays published in this collection.

Aulls, Mark W. "Relating Reading Comprehension and Writing Competency." *Language Arts* 52 (Sept. 1975): 808–12.
Based on observations made in classroom teaching, Aulls formulates six propositions about the nature of the relationship between reading and writing that suggest how they are similar yet independent.

Bailey, Richard W., and Robin Melanie Fosheim, eds. *Literacy for Life: The Demand for Reading and Writing.* New York: Modern Language Association of America, 1983.
A collection of essays treating world literacy, the relationship of literacy to politics, the uses of literacy in vocations and professions, the problems of literacy in various educational settings, and the teaching of literacy, originally presented as papers at the conference on "Literacy in the 1980s" sponsored by the English Composition Board that oversees the writing-across-the-curriculum program at the University of Michigan.

Berthoff, Ann E. *Forming/Thinking/Writing.* Montclair. N.J.: Boynton/Cook, 1981.
Posits Berthoff's theory of reading and writing as acts of composing meaning and describes activities Berthoff uses to teach reading and writing, such as the "dialectical notebook."

———. *The Making of Meaning: Metaphors, Models, and Maxims for Writing Teachers.* Montclair, N.J.: Boynton/Cook, 1981.
Presents a theory of imagination and demonstrates how this theory underlies and gives substance to a pedagogy for writing, reading, and thinking.

Birnbaum, June C. "The Reading and Composing Behavior of Selected Fourth and Seventh Grade Students." *Research in the Teaching of English* 16 (1982): 241-60.
Reports on (1) the procedures for a study of the reading and writing behaviors of eight students who were good readers and writers, (2) the methods of analysis and comparison of data derived from the procedures, and (3) findings about the reading and writing processes of the students as well as the different behaviors that were associated with different levels of their reading and writing proficiency.

Bissex, Glenda L. *Gnys at Work: A Child Learns to Write and Read.* Cambridge: Harvard Univ. Press, 1980.
An account of the author's son's processes of learning to read and write from age five to age eleven.

Bracewell, Robert J., Carl H. Frederiksen, and Janet D. Frederiksen. "Cognitive Processes in Composing and Comprehending Discourse." *Educational Psychologist* 17 (Fall 1982): 146-64.
Building on Carl Frederiksen's earlier work in discourse comprehension, the authors describe their progress in the development of a cognitive theory of discourse processing that is applicable to both composing and comprehending. This theoretical framework, in combination with analysis of task demands and discourse analysis methodologies, provides the basis for the research on the cognitive processes common to both text production and comprehension summarized in this article.

Brannon, Lil, and C. H. Knoblauch. "On Students' Right to Their Own Texts: A Model of Teacher Response." *College Composition and Communication* 33 (May 1982): 157-66.
Reports on research demonstrating that when teachers read student papers the "normal and dynamic connection between a writer's authority and the quality of a reader's attention is altered," often resulting in teachers' denying students both control over their own texts and incentive to write.

Bussis, Anne M., Edward A. Chittenden, Marianne Amarel, and Edith Klausner. *Inquiry into Meaning.* Hillsdale, N.J.: Erlbaum, 1985.
Reports on the ETS Collaborative Research Project on Reading—a six-year investigation of young children learning to read which focused on readers rather than on methods of reading instruction or on subskills presumed necessary for reading.

Chomsky, Carol. "Write First, Read Later." *Childhood Education* 47 (Mar. 1971): 296-99.
This classic work proposes that the natural process of learning to read begins with writing, that through writing children become aware that the written word belongs to them, enabling them to become active participants in teaching themselves to read.

Evanechko, Peter, Lloyd Ollila, and Robert Armstrong. "An Investigation of the Relationships between Children's Performance in Written Language and Their Reading Ability." *Research in the Teaching of English* 8 (Winter 1974): 315-26.
Using a measure of readability to evaluate writing (see also Nystrand), the

authors conduct correlational and regression analyses to identify the aspects of writing that have the strongest relationship to reading ability.

Fader, Daniel, with James Duggins, Tom Finn, and Elton McNeil. *The New Hooked on Books.* New York: Berkeley Books, 1976.
This expanded version of *Hooked on Books* offers a context for teaching the program, expanding the section on writing and adding both essays on the practical environment for the program and an updated reading list.

Ferreiro, Emilia, and Ana Teberosky. *Literacy before Schooling.* Exeter, N.H.: Heinemann, 1979.
Argues that in order to learn to read, the child must explore "the nature, function, and value of written language as a cultural object," an enterprise that begins before schooling and proceeds variously throughout the years of schooling and after.

Flower, Linda. "Writer-Based Prose: A Cognitive Basis for Problems in Writing." *College English* 41 (Sept. 1979): 19–37.
Sets out the distinctions developed by the author between writer-based prose (prose written for writers themselves, recording the workings of their own thoughts in associative, narrative patterns) and reader-based prose (written to communicate something to a reader by a writer who strives to create a shared language and shared contexts in an issue-centered rhetorical structure).

Freedman, Sarah Warshauer, ed. *The Acquisition of Written Language: Response and Revision.* Norwood, N.J.: Ablex, 1985.
A collection of essays based on a theory of how writing is acquired that "takes into account both the writer as a reader of others' writing and the writer in interaction with his or her reader."

Fulwiler, Toby, and Art Young. *Language Connections: Writing and Reading across the Curriculum.* Urbana, Ill.: National Council of Teachers of English, 1982.
Twelve essays and an annotated bibliography written by faculty of the Humanities Department of Michigan Technological University, which has developed a model curriculum in reading and writing across the disciplines.

Goelman, Hillel, and Antoinette Oberg, eds. *Awakening to Literacy.* Exeter, N.H.: Heinemann, 1984.
A collection of papers originally written for a conference on literacy before schooling held at the University of Victoria in 1982. Contributors include Glenda Bissex, Margaret Donaldson, Yetta Goodman, and David Olson.

Hansen, Jane, Thomas Newkirk, and Donald Graves. *Breaking Ground: Teachers Relate Reading and Writing in the Elementary School.* Exeter, N.H.: Heinemann, 1985.
A collection of twenty essays written by teachers at all levels of instruction who teach in environments in which they have been able to translate contemporary theories of composing and comprehending into the instructional practices they report on in this book. The collection concludes with a most useful bibliography covering literacy before schooling, writing and reading, development, classrooms, reading, writing, teachers as researchers, and more.

Harari, Josue V., ed. *Textual Strategies: Perspectives in Post-Structuralist Criticism.* Ithaca, N.Y.: Cornell Univ. Press, 1979.
A collection of essays surveying post-structuralist literary criticism. Contributors are Roland Barthes, Gilles Deleuze, Paul de Man, Jacques Derrida, Eugenio Donato, Michel Foucault, Gerard Genette, René Girard, Neil Hertz, Louis Marin, Joseph Riddel, Michael Riffaterre, Edward W. Said, Michel Serres, Eugene Vance.

Heath, Shirley Brice. "The Function and Uses of Literacy." *Journal of Communication* 30 (Winter 1980): 123–33.
Reports on a five-year study of one community's reading and writing behavior and draws conclusions about both the functions of literacy in society and the ways literacy may be acquired.

——— . *Ways with Words.* New York: Cambridge Univ. Press, 1983.
Reports on a ten-year study of children learning to use oral and written language at home and in the schools in two communities in the Piedmont Carolinas.

Horner, Winifred B., ed. *Composition and Literature: Bridging the Gap.* Chicago: Univ. of Chicago Press, 1983.
A collection of essays which argue that literature and composition cannot be separated either in theory or in teaching practice. Contributors are Robert Bleich, Wayne Booth, Nancy Comley and Robert Scholes, Edward P. J. Corbett, Frederick Crews, E. D. Hirsch, Jr., David Kaufer and Richard E. Young, Richard Lanham, Elaine P. Maimon, Josephine Miles, J. Hillis Miller, and Walter J. Ong.

Jaggar, Angela, and M. Trika Smith-Burke. *Observing the Language Learner.* Newark, Del., and Urbana, Ill.: International Reading Association and National Council of Teachers of English, 1985.
A collection of essays about how children learn language and become literate that grew out of the joint IRA/NCTE Committee on the Impact of Child Language Development Research on Curriculum and Instruction. The collection dramatizes the shift of focus on the part of researchers of children's language development from investigation of form to investigation of process, from concern with linguistic systems to concern with the functions of language, as well as to systematic examination of the contexts in which language is learned and used.

Jensen, Julie M., ed. *Composing and Comprehending.* Urbana, Ill.: ERIC Clearinghouse on Reading and Communication Skills and National Conference on Research in English, 1984.
Nineteen essays about composing and comprehending, divided into three sections—Defining the Relationship, Sampling the Research, and Learning and Teaching—argue that the "more students use reading and writing together, the more they learn from them both." Among the contributors are Arthur N. Applebee and Judith A. Langer, Elizabeth Church and Carl Bereiter, Robert Tierney and P. David Pearson, and Sandra Stotsky.

Jones, Linda. *Theme in English Expository Discourse.* Lake Bluff, Ill.: Jupiter Press, 1977.
Uses tagmemic analyses to demonstrate how readers see certain features as central to an author's message and others as marginal.

Langer, Judith A., and M. Trika Smith-Burke, eds. *Reader Meets Author—Bridging the Gap: A Psycholinguistic and Sociolinguistic Perspective.* Newark, Del.: International Reading Association, 1982.
Part 1 presents five articles, based on current theory and research, that examine how comprehension is affected by what the reader brings to the text, the way the text is structured by the author, and the contextual variables that shape the meaning a reader derives. Part 2 is oriented to the same three aspects of comprehension as part 1, but presents implications for instructional environments. In addition to the editors, contributors include Marilyn Adams, Ann Brown, Judith Green, Jerome Harste, William Hall, Lenore Ringler, Rudine Sims, and Robert Tierney.

Language Arts 60 (May 1983). Theme: Reading and Writing.
A useful collection of essays focused on the theoretical relationships between reading and writing and the implications of these relationships for instruction. In general, reading and writing are viewed as constructive, transactional processes with specific communicative functions. Contributors include Kenneth and Yetta Goodman, David Pearson, Frank Smith, James Squire, Sandra Stotsky, and Robert Tierney.

A Language for Life. London: H. M. Stationery Office, 1975.
Report of the Committee of Inquiry chaired by Sir Alan Bullock that conducted a comprehensive study of attitudes and standards of teaching English in Great Britain. The report makes broad recommendations for instruction and teacher training, calling for schools to develop programs and philosophies that teach oral and written language largely by asking students to talk, read, and write as means of learning. James Britton, whose influential work *Language and Learning* (1970) clearly influences this report, adds a "Note of Extension."

Macrorie, Ken. *Writing to be Read.* Rochelle Park, N.J.: Hayden, 1968.
Emphasizes the value to writers of composing academic prose in their personal voices, which can speak authentically to readers.

Martin, Nancy D'Arcy, Bryan Newton, and Robert Parker. *Writing and Learning across the Curriculum 11–16.* London: Ward Lock, 1976.
Reports on talking, reading, and writing activities implemented in British schools as part of the language-across-the-curriculum programs which were recommended by both the Bullock Report (1975) and the Schools Council Projects' research described in James Britton, Tony Burgess, Nancy Martin, Alex McLeod, and Harold Rosen, *The Development of Writing Abilities (11–18)* (London: Macmillan Education, 1975).

Meyer, Bonnie J. F. "Reading Research and the Composition Teacher: The Importance of Plans." *College Composition and Communication* 33 (Feb. 1982): 37–49.
In support of her contention that organizational plans—e.g., antecedent/consequent, comparison, description—should be taught to readers and writers because such plans help them to use intellectual resources such as memory and attention to comprehend and compose, Meyer cites reading theory and research which indicates that organizational plans (schemes) of texts can either help or hinder readers' comprehension of those texts.

Moffett, James. *Coming on Center: English Education in Evolution.* Montclair, N.J.: Boynton/Cook, 1981.
A collection of Moffett's writing during the decade of the 1970s, with connecting headnotes. The collection analyzes forces at work on education and offers recommendations for teaching reading and writing based upon Moffett's assessment of current theories.

Murray, Donald. "Teaching the Other Self: The Writer's First Reader." *College Composition and Communication* 33 (May 1982): 140–47.
First, Murray encourages writers to develop an "other self" to evaluate their own writing, a sophisticated self who "monitors" writing "before it is made, as it is made, and after it is made"; then, he describes the reading roles this "other self" must fulfill for the writer.

Nystrand, Martin. "Using Readability Research to Investigate Writing." *Research in the Teaching of English* 13 (Oct. 1979): 231–42.
Drawing from psycholinguistic theory, this article considers the relationship between the reader's use of cuing systems within the text in comprehending it and the writer's use of cuing systems in composing text. Within this context, the author proposes the use of measures of readability for writing assessment. (See also Evanechko et al.)

Ong, Walter J., S. J. "Beyond Objectivity: The Reader-Writer Transaction as an Altered State of Consciousness." *The College English Association Critic* 40 (Nov. 1977): 6–13.
Claims that there is no one-way human communication; text created by a writer is merely an object until the human mind of a reader interacts with it.

———. "The Writer's Audience Is Always a Fiction." In *Interfaces of the Word: Studies in the Evolution of Consciousness and Culture.* Ithaca, N.Y.: Cornell Univ. Press, 1977.
Discusses the differences between the concept of audience for readers and writers and the kinds of masks or identities that writers assume; posits that readers can never strip writers' masks away in the way that listeners can strip speakers' masks away.

Oxenham, John. *Literacy: Writing, Reading, and Social Organization.* London: Routledge & Kegan Paul, 1980.
A short, very readable, authoritative statement on contemporary problems of literacy in the world, the future of literacy, and the relationship between reading and writing and social and technological change.

Page, William D. "The Author and the Reader in Writing and Reading." *Research in the Teaching of English* 8 (1974): 170–83.
Drawing on the work of Kenneth Goodman, this article proposes a theoretical model for a "general concept of reading and writing" as a framework for investigating the observable elements of the largely unobservable reading and writing communication process.

Perl, Sondra. "Understanding Composing." *College Composition and Communication* 31 (Dec. 1980): 363–69.
Reporting on a study which examines recursive features of composing, Perl concludes that retrospective and projective structuring are two parts of the same process of composing. The former relies on the writer's attending to

the words on the page to capture meaning; the latter relies on the writer's assessing how the words on the page will affect a reader.

Petersen, Bruce T. "Writing about Responses: A Unified Model of Reading, Interpretation, and Composition." *College English* 44 (Sept. 1982): 459–68.
Relates the work of Britton and Flower in composition, Bleich and Rosenblatt in literary criticism, and Kintsch and Van Dijk in cognitive psychology and linguistics to create a composite theory of composition and comprehension. Petersen also suggests ways to draw upon this unified model in composition/literature courses, demonstrating how literature can enhance the learning of composition and how composition can enhance responding to literature.

Petrosky, Anthony. "From Story to Essay: Reading and Writing." *College Composition and Communication* 33 (Feb. 1982): 19–37.
In support of his claim that making meaning through reading is as much an act of composition as is making meaning through writing, Petrosky presents examples of student writings to demonstrate that students can be helped to comprehend texts they are reading by writing about those texts. In further support of his thesis, Petrosky reviews research and theory in reading and cognitive psychology (Adams and Collins, Anderson, Bartlett, Dewey and Bently, Rumelhart, Schank and Abelson) which posit schemata, plans and scripts, as the material of "active" readers, and in literary criticism (Bleich, de Beaugrande, Holland, Richards, Rosenblatt) which posit transactional and subjective views of reading.

Pratt, Mary Louise. *Toward a Speech-Act Theory of Literary Discourse.* Bloomington: Indiana Univ. Press, 1977.
Demonstrates "how some of the general principles of language use worked out by sociolinguists such as William Labov and Emmanuel Schegloff and of speech theoreticians such as John Searle and H. Paul Grice can be used to describe what readers and writers are doing when they are participating in works of literature."

Scholes, Robert. *Textual Power.* New Haven, Conn.: Yale Univ. Press, 1985.
Argues for empowering students as readers and writers by breaking what Scholes calls the hermetic seal around the text. For Scholes, liberation from the dominance of the text comes when students acquire the capacity to construct their own texts and offer their own interpretations of other texts.

Scribner, Sylvia, and Michael Cole. *The Psychology of Literacy.* Cambridge: Harvard Univ. Press, 1981.
Reports on an empirical study which tested the mental differences between literates and nonliterates among the Via, a small West African group. The study demonstrated that literates showed little or no superiority over nonliterates in tests of memory, conceptual ability, and deductive reasoning, although literates did show superiority in skills closely related to successful reading and writing.

Shanklin, Nancy. *Relating Reading and Writing: Developing a Transactional Theory of the Writing Process.* Monograph in Language and Reading Studies. Bloomington: School of Education, Indiana Univ., 1981.
Shanklin reviews recent research in composition, socio- and psycholinguistics, reading research, and discourse analysis and explores implications for

the writing process of her contention that reading and writing are constructive cognitive processes involving the same concepts.

Smith, Frank. *Reading without Nonsense.* 2d ed. New York: Teachers' College
Press, Columbia Univ., 1985.
Argues that "children become readers when they are engaged in situations
where written language is being meaningfully" and functionally used.

Sommers, Nancy. "Revision Strategies of Student Writers and Adult Writers."
College Composition and Communication 31 (Dec. 1980): 378–88.
Contrasts the revision strategies of student writers who focus on redoing,
scratching out, reviewing, marking out, etc., with the revision strategies of
experienced writers, who "imagine a reader (reading their product) . . .
[who] seems to be partially a reflection of themselves and functions as a
critical and productive collaborator."

Stock, Patricia, ed. *Fforum: Essays on Theory and Practice in the Teaching of
Writing.* Montclair, N.J.: Boynton/Cook, 1983.
Collection of essays on the teaching of writing. Five sections deal with the
history and psychology of literacy, the relationships between speaking and
writing, writing as a way of learning, writing and rhetoric, and the relationships between reading and writing. Those contributing to the reading and
writing section are John Bransford, Nancy Vye, and Lea Adams; Ann Berthoff;
Frank D'Angelo; Jane Hansen; Patricia Harkin; James Moffett; Sandra Stotsky;
Patricia Stock and Karen Wixson; Robert Tierney; and Mike Torbe.

Stubbs, Michael. *Language and Literacy: The Sociolinguistics of Reading and
Writing.* London: Routledge & Kegan Paul, 1980.
Within a discussion of both the formal and functional characteristics of
language in use, Stubbs provides the basis for a theory to explain the relations between reading and writing and between speaking and writing, and
the place of written language in our society.

Tchudi, Stephen N. *The ABC's of Literacy: A Guide for Parents and Educators.*
New York: Oxford Univ. Press, 1980.
Offers an overview of literacy that emphasizes a holistic, rather than piece-
meal, approach to teaching reading and writing, and specifically treats
"Science and Writing 'For Real.'"

Tierney, Robert J., and Jill La Zansky. "The Rights and Responsibilities of
Readers and Writers: A Contractual Agreement." *Language Arts* 57 (Sept.
1980): 606–13.
Argues that implicit contractual agreements exist between readers and
writers governing the roles writers must assume as they create texts and the
roles readers must assume as they work to understand texts.

Tierney, Robert J., Jill La Zansky, Taffy E. Raphael, and Philip Cohen. "Author's
Intentions and Reader's Interpretation." In *Understanding Readers Understanding.* Edited by Robert J. Tierney, Patricia Anders, and Judith Mitchell.
Hillsdale, N.J.: Erlbaum, forthcoming.
The authors adhere to the view that production and comprehension of texts
are social events involving transactions between readers and writers. The
article describes three investigations focusing on the nature of the author-
reader interactions based on this pragmatic view of written communication.

Tompkins, Jane P., ed. *Reader-Response Criticism: From Formalism to Post-Structuralism.* Baltimore, Md.: John Hopkins Univ. Press, 1980.
Although Tompkins's anthology does not represent "a conceptually unified critical position," it does constitute a useful introduction to criticism focusing upon the role of the reader in creating the meaning of literary works. The collection includes essays by Walker Gibson, Gerald Prince, Michael Riffaterre, Georges Poulet, Wolfgang Iser, Stanley E. Fish, Jonathan Culler, Norman N. Holland, David Bleich, Walter Benn Michaels, and Jane P. Tompkins, as well as an excellent annotated bibliography.

Walmsley, Sean A. "On the Relationship between Writing and Reading Processes: A Contextual Perspective." Paper presented at the Annual Meeting of the National Council of Teachers of English, Kansas City, Missouri, November, 1978 (ED 174 938).
Analyzes the relationship between reading and writing from linguistic, social, schematic, and strategic perspectives. Walmsley argues that writers have some control over the clarity or obscurity of the contexts they provide for readers, and that readers have less ability to create those same contexts. He also suggests that future researchers will profit from focusing their studies on (1) the demands which composing places upon writers versus the demands comprehension places on readers, as well as (2) writers' and readers' purposes for writing and reading.

Wilson, Marilyn J. "A Review of Recent Research on the Integration of Reading and Writing." *The Reading Teacher* 34 (May 1981): 896–901.
Reports on research which supports Wilson's argument that children learn to read and write in the same manner as they learn to speak, by forming hypotheses and testing them. Wilson indicates (1) that the processes of reading and writing must be taught integrally because of their mutual dependence upon each other and (2) that children's desire to make meaning must serve as a guide to instruction in those processes.

Contributors

Dorothy Augustine is associate professor of English and director of composition at Chapman College, where she teaches writing and rhetorical theory, linguistics, and literature. She has participated in workshops and panels at national and regional conferences of composition teachers, and she has designed programs in writing across the curriculum for her colleagues at Chapman and for high school teachers in southern California. She is the author of *The Thought of Writing* (1975), and articles on the composing process published in *College English* and *The Rhetoric Society Quarterly.*

Richard Beach is professor of English education at the University of Minnesota, Minneapolis. He is chair of the NCTE Assembly on Research and a former secretary for the Conference on English Education. He is coeditor of *New Directions in Composition Research* (1984) and the author of *Writing about Ourselves and Others* and has published numerous articles and research reports in the areas of composition and response to literature.

June Cannell Birnbaum, a winner of the NCTE Promising Researcher Award in 1981, is an instructional specialist with the State of New Jersey Department of Education. In addition to teaching high school she has formerly been a writing specialist at the Douglass-Cook Writing Center and taught courses at the Rutgers Graduate School of Education. Her publications include articles that have appeared in *Research in the Teaching of English, Theory into Practice,* and *Developing Literacy,* a text published by IRA in 1983.

David Bleich is professor of English at Indiana University. He is the author of numerous articles on language and literary criticism and has authored the books *Readings and Feelings: An Introduction to Subjective Criticism; Subjective Criticism;* and *Utopia: The Psychology of a Cultural Fantasy.*

Deborah Brandt is an assistant professor of English at the University of Wisconsin, Madison, where she teaches writing and studies reading and writing processes. Winner of a 1984 NCTE Promising Researcher Award for a study of context in composing, she is at work on a booklength manuscript called "The Substance of Literacy."

Jill N. Burkland is an instructor at Michigan Technological University. She teaches freshman composition and literature and has tutored in the Language Skills Laboratory. Her publications include articles on tutoring and upcoming articles in *College Composition and Communication* and the *Journal of Teaching English,* and she is presently doing research on evaluation of student writing.

269

Joseph J. Comprone directs a doctoral program at the University of Louisville that includes a degree in rhetoric and composition. His books include *From Experience to Expression; Form and Substance;* and a forthcoming composition anthology, *Interactions: A Thematic Reader for College Writers.* He is at work on a book applying literary theory to the teaching of composition. He has published twenty-five articles on film, modern literature, literary theory, and composition, and given papers at CCCC, MLA, NCTE, and many regional English conferences. He has been a visiting lecturer and professor at the University of South Carolina, Simon Fraser University in Canada, and Harvard, and has conducted workshops for composition teachers at the Universities of Colorado and Vermont. He has held previous teaching positions at the Universities of Cincinnati and Minnesota.

Barbey Dougherty is currently editor-in-chief for Thoughtware, which produces computer software and management training materials for the Institute for Management Improvement in Miami, Florida. She was a founding member of the English Composition Board and cofounder of the Writing Workshop at the University of Michigan. At Michigan, she taught advanced expository writing classes for the English Department and worked extensively with teaching fellows and faculty members charged with implementing the junior-senior writing requirement in content area classes. Prior to teaching at Michigan, she taught at Eastern Michigan University and Ohio University. She is author of *Composing Choices for Writers,* an advanced composition text published in 1985.

Anne Eisenberg directs the graduate program in scientific and technical writing at the Polytechnic Institute of New York. She is the author of *Reading Technical Books* and *Effective Technical Communication,* as well as the film *Technical Writing,* done for the American Chemical Society. Her articles have appeared in *Physics Today,* the *Journal of Chemical Education,* the *Journal of Basic Writing,* the *Journal of Technical Writing and Communication,* and other publications.

Linda Flower is associate professor of English and director of the freshman writing course at Carnegie-Mellon University. "In a previous life," she says, she served as Director of the Business and Professional Communications program at the Graduate School of Industrial Administration and part of the research team on the Document Design Project. With Dick Hayes, she has just completed a National Science Foundation–supported research project on cognitive processes in revision, which looked at how a group of professional writers, writing instructors, and students orchestrated processes of detection, problem diagnosis, and strategy selection in revision.

Maxine Hairston is professor of English and rhetoric at the University of Texas, Austin, where she teaches writing at all levels and graduate courses in rhetorical theory and teaching composition. She was the 1985 chair of the Conference on College Composition and Communication. Her publications include "The Winds of Change: Thomas Kuhn and the Revolution in the Teaching of Writing" and two textbooks: *A Contemporary Rhetoric* and *Successful Writing.*

Margie S. Leys is on the faculty at Riverina College of Advanced Education in Wagga Wagga, Australia, where she teaches courses in reading education for preservice and inservice teachers. Prior to that time she was on the staff at the Center for the Study of Reading at the University of Illinois, where she was involved in research on reading-writing relationships and learning from text. She has also taught social studies and reading in junior and senior high schools.

JoAnne Liebman-Kleine received her Ph.D. from the University of Minnesota and is currently assistant professor of English at the University of Arkansas at Little Rock. She has published articles in the areas of literary theory and composition.

Bruce Thorvald Petersen was an associate professor of English and the director of the Literature Committee at Michigan Technological University, where he taught writing and composition theory, rhetoric, and literary criticism and theory. Petersen served as the chair of the Writing in College Section of the Midwest Modern Language Association (1982–83) and co-directed the Copper Country and Upper Peninsula Writing Projects (1980–81). He published widely in the areas of composition, writing across the curriculum, reading and writing connections, and computer-assisted instruction.

Petersen earned his B.A. from Macalester College in St. Paul, Minnesota (1969), and his M.A. from Indiana University in Bloomington (1979). In 1980, he received his Ph.D. from Indiana University. His dissertation, "No Shadow of Another Parting: Dickens's Concept of the Family," reflected his longstanding love of Victorian literature and life.

Bruce Petersen died in July of 1984 of liver cancer. He was thirty-seven years old. These lines only hint at Bruce's accomplishment as a scholar and value as a colleague. He died when his work was just beginning to receive the national attention it merited. Words cannot express our feeling of loss. Bruce was our friend and companion.

Katharine Ronald is assistant professor of rhetoric and composition at the University of Nebraska, Lincoln. Before taking that position, she was Director of the Writing Clinic at the University of Louisville. Besides connections between reading and writing, her research interests include applications of classical rhetoric to modern classrooms, expressive discourse and personal theories of knowing, and speaking-writing relationships.

Cynthia Selfe is a rhetorician turned technophile. She used to believe in quasi-modals; now she believes that computer fairies inhabit her IBM-PC. She still wonders how reading and writing fit into the cosmic scheme of things. Having moved from Austin, Texas, to Houghton, Michigan, she would gladly trade three hundred inches of snow for one ripe avocado.

Marilyn S. Sternglass is associate professor of English at City College of the City University of New York, where she directs a new master's program in language and literacy. She has published on language and reading/writing relationships and is the author of a freshman composition text, *Reading, Writing, and Reasoning.*

Patricia L. Stock is a lecturer for the English Composition Board at the University of Michigan, where she has taught a variety of composition courses, edited a newsletter for secondary and university teachers of writing, and conducted workshops and seminars for secondary school teachers of reading and writing. She is editor of *Fforum: Essays on Theory and Practice in the Teaching of Writing.*

Patricia Sullivan is director of technical writing at Purdue University and a doctoral candidate in rhetoric at Carnegie-Mellon University. She has published on rhetorical theory and on technical writing.

Stephen N. Tchudi is professor of English and of American Thought and Language at Michigan State University, where he also serves as Director of English Education. A past president of both the National and Michigan councils of teachers of English, he has authored and coauthored a number of books for teachers, including *Explorations in Teaching Secondary English, The English Teacher's Handbook, Writing in the Content Areas, The ABC's of Literacy: A Guide for Parents and Educators,* and *An Introduction to the Teaching of Writing.* He is also a writer of fiction and nonfiction for young adults, including *The Burg-O-Rama Man, The Young Writer's Handbook, Putting on a Play, Gifts of Writing,* and *Jeepers Creepers, Peepers Weepers.*

Robert J. Tierney is a senior scientist at the Center for the Study of Reading at the University of Illinois, where he conducts research on reading-writing relationships, reading comprehension instruction, and teacher problem solving. Tierney was formerly a teacher in Australia and has been a member of the faculty at the University of Arizona and Harvard University.

W. Ross Winterowd is Bruce R. McElderry Professor of English (rhetoric, linguistics, and literature) at the University of Southern California. His books include *Rhetoric: A Synthesis* and *Contemporary Rhetoric: A Conceptual Background with Readings.*

Karen K. Wixson is assistant professor of education at the University of Michigan, where she teaches graduate courses in reading. She holds master's degrees in both reading and learning disabilities and received her Ph.D. from Syracuse University in the area of reading. She is a frequent contributor to journals in education, and her primary area of interest is the assessment and remediation of children's problems in reading and writing.